ANGOLA

Marxist Regimes Series

Series editor: Bogdan Szajkowski,
Department of Sociology, University College,
Cardiff

Further Titles

ANGOLA

Politics, Economics and Society

Keith Somerville

Frances Pinter (Publishers), London
Lynne Rienner Publishers, Inc.
Boulder

© Keith Somerville 1986

First published in Great Britain in 1986 by
Frances Pinter (Publishers) Limited
25 Floral Street, London WC2E 9DS

First published in the United States of America in 1986 by
Lynne Rienner Publishers Inc.
948 North Street
Boulder, Colorado 80302

Printed in Great Britain

British Library Cataloguing in Publication Data
Somerville, Keith
    Angola: politics economics and society.
    — (Marxist regimes)
    1. Angola — History
    I. Title   II. Series
    967'.3   DT611.5
    ISBN 0-86187-394-7
    ISBN 0-86187-395-5 Pbk

967.3
So Sa
141161
Feb. 1987

Library of Congress Cataloging in Publication Data
Somerville, Keith.
    Angola: politics, economics and society.
    (Marxist regimes series)
    Bibliography: p.
    Includes index.
    1. Angola—Politics and government.   2. Movimento
    Popular de Liberação de Angola.   3. Angola—Economic
    conditions.   4. Angola—History.   I. Title.   II. Series.
    JQ3651.A2   1987
    ISBN 0-931477-21-2 (Reinner)
    ISBN 0-931477-22-0 (Reinner: pbk.)

Typeset by Joshua Associates Ltd, Oxford
Printed by SRP Limited, Exeter

Editor's Preface

Over the past decade, Angola has increasingly assumed added importance not only in the context of impending radical change in southern Africa but also in terms of socialist experiments in the Third World. This, the first full account of socialist development of Angola, provides the reader with an indispensible background to the future course of events in one of the most strategically important countries of a region undergoing dramatic transformation.

The study of Marxist regimes has for many years been equated with the study of communist political systems. There were several historical and methodological reasons for this.

For many years it was not difficult to distinguish the eight regimes in Eastern Europe and four in Asia which resoundingly claimed adherence to the tenets of Marxism and more particularly to their Soviet interpretation—Marxism–Leninism. These regimes, variously called 'People's Republic', 'People's Democratic Republic', or 'Democratic Republic', claimed to have derived their inspiration from the Soviet Union to which, indeed, in the overwhelming number of cases they owed their establishment.

To many scholars and analysts these regimes represented a multiplication of and geographical extension of the 'Soviet model' and consequently of the Soviet sphere of influence. Although there were clearly substantial similarities between the Soviet Union and the people's democracies, especially in the initial phases of their development, these were often overstressed at the expense of noticing the differences between these political systems.

It took a few years for scholars to realize that generalizing the particular, i.e. applying the Soviet experience to other states ruled by elites which claimed to be guided by 'scientific socialism', was not good enough. The relative simplicity of the assumption of a cohesive communist bloc was questioned after the expulsion of Yugoslavia from the Communist Information Bureau in 1948 and in particular after the workers' riots in Poznań in 1956 and the Hungarian revolution of the same year. By the mid-1960s, the totalitarian model of communist politics, which until then had been very much in force, began to crumble. As some of these regimes articulated demands for a distinctive path of socialist development, many specialists studying these systems began to notice that the cohesiveness of the communist bloc was less apparent than had been claimed before.

Also by the mid-1960s, in the newly independent African states 'democratic' multi-party states were turning into one-party states or military dictatorships, thus questioning the inherent superiority of liberal democracy, capitalism and the values that went with it. Scholars now began to ponder on the simple contrast between multi-party democracy and a one-party totalitarian rule that had satisfied an earlier generation.

More importantly, however, by the beginning of that decade Cuba had a revolution without Soviet help, a revolution which subsequently became to many political elites in the Third World not only an inspiration but a clear military, political and ideological example to follow. Apart from its romantic appeal, to many nationalist movements the Cuban revolution also demonstrated a novel way of conducting and winning a nationalist, anti-imperialist war and accepting Marxism as the state ideology without a vanguard communist party. The Cuban precedent was subsequently followed in one respect or another by scores of regimes in the Third World who used the adoption of 'scientific socialism' tied to the tradition of Marxist thought as a form of mobilization, legitimation or association with the prestigious symbols and powerful high-status regimes such as the Soviet Union, China, Cuba and Vietnam.

Despite all these changes the study of Marxist regimes remains in its infancy and continues to be hampered by constant and not always pertinent comparison with the Soviet Union, thus somewhat blurring the important underlying common theme—the 'scientific theory' of the laws of development of human society and human history. This doctrine is claimed by the leadership of these regimes to consist of the discovery of objective causal relationships; it is used to analyse the contradictions which arise between goals and actuality in the pursuit of a common destiny. Thus the political elites of these countries have been and continue to be influenced in both their ideology and their political practice by Marxism more than any other current of social thought and political practice.

The growth in the number and global significance, as well as the ideological political and economic impact, of Marxist regimes has presented scholars and students with an increasing challenge. In meeting this challenge, social scientists on both sides of the political divide have put forward a dazzling profusion of terms, models, programmes and varieties of interpretation. It is against the background of this profusion that the present comprehensive series on Marxist regimes is offered.

This collection of monographs is envisaged as a series of multi-disciplinary textbooks on the governments, politics, economics and society of these countries. Each of the monographs was prepared by a specialist on the country concerned. Thus, over fifty scholars from all over the world have contributed monographs which were based on first-hand knowledge. The geographical diversity of the authors, combined with the fact that as a group they represent many disciplines of social science, gives their individual analyses and the series as a whole an additional dimension.

Each of the scholars who contributed to this series was asked to analyse such topics as the political culture, the governmental structure, the ruling party, other mass organizations, party-state relations, the policy process, the economy, domestic and foreign relations together with any features peculiar to the country under discussion.

This series does not aim at assigning authenticity or authority to any single one of the political systems included in it. It shows that depending on a variety of historical, cultural, ethnic and political factors, the pursuit of goals derived from the tenets of Marxism has produced different political forms at different times and in different places. It also illustrates the rich diversity among these societies, where attempts to achieve a synthesis between goals derived from Marxism on the one hand, and national realities on the other, have often meant distinctive approaches and solutions to the problems of social, political and economic development.

University College   *Bogdan Szajkowski*
Cardiff

To my late father, Len, my mother, Joan, and my wife, Liz.

Contents

List of Illustrations and Tables

Map

Figure

Tables

Preface

The attempt by the MPLA to implement its undoubtedly Marxist policies in Angola has taken place against the background of, and has been hindered by, the complex internal and external political and military situation in and around Angola. It is my view that the MPLA–Workers' Party is sincere in its commitment to Marxism–Leninism and that its policies have reflected this. The failure to make any headway in implementing socialist policies has been brought about by the policy of destabilization pursued by the Botha regime in South Africa both through direct military attacks and through extensive support for UNITA. Although UNITA clearly has some lasting support from sections of the mainly Ovimbundu population of southern and central Angola, I feel it is very unlikely that it would today be a major force politically or militarily had it not been for South Africa's assistance, particularly in the wake of the MPLA victory in 1976.

Because of the short life of the MPLA government—a mere decade—it is too early to make profound judgements on the successes or failures of the movement's socialist policies. Rather, this book aims to present as clear an account as possible of the development of the MPLA as a Marxist–Leninist party, the policies formulated by the movement, and its attempts, frustrated though they may have been in many cases, to implement some of its policies.

It will be evident to readers that the evidence available does not allow a detailed evaluation of the development of aspects of Marxist–Leninist structures and policies in Angola. This does not result from any oversight or because I feel that such a task is unnecessary. Rather, the situation of war and mobilization in much of Angola has meant that it is extremely difficult to reach objective conclusions about the creation and role of socialist institutions in a country that is still in a state of flux.

It should be stated from the outset that much of the MPLA's energy has been diverted away from the task of transforming society into the fight against UNITA and South Africa and into the struggle to rehabilitate the economy. Certainly, in the case of the economy, the government has been more concerned with restoring production to pre-independence levels (something still not achieved in most sectors) than with embarking fully on the socialization of production methods. In the political sphere, the rectification campaign within the party has been the most significant move towards Marxism–Leninism. Other socialist objectives have not been pursued as vigorously as they might have been because of the imposed war, the shortage of cadres and the problems of reconstruction. Throughout the book I have made reference to the problems caused by the military situation and the shortage of trained cadres and educated people—I hope that these references will not prove repetitive but will instead serve to emphasize the effects of the factors.

Against this background and because of the scarcity of statistics and up-to-date and reliable information about internal developments, I have, where relevant, concentrated on an elaboration of the MPLA's policies and objectives as laid out in the seminal documents produced by the successive Party Congresses and the vitally important plenum of the MPLA Central Committee in October 1976.

It should be noted from the start that the author's sympathies are with the general aims and direction of the MPLA in trying to build a more equitable society on the ruins of the exploitative colonial system. Furthermore, the author believes that during and after the liberation struggle, the MPLA was the only one of the three liberation groups to follow truly national rather than regionally or ethnically based policies. The South African destabilization has the aim, I believe, of frustrating Angolan attempts to build socialism, to support other liberation groups and to take part in the construction of a southern African region free from racism, minority rule and exploitation. The policies of the regime in Pretoria spring from their 'total strategy' aimed at ensuring the continuation of white minority, capitalist rule in south Africa— the strategy encapsulates domestic, political, social and economic policies and all aspects of foreign policy.

There are many people whom I would like to thank for their help in enabling me to write the book and also their sustained encouragement for a number of years of my interest in southern African affairs and the involvement of the Soviet Union and China in Africa. Firstly, I would like to thank Bogdan Szajkowski and Peter Moulson for their faith in my ability to produce the book and their help along the way. Secondly, this book would never have been written had not David Morison, the Director of the Central Asian Research Centre in London and Editor of *USSR and the Third World*, and Dr Karen Dawisha, formerly of the University of Southampton and now of the University of Maryland, encouraged me to keep up my in-depth study of the Soviet Union and southern Africa following my decision to move into journalism. They have been an inestimable source of support for several years. In the same vein I would like to thank Colin Legum and Dr Johnson Simpson, of Southampton University, for their help, and James Mayall of the London School of Economics for his timely advice on a number of occasions. On a more personal note, I would like to thank a Tanzanian friend and fellow journalist, Marcelino Komba, for his good humour and friendship and the insight he helped to give me into the people of Africa.

Others who cannot be missed out, but whom I do not know personally, are Basil Davidson and John Marcum. Their studies of Angola are invaluable to all who wish to learn about the history of the Angolan people. My attempts to provide a historical background to my study of modern Angola would have been impossible without their works and can in no way compare with them.

Finally, but most importantly, I must thank my family for the support and help without which this book would not have appeared and my determination to continue with my studies and my writing would have waned long ago. I can never repay the debt that I owe my late and much missed father, Len Somerville, for teaching me the basics of politics and instilling in me a healthy scepticism about the motives and sincerity of politicians. To my mother I owe my willpower and determination not to give up. Last and by no means least, to my wife Liz, I must say that I would not have retained my sanity or sense of proportion without her there to help and, when necessary, to cut me down to size.

Keith Somerville
Reading, Berks., 1985

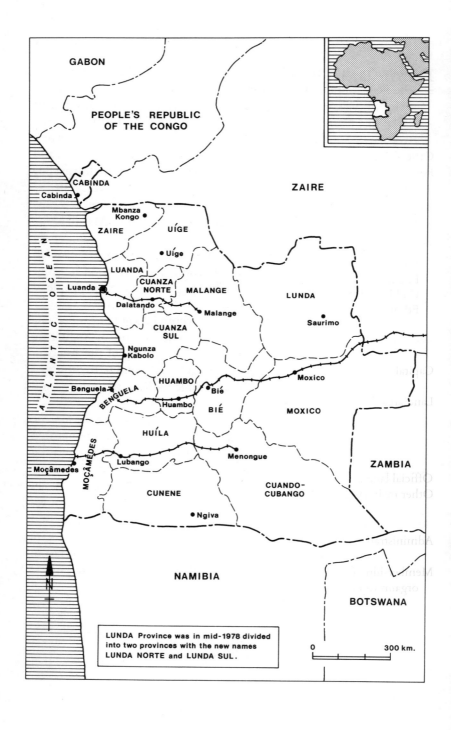

GABON

PEOPLE'S REPUBLIC
OF THE CONGO

ZAIRE

CABINDA

Cabinda

ATLANTIC OCEAN

Mbanza
Kongo

ZAIRE

UÍGE

Uíge

LUANDA

Luanda

CUANZA
NORTE

MALANGE

LUNDA

Dalatando

Malange

Saurimo

CUANZA
SUL

Ngunza
Kabolo

HUAMBO

Benguela

BENGUELA

Bié

Moxico

Huambo

BIÉ

MOXICO

HUÍLA

ZAMBIA

MOÇÂMEDES

Lubango

Menongue

Moçâmedes

CUANDO-
CUBANGO

N

CUNENE

Ngiva

NAMIBIA

BOTSWANA

LUNDA Province was in mid-1978 divided
into two provinces with the new names
LUNDA NORTE and LUNDA SUL.

0   300 km.

Basic Data

Official name	People's Republic of Angola
Population	8.339 million (UN estimate mid-1983)
Population density	6.7 per sq. km.
Population growth (% p.a.)	2.4 (1983)
Urban population	No reliable estimates available since independence
Total labour force	1.98 million (mid-1983)
Life expectancy	42 (1979)
Infant death rate (per 1,000)	No reliable statistics available
Child death rate (per 1,000)	No reliable statistics available
Ethnic groups	Ovimbundu 37%, Mbundu 23%, Kongo 14%, Lunda–Chokwe 9%, Nganguela 7%, *mesticos* 2–3%, others 6–7%
Capital	Luanda (pop. 1.2 million (1982))
Land area	1,246,700 sq. km., of which 6.4% arable, 58.3% forest and woodland, 23% pasture, 12% desert, semi-desert, urban areas and parkland
Official language	Portuguese
Other main languages	Kimbundu, Kikongo, Umbundu, Chokwe, Kwanyama
Administrative division	18 provinces
Membership of international organizations	UN since 1976; OAU since 1976; CMEA observer status; African Development Bank; Southern African Development Coordination Conference

Foreign relations	Embassies in 22 states; diplomatic accreditation for envoys from 51 states

Political structure

Constitution	Adopted in November 1975, amended in October 1976 and September 1980
Highest legislative body	People's Assembly
Highest executive body	Council of Ministers
Prime Minister	None since 1978
President	José Eduardo dos Santos (since 1979)
Ruling Party	Movimento Popular de Libertacao de Angola–Partido de Trabalho (MPLA-PT)
Chairman of MPLA-PT	Jose Eduardo dos Santos (since 1979)
Party membership	34,732 (December 1985)

Trade and balance of payments

Exports	US$ 2,257 million (1984)
Imports	US$ 1,003 million (1984)
Exports as % of GNP	Figures unavailable
Main exports	Oil, diamonds, coffee, sisal, fish products
Main imports	Industrial and agricultural machinery, industrial raw materials, foodstuffs, consumer goods, transport vehicles, medical goods
Destination of exports (%)	Socialist countries under 10%; Western industrial countries 71.7%
Main trading partners	USA, Portugal, France, Sweden, Netherlands, West Germany, USSR, Cuba, East Germany
Foreign debt	US$2.262 billion (1981); debt service ratio 20% (1983–5)
Foreign aid	$43 million (1979)

Main natural resources	Oil, diamonds, iron ore
Food self-sufficiency	Drought and insurgency problems in the 1980s have led to increases in food imports and shortages of grain
Armed forces	39,500 in 1985 (estimated to be 24,000 conscripts); militia forces number 50,000

Education and health
  School system   8 years basic education (1983)
  Primary school enrolment   1.25 million (1981)
  Secondary school enrolment   0.14 million (1981)
  Higher education enrolment   2,666 (1981)
  Adult literacy   Less than 10% (1977)

Economy
  GNP   US$ 3.320 billion (1980)
  GDP   US$ 4.186 billion (1982)
  State budget (expenditure)   US$ 2.78 billion (1983-4)
  Defence expenditure % of
  state budget   25 (1983-4)
  Monetary unit   Kwanza (29.6 kwanzas equal US$1)

Main crops   Cassava, maize, sweet potato, pulses,
                               vegetables, bananas, sugar-cane, citrus
                               fruits, cotton, sisal, livestock.

Main religions   Roman Catholic 40-50%, Protestant 14-
                               18%, indigenous religions 30%

Transport
  Road network   35,800 km. (1975)
  Rail network   2,900 km. (1978)

Population Forcasting

The following data are projections produced by Poptran, University College Cardiff Population Centre, from United Nations Assessment Data published in 1980, and are reproduced here to provide some basis of comparison with other countries covered by the Marxist Regimes Series.

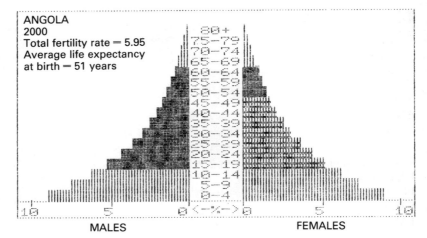

MALES   FEMALES

Projected Data for Angola 2000

Total population ('000)	12,374
Males ('000)	6,124
Females ('000)	6,250
Total fertility rate	5.95
Life expectancy (male)	49 5 years
Life expectancy (female)	52.6 years
Crude birth rate	44.0
Crude death rate	15.2
Annual growth rate	2.88%
Under 15s	45.20%
Over 65s	3.13%
Woman aged 15–49	22.62%
Doubling time	24 years
Population density	10 per sq. km.
Urban population	36.2%

List of Abbreviations

AAPSO	Afro-Asian People's Solidarity Organization
ANC	African National Congress of South Africa
CONCP	Conference of Nationalist Organizations of the Portuguese Colonies
CPSU	Communist Party of the Soviet Union
DISA	Angolan Directorate of Information and Security
EPLA	Angolan Popular Liberation Army (MPLA)
FALA	Armed Forces for the Liberation of Angola (UNITA)
FAPLA	Popular Armed Forces for the Liberation of Angola (MPLA)
FLEC	Front for the Liberation of the Cabinda Enclave
FNLA	National Front for the Liberation of Angola
Frelimo	Mozambican Liberation Front
GRAE	Revolutionary Government of Angola in Exile
JMPLA	MPLA-Youth
MPLA	Popular Movement for the Liberation of Angola
MPLA-PT	MPLA-Workers' Party
NATO	North Atlantic Treaty Organization
OAU	Organization of African Unity
OCA	Organization of Angolan Communists
ODP	Peoples's Defence Organization
OMA	Organization of Angolan Women
PLUA	Party for the United Struggle of the Africans of Angola
SADCC	Southern African Development Coordination Conference
SADF	South African Defence Force
SWAPO	South West African People's Organization
UNITA	National Union for the Total Independence of Angola
UNTA	National Union of Angolan Workers
UPA	Union of the Angolan People
UPNA	Union of the People of Northern Angola
ZANU	Zimbabwe African National Union
ZAPU	Zimbabwe African People's Union

Glossary

aldeamentos	Protected villages established by the Portuguese colonial authorities to prevent guerrilla incursions and recruitment of peasants.
assimilado	Africans and *mesticos* considered by the colonial authorities to have met certain educational standards were given *assimilado* status, which enabled them to assume the privileges and obligations of Portuguese citizens.
degredado	Exiled convicts sent to Angola and other colonies.
donateria	Territorial proprietorship—the holder had the right to colonize a given area.
indigena	Term for the non-*assimilado* Africans and *mesticos* of the Portuguese colonies—in 1961 about 99 per cent of Africans had this status.
kwanza	The new currency introduced by the MPLA to replace the colonial escudo.
mani	Title of the King of the Kongo.
mestico	A person of mixed white and African ancestry—before 1961 most of them had *assimilado* status.
musseque	Slums of Luanda (and other large towns)—in Luanda most of the slums referred to as *musseques* were built of sand.
ngola	King of the Ndongo people—used as basis for the name Angola.
poder popular	The People's neighbourhood commissions (pro-MPLA) which emerged in Luanda and other towns following the Portuguese revolution of April 1974—also used as a general term by the MPLA for the local, provincial and national assemblies set up by the MPLA.

1 History and Political Traditions

Geographical and Historical Setting

Angola is physically a country of contrasts. It stretches from the Cabinda enclave in the north, whose Mayombe mountain range has a generous covering of equatorial rain forest, to the Namib and Kalahari deserts in the south. There is a further contrast between the narrow, dry coastal strip and the high, well-watered plateau. On the coast, and particularly the southern coast, there are few rivers, but as you go inland and climb up the slopes of the central and southern plateaus of Bie and Huila you find the watershed of the Kasai-Congo, Zambezi, Cuanza and Cunene rivers. Many of these rivers have their source in Angola but flow into neighbouring Zaïre and Zambia. The Cubango rises in Angola but flows into Botswana, where it is known as the Okavango.

The inland plateau has a good climate for agriculture, notably the Bie and Huila plateau districts; further north in Malanje and Cuanza Norte there is plateau country with a subtropical climate suitable for plantation-style agriculture. As Angola lies within the tropical climate belt, rainy and dry seasons alternate. The highest rainfall is to be found in the Mayombe forest area of Cabinda, where annual precipitation averages 60–70 inches. The further south one goes the lower the rainfall is, just as the nearer the coast one is the drier it is. At Mocamedes, on the southern coast, rainfall is a mere 2 inches a year. The northern plateau around Uige, the eastern Lunda district, and the central sector of the plateau receive almost as much rain as Mayombe.

Vegetation naturally varies with climatic and altitude variations. Tropical rain forest is more or less confined to Mayombe, grass savannah and relatively dry woodlands predominate on the plateau, though with some rain and cloud forest in the valleys and on sheltered slopes of the northern plateau, while scrub and thorn steppes are characteristic of the coastal strip, which becomes more and more barren the further south it stretches, until it merges into the Namib Desert.

Further inland dry scrub and woodland merges into the northern reaches of the Kalahari desert.

The average height of the plateau is 1,050–1,350 metres, with a few higher ranges climbing to 2,000 metres. The highest point in the country is Mt. Moco in Huambo Province, which reaches 2,620 metres; other peaks include Mt. Mepo in Benguela Province (2,583 metres) and Mt. Vavele in Cuanza Sul Province (2,479 metres). The plateau is separated from the coastal plain, whose width varies from 160 kilometres in the north to 25–40 kilometres in the centre and almost nothing at Mocamedes in the south, by a gradually rising subplateau marked by a series of escarpments, which form sheer drops of thousands of feet in some places.

Although Angola is the birthplace of a number of important rivers, the only one of great importance to the country itself is the Cuanza. The river flows north from its source in the central plateau, reaching the sea just south of Luanda, the capital. It is navigable as far as Dondo, 193 kilometres from the sea. The Cuanza has significant hydro-electrical-power-generating potential, as do some of the rivers flowing out of Angola. In the far south the Cunene river forms the border with Namibia (South West Africa) and is sufficiently powerful to enable the generation of electricity at Ruacana (where the power station is operated by South Africa and supplies power for mining and other economic sectors in Namibia).

Geo-politically, Angola is bordered by South African-occupied Namibia in the south, moderate Zambia in the east, conservative and periodically hostile Zaïre in the north-east and north, and radical and friendly Congo (Brazzaville) on the northern border of the Cabinda enclave. This geo-political position has exerted an almost overwhelming influence on Angola's post-independence political and economic development and has been largely responsible for thrusting the country, at times, into the forefront of global rivalry between the United States and the Soviet Union.

Related to Angola's geographical position and the influences of neighbouring states is the ethnic make-up of the population. Several of the larger ethnic groups are not limited to Angola and extend into neighbouring Zaïre, Zambia and Namibia. This has led to numerous problems, notably in northern Angola where the large and important

Kongo tribe stretches into Zaïre, creating the opportunity for conflicts of loyalty, porous borders and possible interference in Angolan affairs via the Kongo peoples. In the early stages of the rise of African nationalism within Angola, Kongo separatism and nationalism was a strong and divisive influence which detracted from the national liberation, struggle. The Lunda–Chokwe group also spans the borders with Zaïre and Zambia, and the Ovambo people are to be found on both sides of the border with Namibia.

The majority of the Angolan people live on the plateaux, where the best agricultural land is situated, although there are tendencies towards expansion of urban populations around Luanda, Huambo and Malanje. The largest ethnic group is the Ovimbundu of the central and southwestern plateau. They make up around one-third of the population. Many members of this group have moved north to the coffee-growing area around Uige. The Mbundu (north-central plateau area and around Luanda) and the Kongo (north-western Angola) are the next largest groups. Between them, the three groups account for nearly three-quarters of the entire population. Other groups include the Lunda–Chokwe, Mbunda–Luchazi–Luvale, the Nganguela, Herero, Ovambo and Bushmen. People of mixed race, *mesticos*, make up approximately 2–3 per cent of the population. A very small population of Khoisan (Bushman/Hottentot) people inhabit remote areas of southern Angola, particularly the Kalahari areas. Estimates of the total population differ slightly. Figures from the Angolan Instituto Nacional de Estatistica put the population in 1981 at 8.2 million, while UN estimates put the 1981 population at 7.26 million and the 1982 population at 7.45 million. The difference may result from the Angolan estimate including Angolan refugees living temporarily in Zaïre and Zambia (a few Bushmen and Ovambo people from Angola are to be found in northern Namibia). Population density is 6.0 per square kilometre.

Luanda is the country's capital, largest city and major port. Its population was estimated at 1.2 million in 1983, but growth since then has not been computed—though continuing internal conflict and external aggression will have encouraged faster growth than would normally be expected as people flock to the capital in the expectation of greater security. The largest ethnic group in the capital is the Mbundu, though there are a disproportionate number of *mesticos* in comparison with the rest of the country. The other major cities are Lobito (a growing port and the terminus of the Benguela Railway), Mocamedes (the main southern port), Huambo (the chief town in the central plateau area), Bie (also in the central plateau), Malanje and Uige (the centre of the coffee-growing region). The populations of these smaller towns and cities are hard to estimate as internal migration as a result of the liberation war, civil war and South African-backed UNITA insurgency (and South Africa's occupation of Cunene) have made a statistical analysis of the population or a nationwide census impossible.

The main economic areas are the Cabinda oilfields, in the enclave which is physically separated from the rest of the country by the Congo (Zaïre) river, coffee-growing around Uige, diamond-mining around Cafunfo in Lunda Province, iron-ore-mining at Cassinga, maize and other food-crop production in the central plateau area and cattle-raising in the south. A fishing industry is being built up, with extensive Soviet assistance, at the ports scattered along the coast, and a major hydro-electric-power complex is being built with Soviet and Brazilian aid at Capanda on the Cuanza river. The country has over 2,000 miles of railway track. The longest line is the Angolan section of the Benguela Railway, which links the copper-producing areas of Zambia and Zaïre with the Atlantic seaboard at Lobito. The other two lines link Malanje with Luanda, and Menongue with Mocamedes. The country has well over 2,200 miles of paved roads and over 15,000 miles of provincial roads.

Pre-colonial History

Accounts of the early history of Angola shed little light on the first, aboriginal inhabitants of the area. What evidence there is of the first inhabitants suggests that they belonged to the hunter–gatherer culture which was spread thinly across southern Africa in the middle and late Stone Ages (Davidson, 1975, p. 61). The Khoi, or Bushmen, are descendants of these people and scattered groups of them are still living in the Kalahari desert in south-east Angola and in the far south of the country near the border with Namibia. Examples of Bushman art from very early periods can still be found in Angola, as well as Namibia. It is hard to put a date on the earliest evidence of Bushmen in Angola, but rock paintings in neighbouring Namibia have been dated at between 25,000 and 27,000 years old (Van der Post & Taylor, 1984, p. 31). Ancestors of the present Bantu-speaking peoples of Angola (the Kongo, Mbundu, Ovimbundu, Lunda–Chokwe, etc.) expanded into the area from their nucleus around the Cameroon–Nigeria border via the Congo basin around AD 500. Davidson says that the cultures which they developed were partly shaped by the absorption of the Bushman peoples in the areas into which they moved. He adds that the new arrivals had made the 'long revolutionary leap' into crop production, cattle-rearing and the manufacture of metal implements. This development made it possible for them to establish more fixed dwelling-places rather than relying on nomadic hunting and gathering, like their Bushman predecessors. The more advanced form of subsistence and the growth of larger settlements in their turn led to more sophisticated social structures and the advent of forms of chieftaincy and kingships.

Bantu-speaking groups continued to move south into the Congo basin and on into Angola, with extensive migrations occurring between 1300 and 1600 (Kaplan, 1979, p. 10). It is thought that the Bantu peoples introduced iron-working to the area.

The earliest unified kingdom in the region was that of the Kongo, situated near the Atlantic in an area straddling what is now the Angola–Zaïre border. The kingdom grew up between the mid-fourteenth and fifteenth centuries. By the middle of the fifteenth century it was the most powerful kingdom in the west-central African area and exerted a strong influence over neighbouring peoples and emerging kingdoms. By the time of the arrival of the first Portuguese sailors at the mouth of the Congo river in 1483, seven kings had governed the Kongo. The Kongo kings had as their vassals numerous smaller ethnic groups and claimed hegemony over the large Ndongo groupings (Mbundus) to the south, although the Ndongo rulers maintained that they were independent of Kongo control. In the late fourteenth century the Kongo capital was at Mbanza Kongo in present-day Angola.

Kongo kings had religious as well as political power over their subjects and the line of command in the kingdom was transmitted down through the district rulers to village chiefs and the heads of extended families. The king's power rested in spiritual terms on his descent from what were considered to be the 'national' ancestors of the Kongo people. Each king or district ruler or chief subsumed in their persons 'the total sum of all the ancestral lines of Kongo authority' (Davidson, 1975, p. 69).

The Ndongo people lived south/south-east of the Kongo in an inland area between the Dande and Cuanza rivers. They were ruled by a king known as the *ngola a kiluanje*, from whom the Portuguese developed the name Angola for the whole region. At the time of Kongo supremacy the Ndongo were subject to influence, though probably not direct control, from that quarter, but by the early sixteenth century a strong, centralized kingdom had been built up around control of iron and salt deposits. As with many African kingdoms at this time, the boundaries of the Ndongo area were fairly flexible and were subject to change as a result both of the absorption or movements of other peoples and of economic factors such as soil exhaustion.

In the late sixteenth century the Lunda Kingdom emerged in the grassland areas of the upper reaches of the Kasai river. Along with the Kongo and Ndongo kingdoms, it was set apart from other ethnic groups in the area by its size, the number of its subjects and the level of its centralization. Although the rulers of each of the kingdoms could not necessarily exercise absolute and direct control over vassal peoples or even over all of those speaking the same language, they had sufficient power to be strong sources of influence and to exact tributes and allegiance from the less powerful of their vassals and neighbours.

Prior to the arrival of the Portuguese on the scene, the main trading routes were directed inland rather than towards the Atlantic—mainly because the best agricultural and hunting land was in the hinterland and because of the existence of economically strong kingdoms such as the Monomotapa (a Shona-based empire in present-day Zimbabwe) further inland and towards the Indian Ocean coast.

By the sixteenth century the Kongo kingdom had become large enough to be divided into six provinces, each under a governor responsible to the Kongo ruler, who was known as the *mani*. The kingdom had no standing army. The Kongo currency consisted of a type of shell found only in the royal fisheries, thereby ensuring total royal control over the means of exchange. The Kongo king was traditionally chosen by a council of elders, some of them provincial governors, from among the male descendants of previous kings.

Arrival of the Portuguese and Establishment of Colonial Rule

The earliest Portuguese contact with the peoples of Angola occurred in 1483 with the arrival at the mouth of the Congo of the Portuguese explorer Diogo Cao. Following his first visit, Cao returned to the Kongo kingdom a number of times during the 1480s and relayed a request to Portugal from the king of the Kongo asking for missionaries and advisers in return for ivory and other goods (Kaplan, 1979,p. 15). The king with whom Cao first came into contact did not convert to Christianity, but in 1506 he died and his brother, Affonso, who had become a Catholic, won the struggle for succession.

Affonso accepted a Portuguese adviser at his court and in 1530 the capital of the Kongo kingdom was renamed São Salvador. Under Affonso contacts and trade with the Portuguese increased. Much of the trade was in slaves and this rapidly became a destructive and conflictual factor in bilateral relations. Another cause of conflict was the superior attitude towards Africans adopted by some Portuguese missionaries and advisers who were sent to the Kongo. There was also conflict between different groups of Portuguese who came into conflict with the Kongo. This conflict arose between Portuguese traders based on São Tomé and representatives of the Crown. The traders sought to take a share of the trade and the resulting rivalry led the groups to seek allies from among the Kongo. This exacerbated tensions already apparent within the kingdom, due partly to the system of choosing a new king and the existence of different factions which could claim to be descendants of previous kings.

The slave trade, though, was by far the most negative aspect of early Portuguese–African interactions in Angola. The trade had started almost as soon as the Portuguese had first arrived. Once begun it was hard to stop, even though Affonso complained in 1514 to the Portuguese of the effect it was having on his people. In 1526, King Affonso wrote to his Portuguese counterpart that slaving was disastrous for his kingdom (Kaplan, 1979, p. 17). The slave trade was leading to depopulation and also to signs of rebellion by some Kongo against Affonso because of his ties with the Portuguese. As a result Affonso tried to ensure that only non-Kongo people were sold to the Portuguese as slaves; this of course led to conflict with neighbouring peoples who became the primary source for captives to be sold to the Portuguese.

But rather than pushing the Portuguese into curtailing the slave trade, declining willingness of peoples such as the Kongo to sell or trade in slaves, combined with a shortage of attractive Portuguese goods available for trading, meant that gradually the Portuguese began to look to war as a means of capturing slaves. The dynamic factor that led to the growing need for slaves was the expansion of Portugal's colony in Brazil and, in particular, the establishment of massive sugar-cane plantations that needed huge quantities of cheap labour. Basil Davidson has pointed out that by 1580 the colonial population of the Portuguese-controlled part of Brazil was 57,000, 29 per cent of which was African; and the African population was growing rapidly (Davidson, 1975, p. 82). Angola was an important source of slaves for Brazil, partly because it was sited conveniently for the transatlantic trade.

King Affonso died in about 1540 and his successors managed for a number of years to maintain sovereignty over their kingdom. However, in 1568 an assault on the Kongo capital by the Jaga tribe, possibly with support from some discontented Kongo factions, drove the King into exile on an island in the Congo river. The King, Alvaro I, called on the Portuguese to help him restore his throne. The Portuguese response was to send the governor of Saõ Tomé at the head of a force to drive out the invaders. The governor fought the Jaga from 1571 to 1573 and then occupied the country until the mid-1570s. Following the campaign in Kongo, the Portuguese forces moved south and seized an area of Mbundu country that came to be known as the Angola colony. The future capital of Luanda was founded in 1576.

King Alvaro was restored to power with Portuguese aid but his rule was less strong and some Portuguese forces remained in the Kongo kingdom. The kingdom also began to lose control over vassal peoples on the coast, who were linked closely to São Tomé slave merchants. Alvaro managed to keep the Portuguese from extending their Angola colony into his lands, but the continuation of the slave trade, the disruption caused by the Jaga invasion, and his partial dependence on Portuguese troops led to the gradual disintegration of Kongo hegemony. The disintegration became most marked after the death of King Alvaro II in 1614, by which time tension between the Kongo and the colony of Angola had became more acute. In 1622 the Portuguese governor of Angola launched an attack on the kingdom. It did not succeed totally but, importantly for the Portuguese slave merchants, it led to the capture of large numbers of slaves.

In the Angolan colony Portuguese efforts to establish their authority were aided by the absence of a strong paramount chief like the Kongo king. Control was established through armed force—in contrast to the trade and diplomatic approach used with the more powerful Kongo. In the early sixteenth century, merchants from São Tomé had visited the future site of Luanda and had attempted to initiate trade with the Mbundu peoples around Luanda. However, the Mbundu had been suspicious of Portuguese intentions and had not responded. The area had then been virtually ignored by the Portuguese Crown for around thirty years, although local Portuguese traders and Mbundu factions became involved in localized conflicts. In the 1550s, one *ngola* had allied himself with a group of Portuguese merchants and attacked part of the Kongo kingdom. The attack led to a battle around the area of Caxito in which the Kongo were defeated.

The main Portuguese attempt at gaining control of the Mbundu territory followed the allocation of the *donataria* (territorial proprietorship—giving the holder the right to colonise a given territory) by the Portuguese Crown to Paulo Dias de Novais in 1571. Dias established Luanda and several forts along the Cuanza river but was unable to penetrate very far inland. Under his control the slave trade expanded and his forces became involved in small local wars. In 1579 Dias tried to advance up the Cuanza and came into conflict with the *ngola* of the Ndongo people. In 1580 he received reinforcements from Portugal and mounted a second expedition. Eventually Dias was able to advance seventy miles up-river after an expensive, ten-year campaign (Duffy, 1959, p. 56). Dias died in 1589 and Dom Francisco d'Almeida was appointed governor general of Angola. Duffy says the governor was accompanied to the new colony by 450 troops and a few Portuguese craftsmen. Those Portuguese soldiers already in Angola were heavily involved in the slave trade and the new governor had little success in trying to control their activities on behalf of the Crown. Around this time a small Portuguese settlement had been set up at Benguela, on the coast nearly 300 miles south of Luanda. Although at first relatively independent, it soon came under Luanda's influence (it was eventually taken over by the Angola colony following the Dutch invasion in 1641).

The area of Portuguese control over Angola gradually widened in the seventeenth century with forts being set up further inland. As the area to be administered increased, so the problems of the governor increased, since he was given little financial backing from Lisbon, with the result that his soldiers and administrators became little more than freebooters. The Portuguese in Angola relied on the slave trade for the colony's and their own enrichment, though the latter usually came first.

In 1617, Portuguese expansion led to a war with the *ngola* of the Ndongo, Nzinga Mbandi. He had objected to the building of fortresses further and further inland, seeing them as encroachments on his kingdom, which was an even looser political and economic system than the Kongo kingdom. The war with the Ndongo was used primarily by the Portuguese as a means of seizing even more slaves. According to Duffy (1959, p. 64), Mbandi was killed in 1623 and succeeded by his sister, Jinga, who allied herself with the Jaga and fought the Portuguese for three years. This war was followed by a series of minor wars which lasted until 1636.

Minor conflicts occurred around the Benguela colony in the south as a result of attempts to capture slaves. Benguela itself became a major slave port fairly soon after its establishment in 1617. It was situated adjacent to country occupied by the Ovimbundu peoples who, unlike the Kongo or Mbundu, did not have a single kingdom or political entity but twenty-two separate kingdoms.

As for the Kongo kingdom, the early 1600s marked a period of disintegration and factionalism. Competition between different claimants to the throne and the formation of alliances between Kongo factions and different groups of Portuguese traders led to a further decline in the power of the king. One result of this was that vassal peoples and some sections of the Kongo themselves became increasingly autonomous. The last really effective years of the Kongo monarchy were from 1641 to 1661 under Garcia II (Kaplan, 1979, p. 19).

A factor that temporarily threw a spanner in the works of Portuguese aggrandizement was the arrival of the Dutch, first as rival traders and later as invaders. In 1641, the Dutch captured Luanda and the Portuguese governor was forced to retreat to Massangano. The Ndongo leader, Jinga, and King Garcia II of the Kongo allied themselves with the Dutch against the Portuguese. However, the Dutch had no great interest in holding the small coastal strips previously controlled by the Portuguese and they failed to maintain their defences. In 1648, a Portuguese fleet was sent from Brazil to retake Luanda and reestablish control in Angola. The short period of Dutch control had cut the supply of slaves to the Portuguese rulers of Brazil and they were keen to get back their major source of manpower.

The return of the Portuguese was hardly welcomed by the Ndongo or the Kongo. A new campaign was launched to conquer Ndongo territory and increasing pressure was exerted on the Kongo. In 1649, the Portuguese force which had driven out the Dutch forced peace on Jinga and Garcia, a peace which prevailed throughout the 1650s. Garcia died in 1661 and four years later the Portuguese invaded the Kongo kingdom. A major battle was fought at Mbwila which was won by the Portuguese. They captured Garcia's successor, Antonio, and executed him. The great kingdom did not recover from this set-back, although some local loyalties and political/religious structures remained (Davidson, 1975, p. 85). One result of the decline of the Kongo was that Mbundu groups to the south began raiding their former overlords for slaves to sell to the Portuguese. The Mbundu statelet called Kasanje became important as a middleman in the slave trade, this served to delay Portuguese attempts to secure control further inland. In 1680, the Kasanje were defeated by the Matamba tribe, who gave the Portuguese a trade monopoly and continued to supply them with slaves. Both the Kasanje and Matamba seized their slaves from peoples further inland to the east. The practice of raiding neighbouring groups for slaves was one factor that built up a long history of conflict between different ethnic groups within the area now occupied by Angola. The Mbundu and Kongo clashed frequently, as did the Ovimbundu and their neighbours further inland (Davidson, 1975, p. 53). Much of the conflict was generated by Portuguese pressures for slaves and a policy of divide and rule pursued by the colonists.

In the eighteenth century there was further disintegration of African political systems as the slave trade exerted its influence on the African peoples of the region. Individuals and small groups who could act as middlemen and slaving agents became increasingly important. Duffy estimates that between 1580 and 1680 around one million slaves were shipped out from the Angola colony and half a million from the Kongo kingdom (Duffy, 1959, p. 138). Luanda became quite a prosperous port as a result of its important role in the trade. Few attempts were made by the colonial rulers to set up agricultural settlements or find an alternative to slaving. One major problem regarding Portugal's colonization of Angola was that those sent out to settle were, as a rule, exiled convicts (*degredados*) who had little interest in developing the territory they had conquered. The same was generally true of the free immigrants from Portugal who, as Gerald Bender has pointed out, 'were drawn from among the lowest elements in Portuguese society' and who had few if any educational or occupational skills with which to contribute to the development, rather than the naked exploitation, of the colony (Bender, 1978, p. 94).

Although in the twentieth century the Portuguese expounded theories concerning the basis for their colonial rule that denied the existence of racism in colonial administration, throughout the development of Portuguese rule in Angola the attitude towards the Africans 'was little different from that of colonists from other European countries, but the form in which that prejudice was expressed was shaped by Angola's particular circumstances' (Kaplan, 1979, p. 28). These circumstances included the overriding importance of slaving and the nature of the majority of Portuguese colonists, many of whom had to compete with Africans and *mesticos* for work as skilled workers, traders and minor colonial officials. The only way that many colonists could maintain some sort of higher status was for them to adopt a (racially) superior attitude towards the Africans.

Desultory attempts were made to diversify away from slaving in the late eighteenth century and early nineteenth centuries. Governor Tovar de Albuquerque tried to encourage the planting of cotton and coffee, but with little success. In the early nineteenth century, the colony was viewed by the Portuguese as the source of one commodity only—Angolan slaves. This was still the case when in 1836, under great pressure from Britain, the Portuguese Prime Minister Sa da Bandeira, forbade the slave trade, although the institution of slavery still lived on in Angola for over forty years. The ban on the trade was not universally adhered to and at least one governor took bribes in return for turning a blind eye (Duffy, 1959, p. 76). The trade only came to an end in mid-century when Governor Pedro de Cunha cooperated with British efforts to stamp out slaving. In 1858 a law was passed in Angola under which all slaves would become freemen in 1878.

By the mid-nineteenth century, there were only about 2,000 Portuguese settlers in the colony, the vast majority of them men. Few women settled in Angola, one result of which was the growth of the *mestico* population. As far as the African population was concerned, there had been massive depopulation as a result of slaving and migrations to avoid Portuguese expansion. At least two million slaves reached the New World from Angola and a similar number died in transit. To make matters worse, those sold as slaves were often among the youngest and strongest of their peoples.

Throughout the seventeenth, eighteenth and nineteenth centuries, small wars were in progress as the Portuguese tried to extend their control over the Kongo, Mbundu and Ovimbundu peoples. The wars were one factor in increasing the Portuguese population, as soldiers who went out to fight often stayed after their military service. In the 1870s there were 3,684 officers and men stationed in Angola. By 1901 this had increased to 4,895. This relatively small number of troops was fleshed out by African soldiers and irregulars from ethnic groups willing to assist the Portuguese to fight their neighbours. Boer immigrants who settled around the Humpata area of southern Angola also fought with the Portuguese against the Ovimbundu and tribes in the south (Newitt, 1981, p. 51-2).

In 1856, the Portuguese attempted to extort high taxes from Africans in areas they controlled to help them pay for military campaigns. This led to tax raids by Portuguese troops and depopulation as population groups tried to move out of Portuguese-controlled areas. The campaigns and the failure of the colonists to develop the colony meant that financial resources of the colonial administration became depleted in the 1860s and for several years military campaigns (to spread control further inland) had to be put off and attention concentrated on the coastal regions. In 1883, the Portuguese occupied Cabinda and Massabi, north of the Congo river, and also annexed the areas of the old Kongo kingdom which now form part of northern Angola. The exact area of Portuguese control over the Kongo territories was delineated in treaties with France and Belgium, who also claimed areas around the Congo river. The limits of Portugal's claims to Angola, as well as its other African colonies, were established at the Berlin Conference of 1884–5.

One effect of the decisions of the Berlin Conference, which carved Africa up between the colonial powers, was to force the Portuguese into establishing control over all the territory which it claimed. The documents signed by the colonial powers in Berlin recognized colonial possessions only if the colonizing power actually exercised control over the possessions. This the Portuguese certainly did not do, with the exception of the narrow coastal areas around Luanda, Benguela and Mocamedes. The rest of Angola would have to be subjugated (or pacified as the Portuguese called it) and economic development would be accelerated in order to pay for the campaigns and subsequent administration.

The ban on the slave trade and the subsequent abolition of slavery also had their effect on developments in Angola. The end of the slave trade resulted in a glut of slaves in the colony and this in turn led to experiments with plantation agriculture, notably coffee, cocoa and cotton-growing. The latter two crops did not take off at all but coffee became an important cash-crop. One reason for the failure of cotton and cocoa experiments was the inadequacy of the administrative and transport infrastructure (Newitt, 1981, p. 19).

The total abolition of slavery in 1878 in its turn had important repercussions for the Angolan economy. The main one was that some means had to be found to maintain a supply of cheap labour for the coffee farmers, for the gradually expanding colonial administration, and for tasks like building roads. The Portuguese answer was forced labour, also called contract labour. This device was used from 1878 until 1961 as a means of ensuring that the colonial authorities and

Portuguese settlers could continue to exploit Angolan labour power at minimal cost. Various regulations were introduced in the eighty-three years that the system operated, ostensibly to protect African workers and to create a free labour market, but the day-to-day operation of the forced-labour process remained little changed.

The basis of the labour system was that Africans deemed to be vagrants were liable to labour contracts involving no pay and few restrictions on working conditions or length of contract. The Portuguese proved to be extremely liberal in their interpretation of the term 'vagrant'. Vagrant came to mean someone not working for the Portuguese in some form or another. This, of course, meant that almost any African could be pressed into the service of the government or a settler and receive no pay. If anything, the system was worse than slavery, because at least a slave had a price and was an economic asset. If a slave died you had to buy another. If a forced labourer died you could just apply to the colonial authorities for the supply of another.

The end to slavery also had an effect on the Ovimbundu. During the slave trade period they had acted as agents, supplying slaves from the interior. When the trade ended, they became agents for ivory, wax and honey from the interior. They are also thought to have conducted a lucrative trade in firearms with the Chokwe peoples of eastern Angola, acquiring arms themselves in the course of trading.

At the end of the nineteenth and beginning of the twentieth century, there was a boom for the rubber industry. In Angola wild rubber grew well and there was a great market for the latex that could be collected. The result was that huge numbers of Africans were compelled through labour contracts to move hundreds of miles, usually by foot, to collect latex for the Portuguese. In 1899, a labour code was introduced to clarify the contract regulations but they had little effect on the conditions under which Africans such as the rubber collectors had to work. The regulations set out that all Africans were obliged to work, either producing goods for export, through working a plot of land of a given size, or through earning a wage for a certain number of months of the year. The regulations did nothing to improve conditions or relieve the oppressive forced-labour system.

Post-Berlin Expansion, African Resistance and the New State

For around thirty years after the Berlin Conference, the Portuguese were engaged in a series of wars whose objective was to subjugate the peoples of Angola. Euphemistically called 'pacification campaigns', they involved using military force to extend colonial rule and to stamp out all resistance among the indigenous peoples. The Kongo and Dembos areas north and north-east of Luanda and the Ovimbundu territories east of the Cunene river were the most defiant areas. In places such as Moxico, the population was so sparse that extensive resistance was not possible.

In 1906, attempts to collect hut tax in Kongo areas led to open revolt and a seven-year military campaign to crush the resistance. Many of the Kongo fighters were led by a mission-educated chief, Alvaro Tulante Buta, who was eventually tricked into surrendering to the Portuguese in 1916. The Kongo resistance was strengthened by deep resentment towards the system of forced labour (Newitt, 1981, p. 66). In the Huila area towards southern Angola, Ovimbundu resistance was fought with the help of Boer settlers. It took the Portuguese nearly twenty-five years after the Berlin Conference to establish more or less full control over the central and southern plateau areas inhabited by the Ovimbundu. It took until 1915 to bring the Humbe plateau in the south under control. The offensive in the Dembos area north-east of Luanda was launched in 1905 and lasted two years. Its success was only partial as the area remained militantly anti-colonial and later became an important centre for guerrilla activities by the MPLA and FNLA. Although by 1915 most areas were more or less 'pacified', a campaign was necessary in 1917 to ensure Portuguese rule in distant Moxico. The defeat of the German colonists in South West Africa in 1915 enabled the Portuguese to suppress resistance in the south as Angolan fighters could no longer slip easily across the border into German territory to avoid anti-insurgency drives. In the far south it had been resistance by the Ovambo peoples, who straddled the southern borders, that had held up the Portuguese victory. The Ovambos traded in cattle and had been able to get access to modern weapons in return for cattle.

There was a transition to civilian administration in the early twentieth century, notably during the period following the formation of the Republican government in Lisbon in 1910. The first governor appointed by the Republicans tried to fight against some of the abuses of the colonial system and to end forced labour, but he was fighting a losing battle and resigned in 1912 (Wheeler & Pelissier, 1971, pp. 109–10). The new governor appointed was José Ribeiro Norton de Matos, who was to be 'the chief architect of the extractive system's extension through Angola,and of its regulating principles and practices' (Davidson, 1975, p. 120). His efforts resulted in an increase in the numbers of Portuguese settlers and an entrenchment of their privileges in relation to the Africans. De Matos built up a colonial administration and a staff of district governors to carry out his directives. He was opposed by the conservative settler–trader class in Angola but, if anything, his work was for their benefit at the expense of the already exploited Africans. He stated his opposition to forced labour, but the system outlived his governorship by decades. More importantly, in terms of achievements, De Matos sought to develop the diamond, sugar and palm-oil industries and to put the entire economy on a more modern footing. However, he increased administrative expenditure massively and eventually bankrupted the colonial government, a situation that led to his dismissal and charges of corruption being brought against him. In essence, De Matos had been, in Duffy's words, a 'benevolent imperialist, firm in his faith in the white man's burden' (Duffy, 1959, p. 253). Unfortunately for the Angolan people, his benevolence did not extend to improving the living conditions of the Africans.

One of the administrative effects of De Matos's period of rule was the destruction of all remaining African traditional authority through the establishment of controlled villages and the fostering of differences between the ethnic groups in Angola. Trusted Africans were appointed by the Portuguese to head the new-style villages and the whole system was used to fragment traditional links and customs and to weaken as far as possible any indications of unity (in the form of common religious beliefs or linguistic ties) between African communities. The regulations controlling African villages and dwelling-places in towns had the ring of apartheid to them, as they segregated the Africans from the white and from *assimilados* (those Africans deemed to have reached an educational level sufficient for them to have the right to Portuguese citizenship) and *mesticos*.

Under the Republic, administrative changes took place which gave the colony greater autonomy, including financial autonomy. The high commissioner or governor had great powers and under the expansionist Norton de Matos this led in the end to virtual bankruptcy for Angola. However, under his control a number of important economic developments took place in the colony, some of them financed by foreign capital. Much of the work on the Benguela Railway, which links the copper mines of Katanga and Zambia with the Atlantic, was carried out during his period of rule. There were many problems connected with the line and it did not cross the border into Katanga until 1928, although the agreement for its construction had been signed in 1902.

In 1917,the Companhia de Diamantes de Angola (Diamang) was formed to exploit the diamonds that had been discovered in the Lunda region in 1912. The colonial government granted Diamang a concession which covered much of the north-eastern quarter of the colony. Diamang was essentially the Portuguese subsidiary of the Anglo-American mining conglomerate of South Africa, though initially 40 per cent of the shares were in British and Belgian hands, with 5 per cent for the colonial authorities (this holding later rose to 11.5 per cent, where it stayed until independence).

The colonial government in Angola relied on taxes and customs dues for its finances: Africans benefited little from colonial administration but paid heavily for it through hut taxes. Many of the expansion programmes of Norton de Matos were financed by borrowing from the Portuguese Banco Nacional Ultra-marino. The debts built up were such that, following the fall of the Republic in1926, the Lisbon government had to assist Angola in meeting foreign payment obligations until 1930. Angola had a trade deficit of 10–12 per cent of total trade in two years out of three. Far from becoming an economic asset for the colonizing country, Angola was undeveloped and a potential drain on resources. Few effective development projects were launched and attempts to encourage substantial settlement by Portuguese nationals were unsuccessful. In 1929–30, Angola had a population of around 3,000,000 of whom only 50,000 were white or *mestico* (Duffy, 1959,

p. 265). Because of the low level of settlement there was less competition for land than in other African countries colonized by Europeans, although Boer settlers in the Huila plateau area drove out local African farmers and the coffee boom of the early twentieth century led to a scramble for land in northern Angola. Where African land was required by settlers or the colonial authorites, force was used to dispossess the African owners, even though laws nominally protected Africans against such actions.

The overthrow of the Republic in 1926 and the subsequent rise of the New State under Dr Salazar led to changes in the economic relationship between Portugal and its colonies. Absolute self-sufficiency became the order of the day but no assistance was given to enable the colonies to achieve this goal. Little thought was given to investment in infrastructure. The African population was still viewed as nothing more than a pool of cheap (or even free) labour and no encouragement was given to African farmers or craftsmen. Some attempts were made at establishing planned settlements populated by Portuguese peasants. The aim was to 'transplant' peasants from Portugal to Angola. Very few Portuguese were interested in such plans and the few who went got African labourers to do all the work. Land was taken from the more productive Africans to provide farms for the settlers. Most settlement schemes were costly economic failures (Bender, 1978, p. 131).

Under Salazar's rule (1932–68) much of the emphasis in colonial policy was on integrating colonies with Portugal. Foreign investment was no longer encouraged, except in the Benguela Railway and Diamang. In the 1950s the Angolan currency, the angolar, was replaced with the Portuguese escudo. Salazar wanted to make Angola self-sufficient while at the same time turning it into a market for Portuguese goods. But only the post-Second World War coffee boom lifted Angola's economy from its normally stagnant position. One reason for stagnation was the unwillingness of Portuguese settlers to put much effort into development combined with measures that restricted African and *mestico* advancement—in 1929 laws were passed limiting *mesticos* and *assimilados* to the level of clerk within the colonial civil service. Differential pay rates were also established to reward whites more than *mesticos* or blacks. Although reforms of the forced-labour system were introduced in the 1940s and 1950s, little change resulted.

One of the main characteristics of Salazarist rule was the mystique created about the colonies. Central to this mystique was the idea of a 'pan-Lusitanian community' unified by Portuguese culture. The colonial authorities stressed equality of all the peoples of the colonies (despite the division of Africans into *assimilados* and *indigenas* and the promotion bar for *mesticos* and *assimilados*, let alone the racist attitude of Portuguese officials and settlers). The theoretical basis for the colonial policy became known as Lusotropicalism and was founded on the false premise of the 'historically unique absence of racism among the Portuguese people' (Bender, 1978, p. 3). Efforts were made to glorify the imperial past and to stress the concept of a Portuguese 'mission' in Africa. But despite all the high-flown speeches about equality and the role of culture in unifying Portugal and its colonial subjects, racism and superior attitudes still governed the relations between rulers and ruled. In 1933, Salazar's Colonial Minister, Monteiro, said that the colonial mission required 'boundless tolerance and pity for the inferiority of the blacks in the bush' (Bender, 1978, p. 7). This outlook towards Africans was accompanied by educational and class barriers which kept the races apart and ensured white control of the economy and the colonial machine. What little racial integration there was took place as a result of Portuguese downward mobility rather than African or *mestico* advancement. The whole system is summed up by Gerald Bender as follows: 'Whites in Angola rarely needed to resort to explicit or legalistic forms of racial discrimination because the virulent system of cultural or class discrimination effectively precluded Africans from participating as equals in Portuguese social, economic or political institutions' (Bender, 1978, p. 213). The whole system dominated Africans and exploited them economically without making them an integrated part of the system.

By 1950, there had been little progress economically or socially in Angola. The white settler population had only reached 78,826 and there were only about 30,000 *assimilados*. Few Africans were interested in the status and in any case the poor provision of education meant that few could actually reach the required educational level. In 1956, only 68,759 Africans attended schools, chiefly mission schools. Agricultural production grew 146 per cent between 1950 and 1964, but the demand for rural labour fell although the population was increasing.

One alternative source of employment was migrant labour in the diamond mines but this was limited in scope. However, in the 1950s and early 1960s, the African peasants came to assume a greater role than previously in coffee production and by 1964 were producing 26 per cent of the crop—many workers on coffee plantations in Cuanza Norte and Uige were migrant workers from central and southern Angola. Of the economically active population in the early 1960s, 86 per cent were small-scale (generally subsistence) farmers and the number of wage-earners was extremely small, though there were signs that peasant farmers were adapting to the demands of capitalist agricultural production and the cash-crop economy (Newitt, 1981, p. 135).

Overall, though, the Africans had no political or economic stake in Portuguese colonialism. Their armed resistance had only been ended in the second decade of the 1900s and there was considerable resentment and opposition to colonial rule and exploitation. This was to prove the breeding-ground for African nationalism, spurred on by rapid developments in other African states in the 1950s and 1960s.

African Nationalism and the Liberation Struggle

Although resistance to Portuguese rule had been consistent ever since the first attempts were made to establish a colony, it had taken the form of more or less spontaneous, defensive uprisings or scattered revolts sparked off by particular instances of Portuguese oppression, such as tax-collecting raids or attempts to force Africans to grow cash-crops for the colonial authorities. African nationalism as a coherent set of ideas and with an organized movement to promote it did not really surface in Angola until the mid-1950s.

However, in the Republican period (1910–26), the freer political atmosphere both in Portugal and Angola had led to the establishment of the first African political movements. The Partido Reformista de Angola was formed in Luanda in 1910 by assimilated *mesticos* and Africans. The reform-orientated Liga Angolana came into being in 1912. In Lisbon *assimilados* and *mesticos* established a number of organizations, 'each claiming to repesent and promote the progress, rights and interests of the masses in all five Portuguese African colonies' (Henderson,

1979, p. 162). The parties in both Luanda and Lisbon were strictly constitutional and promoted only ideas of advancing African interests in the colonies rather than decolonization: in this sense they were hardly different to the African National Congress of South Africa, which was formed in 1912 to advance African rights but not to overthrow the existing order. Among the organizations set up in Lisbon were the Liga Africana, which supported the Pan-Africanism of W. E. Du Bois, and the Partido Nacional Africano, which leaned towards the black nationalism of Marcus Garvey and defended the African personality of Portugal's colonial subjects.

One of the main aims pursued by the African groups was the abolition of forced labour. They also opposed racial discrimination and sought to better the lot of Africans as a whole and *assimilados* in particular. Although hardly revolutionary in aims or outlook, the groups did set a precedent of political organization and national/cultural identity that was to be taken up decades later with great fervour.

The establishment of the Fascist New State in 1926 brought about the end of autonomous existence for the African organizations. Although they were not banned by the new regime, they were reorganized and brought under state control. They were reduced from being nascent African political movements to the status of cultural clubs. Official control was tight and members were under close police surveillance. It was perhaps as a reaction to official control that younger members of some of the groups began to cast off the reformist attitudes and to advocate anti-colonialist ideas (Henderson, 1979, p. 163).

Portugal's non-participation in the Second World War and the continuation of the Salazarist dictatorship in the post-war period meant that, unlike British and French colonies in Africa, Angola and the other Portuguese possessions were relatively unaffected by growing anti-colonial sentiments and signs of acceptance by the colonial power that independence might be a possibility. If anything, after the war Portuguese rule became even more oppressive. However, the colonies could not be isolated totally from the rest of Africa or developments in the wider world and educated Angolans began to think more and more of the inequities of the colonial system. In the 1940s and 1950s, Angolans living in Luanda and in the areas bordering the then Belgian

Congo became more and more aware of changes in the rest of Africa and their aspirations became heightened. In 1950, a group of Luanda Africans sent a document to the United Nations criticizing Portugal's administration of Angola. Pointing out that Portugal had demonstrated 'incontestable incompetence in administration of the colony of Angola, practising acts of slavery, robbery and homicide', the document called for the government of Angola to be handed over to the indigenous population under some form of protectorate (Henderson, 1979, p. 163).

One of the precursors of the modern nationalist and revolutionary movements in Angola was the Movement of Young Intellectuals of Angola founded in the early 1940s by educated Angolans, including a future MPLA leader, Viriato da Cruz. The movement proclaimed the importance of Angolan, as opposed to Portuguese, culture. The emphasis on culture was partly due to colonial restrictions on any form of political organizations, although it was also a logical point of departure for establishing a nationalist, Angolan ideology on which to build a nationalist movement. Da Cruz was also a member of a legal *assimilado* group called the Associao do Naturais de Angola which applied for and received permission to publish a journal called *Mesagem* ('The Message'). The first issue was produced in 1948, but when the second copy appeared in 1950 the authorities decided that it was too 'alarming' and cancelled permission for publication. The journal had concentrated mainly on poetry, but much of the verse contained strong nationalist sentiment (Davidson, 1975, p. 152). A principal aim of the association was the promotion of African culture and historical traditions.

These developments in Luanda were paralleled by the establishment of associations in Lisbon (and Paris) involving educated Africans from Portugal's colonies. Among those connected with such groups in Lisbon were Agostinho Neto, Mario Andrade, Lucio Lara and José Eduardo dos Santos (all future leaders of the MPLA) from Angola, and Amilcar Cabral from Portuguese Guinea. At the initiative of these educated Africans, and with official permission, a Centre for African Studies was established in Lisbon. Mario Andrade, later to be the first President of the MPLA, said of the centre that its aim was 'to evoke the sense of belonging to an oppressed world and awaken a national consciousness' through studying African cultures (Davidson, 1975, p. 155). The Salazar regime soon suppressed the centre.

Another strand in the developing nationalist movement in Angola was the formation soon after the war of the Angolan Communist Party (ACP). The party was an offshoot of the clandestine Portuguese Communist Party (PCP). The Portuguese CP had established a cell in Luanda in 1948 and the ACP had developed from that cell. The future ideologist of the MPLA, Lucio Lara, was connected with the party. He later described it as 'much more an ideological study centre' than a proper party (Ottaway, 1981, p. 100). In Lisbon, Neto, Andrade and other politically-aware Angolans came into contact with the Portuguese communists and other radical anti-Salazarist groups, all of which had to operate in secret. Unlike the nationalists from British and French colonies, the Angolans had no legal opposition parties with which to cooperate. Basil Davidson has said that it was partly through contacts with Portuguese communists that the Angolans 'approached the ideas of Marxism, and these became a powerful strand in the developing fabric of their post-reformist and therefore revolutionary ideas' (Davidson, 1975, p. 156). Davidson added that even in the early years of Marxist development the Angolans were aware that Marxist ideas needed to be reapplied in the African context if they were to be efficacious in advancing the nationalist cause.

In the mid-1950s, a small, clandestine nationalist party, the Partido da Luta Unida dos Africanos de Angola (PLUA), was founded in Luanda. Some reports say it was founded in 1953, others say 1955 or early 1956. Whatever the exact date of its establishment, PLUA, along with the ACP, was a component of what later became the MPLA. One observer has described it as the first 'revolutionary political party' which planned to operate as a mass organization (McGowan, 1962, p. 108). PLUA issued a manifesto calling on Africans to join underground groups and unite in a broad movement for liberation, using armed struggle as a means of defeating colonialism.

In December 1956, PLUA and a number of other small Angolan political groupings (based mainly in Luanda and including *mesticos* as well as blacks) came together in Luanda to form the Movimento Popular de Libertacao de Angola (MPLA—Popular Movement for the Liberation of Angola). It was basically a front of nationalists aimed at uniting efforts in the struggle against colonialism. Initially, the MPLA was led by Mario de Andrade, who held the post of President, and Virato da Cruz, who was Secretary General. The MPLA claimed to be 'truly the first party of the masses'.

The main competition to the MPLA for nationalist support in the late 1950s came from a movement based among the Kongo people of northern Angola (and the Congo). The movement was founded in July 1956 as the Uniao das Populacoes do Norte de Angola (UPNA—Union of the People of Northern Angola). It was led by Kongo families belonging to the traditional power structure of the old Kongo kingdom. The moving spirits behind UPNA were Manuel Nekaka, Eduardo Pinock and Holden Roberto. In May 1956 they had written to the US State Department asserting that the Kongo kingdom was historically separate from Angola (Marcum, 1969, p. 62). Shortly after, an anonymous petition was sent to the UN from the former Kongo capital of São Salvador detailing the grievances of the Kongo people. UPNA was founded by the Kongo nationalists in the Belgian Congo, where Roberto and his colleagues were resident. Nekaka was President of UPNA.

In 1958, Holden Roberto represented UPNA at the All-African People's Congress in Accra. Although he was elected to the steering committee for the next congress to be held in Tunis, the African delegates in Accra felt that UPNA's strictly Kongo nationalism was a 'tribal anachronism' (Davidson, 1975, p. 200). On his return from the congress he persuaded the other UPNA leaders to drop 'Northern' from the movement's name and just call it the UPA (Uniao dos Populacoes de Angola). Holden Roberto took over the presidency from Nekaka, who was his uncle, when the movement was renamed. Roberto was violently opposed to the MPLA, which he termed 'the long arm of Russian communism'. The UPA also criticized the membership of *mesticos* in the MPLA and tried to brand it as a movement representing only the elite of Luanda: in fact it was widely supported by the Mbundu people of Angola as well as by intellectuals, *mesticos* and Africans resident in the capital. The UPA, on the other hand, was very strictly a Kongo group concerned only with the liberation of northern Angola. Despite the tribal and regional nature of his movement, Roberto was initially able to maintain a high profile in

Africa and to get support from states such as Guinea and from the National Liberation Front of Algeria, which in the late 1950s and early 1960s was fighting for independence from France. UPA members were given military training at NLF camps in Algeria. After the independence of the Congo (Léopoldville), Roberto and the UPA used the country as their base and were able to get broadcasting facilities in order to beam their message to the Kongo people in northern Angola.

In the late 1950s, the Angolan nationalist leadership within the colony was crushed through a Portuguese campaign of arrests and forced exile. Many politically-conscious young Angolans who succeeded in fleeing abroad established the breeding-ground for MPLA and UPA exile organizations. The MPLA set up shop in Paris, then Conakry, and finally Léopoldville. Mario de Andrade, Viriato da Cruz and Lucio Lara formed the nucleus of the MPLA leadership in exile. In June 1960, the MPLA received another blow when Andrade's brother, a priest, and Dr Agostinho Neto, a respected MPLA supporter, were arrested. Neto had been born the son of a Methodist pastor and had been educated at a high school in Luanda. He later worked as Secretary to the Methodist Bishop in Luanda, Ralph Dodge. In Luanda he took part in the activities of Angolan cultural groups. In the early 1950s he was awarded an American Methodist scholarship which enabled him to commence the study of medicine in Coimbra, Portugal. He was soon in trouble with the authorities because of his involvement in politics. In 1951 he was imprisoned for three months for signing the Stockholm Peace Appeal. After his release he became active in the anti-Salazar youth movement, the Movimento de Unidade Democratica-Juvenil (MUDJ). In 1952 he was arrested for taking part in a MUDJ demonstration. Neto was arrested again in 1955 and 1957 for political activities. In 1958 he passed his medical examinations and in 1959 completed a course in tropical medicine.

Neto returned to Angola in 1959, a few months after the arrest of the MPLA leader, Ilidio Machado, together with fifty-four whites, *mesticos* and Africans on charges of subversion. Neto himself was arrested on 8 June 1960 along with fifty-one other activists. Neto's arrest sparked off one of the first modern manifestations of Angolan defiance of the Portuguese colonial system. Peasants in the Catete area, Neto's birthplace, staged a protest demonstration, prompting the

Portuguese security forces to fire on the demonstrators. At least thirty Angolans were killed and 200 wounded. Following his arrest, Neto was held in Lisbon, then Cape Verde, and then Lisbon again, where he was released but only allowed restricted freedom. He was helped to escape from Portugal and in July 1962 arrived at the MPLA headquarters in Léopoldville.

During the period of Neto's detention much happened in Angola to sharpen the contradictions between growing Angolan aspirations and the intention of the Portuguese to keep the country under the yoke of colonialism. In early 1961, a dissident Christian sect, known as Maria, launched a spontaneous rising against Portuguese authority, aimed in particular at the enforced cultivation of cotton around Malanje. Property and livestock were destroyed and the European planters and officials were driven from the region. Portuguese rule was re-established at huge cost to the Angola peasants around Malanje. Hundreds, if not thousands, were killed as the Portuguese army moved in to crush the revolt (Marcum, 1969, pp. 124–57). The peasant uprising, itself a significant indication of the depth of opposition to Portuguese rule among the Angolan people, was followed swiftly by an insurrection in Luanda itself.

The Luanda events of February 1961 involved an attack by Africans from the capital's slum areas on the main prison in an attempt to release political prisoners, many of them members or supporters of the MPLA. The MPLA played a role in the attack, and the movement dates the start of the liberation struggle from the 4 February uprising. The action was totally unsuccessful, over forty Angolans being killed. Simultaneous, and equally unsuccessful, attacks were launched against two other prisons. In retaliation for the attacks white Portuguese settlers raided the African slum areas of Luanda, killing over 400 people, according to eyewitnesses (Davidson, 1975, pp. 183–4). The MPLA supporters who survived the prison attack and the subsequent revenge killings fled from Luanda to the Dembos forest area north-east of the capital, where they continued to carry out attacks on Portuguese officials and government facilities. The forest remained an area of MPLA military activity right up until the Portuguese revolution of 1974. Szajkowski has noted the establishment in February 1961 of the People's Socialist Republic of Nambuangongo in the Dembos forest, north-western Nambuangongo. Little is known about this transitory development and what little evidence is available suggests that it was established in the wake of the Luanda uprising by fleeing supporters of the MPLA. Because of a total lack of data on the incident, it is not possible to elaborate further on the Republic or its fate (Szajkowski, 1982, p. 4).

Internationally, the MPLA had a lean time in the late 1950s and up until the Luanda fighting. The movement was not represented at the Afro-Asian People's Solidarity Organization (AAPSO) meetings at the end of the decade and the first major gathering it attended was the Second All-African People's Conference in Tunis in January 1960. In Tunis, the MPLA delegation made an unsuccessful attempt to unite with Roberto's UPA. Both the Soviet Union and China were represented at the conference and it is possible that the initial contacts with the communist countries were made there; although the MPLA's links with the Portuguese Communist Party may already have facilitated communications between the Angolan nationalists and Moscow.

Shortly before the February uprising in Luanda, the then Soviet leader, Nikita Khrushchev had made an important speech at the UN in New York calling for an end to colonialism and had referred to the struggle of the people of Angola. Two days after the February events, the Soviet Communist Party newspaper *Pravda* published an article by the MPLA President, Mario de Andrade, in which he described the background and outlook of the movement and stressed the growing opposition to colonialism in Angola. On 10 March 1961, the Soviet government newspaper *Izvestiya* published a correspondent's report referring to the killings in Luanda and to the 'fire of the national liberation movement in Angola'. The following day *Pravda* published a telegram from Andrade to Khrushchev appealing for Soviet solidarity with the struggle of the Angolan people. The Soviet leader replied in June with a message of support for the MPLA (it is not clear whether the declaratory support was at that time matched with material or financial assistance).

At the time of the exchange of messages between Andrade and Khrushchev, events were taking place in Angola that brought the country's plight to greater world attention. On 15 March 1961, a major peasant uprising started in the Kongo areas of northern Angola. UPA organizers who had infiltrated into the area from the neighbouring Congo had helped to incite peasants to attack Portuguese farms, houses, plantations and government property. But the violence did not end there. Over 300 Portuguese men, women and children were killed in an orgy of disorganized destruction. Educated Africans, *assimilados* and *mesticos* were also attacked. In May, the Portuguese military launched a large-scale counter-offensive using bomber aircraft to support ground troops. Again, educated Africans were a target for attacks, this time reprisals by the Portuguese. Although the Portuguese campaign restored control for the colonial authorities, pockets of UPA and MPLA fighters continued to control small pockets of forested country in north and north-east Angola.

An attempt in 1961 to reinforce its guerrillas in the Dembos forest ended in disaster in a way that indicated the massive split within the Angolan nationalist movement. A column of twenty-one MPLA fighters had been dispatched from Congo to infiltrate through northern Angola. On its way to Dembos it was discovered by UPA forces. All twenty-one MPLA cadres were murdered by Roberto's men. Although the UPA leader denied MPLA accusations at the time, in 1963 he admitted that he had ordered the interception and annihilation of MPLA units trying to reach their comrades inside Angola (Davidson, 1975, p. 186). The UPA policy of total opposition to the MPLA was implemented in spite of an agreement reached in Monrovia in 1961 between Andrade and Roberto on cooperation.

Despite UPA opposition, the MPLA continued to mount sporadic operations against the Portuguese. In October 1961, Andrade claimed that MPLA units had occupied the region between Tombocco southwards through Nambuangongo to Ucua (in north-west Angola) for a period of five months (Marcum, 1969, p. 210). The Portuguese reaction to the events of January to May 1961 and to the guerrilla attacks was to tighten security, adopt forced resettlement as a means of combatting rural guerrilla warfare and introduce a number of reforms aimed at buying off the less militant Angolans and at convincing international public opinion that changes were taking place in Portugal's colony (Portugal had been coming under increasing pressure at the UN over her continued role in Angola, Mozambique and Guinea-Bissau). The reforms included the total abolition of forced labour, the scrapping of distinctions between *assimilados* and other Africans and improvements in the education system. The reforms were rejected totally by the exiled nationalists of the MPLA and UPA. To combat guerrilla activities in rural areas, the Portuguese set up protected villages known as *aldeamentos*. Peasants were forced to move from their villages into the *aldeamentos*, which were controlled by the military.

Following Agostinho Neto's arrival in Léopoldville in 1962, an MPLA conference was organized at which Andrade stepped down from leadership and Neto was elected President. Far from helping to strengthen the movement, this served to weaken it considerably for several years to come, as Neto's appointment and his style of leadership was bitterly opposed by the Secretary General, Viriato da Cruz. Da Cruz and his supporters were criticized by Neto and other MPLA leaders for faulty work by the MPLA secretariat and for failures in planning. As a result changes were wrought in the MPLA's structure, something else opposed by the Secretary General who, arguing from a Maoist position, accused Neto of revisionism. Da Cruz and his faction tried to set up an alternative MPLA leadership. This led to their expulsion in July 1963 by the majority group within the MPLA on the grounds that they had carried out 'acts of indiscipline tending to undermine the movement's unity and inspired by personal ambitions for power'. This was to be the first of a number of splits in the MPLA over the next decade and a half. At the time it served to destroy much of the MPLA's credibility and its standing in Africa and elsewhere.

The movement received another body-blow in September 1963 when Agostinho Neto was arrested by the Congo authorities, along with Lucio Lara. Two months later Neto and other leaders were expelled from Congo (Léopoldville). Fortunately, they were able to move to neighbouring Congo (Brazzaville), where the Messemba–Debat regime, which was sympathetic to the movement, had just taken power. In January 1964, an MPLA conference was held in Brazzaville to examine past mistakes and to chart a course for the future. The work of this conference, combined with the structural and organizational changes that had been set in motion after Neto's election, helped to prepare the MPLA to reassert itself internationally and as a viable political and military force. At the Brazzaville conference the MPLA leadership criticized itself for having failed to establish a military base in the Cabinda enclave (an attempt to do so in the early 1960s had ended in failure), for having tolerated the existence of factions, and for generally failing to provide leadership during the February 1961 events and during subsequent guerrilla operations.

One of the conclusions of the meeting was that

the installation of the movement in the interior calls [now] for the rooting into our national territory of one or several groups of Angolan nationalists linked to common principles, inspired by the same revolutionary ideas, and capable of transmitting and spreading these among the masses of the population.

The MPLA documents on the meeting stated that centralization of command and greater coordination was also necessary (MPLA documents, cited by Davidson, 1975, p. 227).

Following the meeting a more successful attempt was made to establish a bridgehead in Cabinda and military assistance began to arrive from the Soviet Union and Czechoslovakia. These developments enabled the MPLA to begin to pull itself back from the brink of fragmentation and decline. Shortly before the Brazzaville conference a well-informed and sympathetic observer of Angolan affairs, Basil Davidson, had written of the MPLA that it was 'fractured, split' and that it had 'reduced itself to a nullity. With Holden Roberto's UPA steadily gathering strength and allies, the MPLA has ceased to count' (Davidson, 1963).

Under Neto's leadership, the MPLA now set itself the task of giving action inside Angola priority over exile activities and of asserting political control over all military operations. A ten-member Steering Committee, set up after the December 1962 conference, assumed authority for day-to-day operations and the party cadre school (Escola de Quadros—set up on 28 February 1963 by Lucio Lara) set about educating and preparing cadres for taking on the roles of political commissars, whose task would be to heighten the political consciousness of peasants in operational zones inside Angola. A primary aim of the cadre school was to reinforce political control over the military. Military and security matters were to be controlled by a six-member politico-military committee consisting of six members of the Steering Committee. Prior to the organizational changes the MPLA forces (the

Exercito Popular de Libertacao de Angola—EPLA) had been uncoordinated and more or less uncontrolled by the political leadership.

Roberto's UPA also underwent a series of political crises in 1962 and 1963, although these were better camouflaged by Roberto through his personal control over all decision-making. During 1962 there were a number of defections from the UPA but Roberto made no attempt to change the autocratic nature of his leadership. Although in March 1962 Roberto formed the UPA and a number of smaller groups into the Frente Nacional de Libertacao de Angola, comprising a complicated organizational structure incorporating an Executive Committee, a National Council and a Control Commission, there was essentially no change in the make-up, nationalist aims or *de facto* command structure. Roberto was no more than theoretically accountable to any of the ruling bodies. Around the time of the FNLA's formation, Roberto announced the establishment of an Angolan government-in-exile (Governo Revolucionario e Angola no Exilio—GRAE). On 29 June 1963, GRAE was officially recognized by the Adoula government in Congo (Léopoldville). As a result of the MPLA's difficulties in 1963, an OAU mission recommended to the OAU Council of Ministers in Dakar in August 1963 that Roberto's GRAE should be recognized as the only significant liberation force in Angola. The meeting accepted the mission's report and recommendations and accorded GRAE official diplomatic recognition, leaving the then embattled MPLA out in the cold.

At the time the FNLA/GRAE seemed more unified and had a larger fighting force (which had been trained in Algeria) and access to Angola across the northern border with Congo (Léopoldville). Throughout 1963 and 1964 the FNLA/GRAE issued military communiqués reporting alleged military actions against the Portuguese, many of which were thought to be fictitious and issued for purely propaganda purposes. The FNLA forces were active, though, in preventing the MPLA units from entering northern Angola and reinforcing stranded guerrilla groups deep inside the country.

Following the MPLA's efforts at reorganization, military operations in Cabinda and attempts to reinforce the units in the Dembos area began to bear fruit. Signs of more efficient political and military operations led to an improved image in Africa and further support from outside the continent. In 1964, Neto met Che Guevara in Brazzaville and as a result the movement began to receive assistance from Cuba. During 1964, the OAU started to help the MPLA, something it had refused to do at the time of the recognition of GRAE because of the MPLA's internal problems. Successes in Cabinda in 1964 and the experience gained in the fighting there, combined with support from President Kaunda of Zambia, enabled the MPLA to open a new military front in eastern Angola in 1965. The first scouts were infiltrated into Moxico Province in 1965 and the main offensive launched the following year.

In 1964, the MPLA opened an office in Dar es Salaam and in the following year one was opened in Lusaka. The support of the Tanzanian and Zambian governments was essential for the opening-up of the Moxico front, as all the weapons used by the MPLA had to be transported across Tanzania and Zambia to the Angolan border (Burchett, 1978, p. 50). Tanzania became an important entry point for arms supplies from both China and the Soviet Union, although in the 1960s such supplies were modest in scale. The improved political and military organizations of the MPLA, better supplies of weapons, and greater support from African countries enabled the movement to increase its effectiveness and to overhaul the FNLA as the most serious threat to Portugal's colonial rule. An example of the more efficient military organization was the successful reinforcement of the isolated guerrilla group in the Dembos forest in early 1966. The period from 1966 to 1970 marked the highpoint in the MPLA's guerrilla struggle and military effectiveness.

Linked to the growing standing among African countries and the improved political and military performance was the growth of a broad yet fairly coherent ideological position. The MPLA leadership sought to imbue the struggle with a definite direction and set of objectives, in contrast to the crudely nationalist, almost tribalist, approach of the FNLA. The MPLA's Major Programme, the main policy document in the 1960s, set out ten basic aims for the movement: (1) immediate and complete independence and the 'liquidation of colonialism'; (2) national unity and the guaranteeing of equality to all ethnic groups; (3) African unity—'solidarity with all African peoples who are fighting for complete independence'; (4) the formation of a democratic regime and 'republican, democratic and secular government for Angola'; (5) economic reconstruction and the planning of production involving the abandonment of one-crop agriculture, establishment of state control over foreign trade' (6) agrarian reform and the nationalization of land belonging to 'enemies of the revolution'; (7) just political and social policies; (8) the development of instruction, culture and education; (9) a commitment to national defence; and (10) an independent and peaceful foreign policy—mutual respect for national sovereignty and territorial integrity, non-aggression and non-interference in others' affairs and peaceful coexistence (MPLA, 1962, p. 112–17).

The programme avoided a clear commitment to socialism or Marxism, but the objectives and some of the terminology foreshadowed the MPLA's commitment to Marxism–Leninism and its adherence to the principles of the non-aligned movement. A more clearly socialist approach was apparent in a statement printed in the MPLA's internal publication, *Boletin do Militante*, in February 1965. The statement said the following of the role of the worker in Angolan society and of the country's class structure:

Our experience from the evolution of human society teaches us that the worker can only obtain his demands by uniting with other workers in the daily struggle against capitalist exploitation ... Workers are all those who, deprived of the means of production (land, machines, tractors, etc.) are forced to sell their labour (physical or mental) to the capitalists in exchange for a miserable wage ... Angolan society is made up of the following groups: peasants, wage workers (i.e. workers in railways, ports, mines, factories, etc.), a small national bourgeoisie, and an insignificant intellectual class. The wage-earning class is one of the most developed and dynamic ... the peasant class is also one of its natural allies since both classes share a common enemy—capitalist, colonialist and neocolonialist exploitation ... It is not by chance that the Angolan revolution has had its beginnings in the cities ... [MPLA, 1965.]

The analysis contains within it the major elements of Marxist-Leninist thinking on anti-imperialist struggles, notably the worker–peasant alliance and the leading role of urban workers. This was combined with a strong emphasis on the importance of the armed struggle as the means of achieving independence. An MPLA document published in 1969 said that the only possible form of struggle in Angola is armed struggle . . . Armed struggle is not simply a sacrifice to those who are fighting on the side of justice . . . It is also a school . . . a means of ensuring that the people will continue that struggle in the future, after political independence, so as to be completely free: politically, economically and socially. [MPLA, 1969.]

The MPLA resurgence in the mid–1960s and its clearly socialist outlook explain the Soviet willingness, mirrored by Cuba and several Eastern European states, to extend material support to the movement. In May 1965, Neto gave an interview for *Pravda* in which he expressed his gratitude to the Soviet party, government and people for their solidarity with the MPLA and for their 'lofty internationalist sentiments' (Ignatyev, 1977, pp. 8–9). Cuban forces involved in training the Congo–Brazzaville militia also gave assistance to the MPLA in training its military cadres and some material assistance was forthcoming from China (Marcum, 1978, p. 172). Support from the OAU had followed the resumption of recognition in 1964. The MPLA also cooperated closely with the Mozambican liberation movement Frelimo and the Guinea-Bissau movement, the PAIGC, through the Conferencia das Organizacoes Nacionalistas das Colonias Portuguesas (CONCP), of which the MPLA had been a founder member.

At the time of the movement's growing ascendancy among Angolan nationalists in 1966 another challenge arose, one which was to assume far more serious dimensions following the Portuguese revolution and then again following Angola's independence. It took the form of the formation of a third liberation movement, the National Union for the Total Independence of Angola (UNITA), by a disgruntled member of the FNLA/GRAE, Jonas Savimbi. Savimbi had been the main representative of the Ovimbundu people within the FNLA and had gained the position of GRAE Foreign Minister. For a time he was a strong force within the movement. However, in 1964 he began to differ sharply with Roberto over policy matters and Savimbi used his influence over the Ovimbundu and some other non–Kongo members of the FNLA to organize a faction to challenge Roberto. Although Savimbi remained GRAE Foreign Minister, he and Roberto began to manœuvre for position in a growing power struggle. Roberto tried to outflank Savimbi by admitting the former MPLA Secretary General, Viriato da Cruz, and his supporters to the FNLA. Savimbi reacted by trying to organize opposition to Da Cruz within FNLA-related student groups and within the FNLA and GRAE itself. His position was not strong enough to oust Roberto and in July 1964, on the eve of the second meeting of OAU heads of state, Savimbi resigned from GRAE.

During his last few months in Roberto's fold, Savimbi had made contact with the MPLA but had been unable to reach agreement on joining the movement, and he is said to have visited Moscow, Prague, Budapest, Berlin and China in an attempt to elicit support. The Soviet Union and the Eastern European states rebuffed his approaches, preferring to stick with the MPLA, while China kept him at arm's length and only provided material support in the 1970s (Marcum, 1978, pp. 134 and 160). In March 1966, however, Savimbi and a group of supporters entered Moxico Province in Angola and established UNITA. Small guerrilla operations against the Portuguese were launched by the movement at the time of its formation. UNITA's ideology was essentially nationalist, although at times Savimbi flirted with Maoist ideas.

During the late 1960s, the MPLA continued to grow in stature and military effectiveness, although its main areas of operation were still limited to Moxico, Cabinda and the Dembos forest. Internationally, it was busy cementing links with other African liberation movements and with the socialist countries and the Scandinavian states. In 1969, the MPLA attended a Soviet-sponsored conference in Khartoum entitled the International Conference in Support of the Liberation Movements in the Portuguese Colonies and Southern Africa. Also present were Frelimo, the PAIGC, the African National Congress of South Africa, the Zimbabwe African People's Union of Zimbabwe, the South West African People's Organization of Namibia, and the Movement for the National Liberation of the Comoros. The MPLA's presence confirmed its status as the favoured movement of the Soviet Union in Angola and also enabled it to join in a loose alliance with the other movements, something which was later instrumental in enabling the ANC, SWAPO and ZAPU to set up training camps in Angola and SWAPO to use southern Angola as a staging-post from which to infiltrate Namibia.

One problem that did affect the MPLA in the late 1960s and that was later to split the party was that of running military and political affairs from scattered exile offices (chiefly Brazzaville and Dar es Salaam) and having three widely dispersed fronts within Angola (Cabinda, the eastern front based on Moxico, and the Dembos area). This led in 1970 to the formation of a Political and Military Coordinating Committee, which became responsible for organizational matters. It initially consisted of Neto, Iko Carreira, Daniel Chipenda, Lucio Lara and 'Spartacus' Floribert Monimambu. The conflicts that developed within the MPLA in the early 1970s divided the committee and for a time rendered the movement ineffective.

But prior to the factional struggle things appeared to go smoothly and the movement continued to develop its basically Marxist ideology. A conference was held at Dolisie in Congo–Brazzaville in February 1968 at which it was decided that the MPLA would be converted into a revolutionary party once sufficient cadres had been educated; it was also decided that at some time in the future the movement would be transformed into a 'vanguard party' (Marcum, 1968, p. 199). Shortly before the February conference Neto had disclosed that the MPLA was moving its headquarters into Angolan territory.

The decision to create a vanguard party was of vital importance to the MPLA, according to Daniel Chipenda, the main organizer of the eastern guerrilla front, during an interview in 1968. He said such a party would 'provide the direction and general orientation of our people'. Referring to the MPLA's relations with the Soviet Union and China and the movement's general ideological stance, Chipenda said:

When people say the ideology of the MPLA is Moscow-orientated . . . they not only help the imperialists confuse things, they are simply wrong. The divisions which have emerged within the Angolan liberation struggle have not come about because of the split between China and Russia . . . in 1961 the MPLA was supported by both China and Russia. The Chinese continued to support the MPLA in 1962 . . . when we expelled our General Secretary, Viriato da Cruz . . . It was this man who went to China and spread his poison that the MPLA was pro-Russian, anti-Chinese and so on. This is when our difficulties with the Chinese began . . . The MPLA does not blindly follow any socialist country, either the Soviet Union or China. It is the MPLA, the Angolan people, who decide on and organise everything . . . [Barnett & Harvey, 1972, pp. 257–9.]

Relations with China had been poor in the late 1960s, particularly following the establishment of UNITA, which gained pride of place in Chinese accounts of the fighting in Angola. However, in the early 1970s the MPLA began to be mentioned favourably once more and in July 1971 Neto visited Peking. Chipenda, to a greater extent than other MPLA leaders, got on well with the Chinese, and following his split from the MPLA he looked to the Chinese for material support (Klinghoffer,1980, p. 149).

By 1972, the leadership of the MPLA was following a clearly Marxist line, the formation of a vanguard party being a step towards the creation of a fully-fledged Marxist–Leninist party. But when questioned in public on ideological matters, MPLA leaders played down the Marxist aspect of the movement's policies, perhaps in the hopes of maintaining a non-aligned image and preventing Western hostility, even though NATO states such as the United States, Britain and West Germany were materially supporting the Portuguese war through NATO's military structures. In an interview with the *Sunday News* of Tanzania in August 1972, Neto said of the MPLA's ideology:

... we consider that in our movement it is not possible at this stage to have this kind of classification (socialist or communist). For a single party it is possible but when a movement consists of people who are different politically and ideologically it is not possible to say that this is, for example, a communist movement. Not all our people are communists or socialists ... Our movement has a programme not only for the present stage but also for after independence ... After independence it will be necessary to organise a popular state. By popular I mean democratic ... About the organisation of the economy, we say that the Angolan people must have the riches of our country, we must give fair wages to avoid exploitation of the workers ... This is what is normally called the socialist way. It is socialist because we don't intend to allow either Angolans or foreigners to exploit others in the country ... We think that ideologically we follow not necessarily the communist or Marxist line but we follow the socialist line, with justice for everyone. [De Braganca & Wallerstein, Vol. II, 1982, p. 107.]

Between 1972 and 1974, the MPLA had little time to reflect on the exact nature of its ideology because of an internal conflict which posed an even greater threat to the movement's existence than had the earlier Neto–Da Cruz split.

The conflict, between MPLA President Agostinho Neto, and the leader of the eastern front and Vice-Chairman of the movement, Daniel Chipenda, seems to have developed as a result of shortcomings in communications and logistics between the movement's leadership and the operational areas, military setbacks and a clash of personalities and styles between Neto and Chipenda.

Calls for improved communications between the leadership and the guerrilla fronts had begun to be voiced in 1971. At a meeting in Angola in mid-year, the MPLA Steering Committee decided to enlarge itself and the Political–Military Coordination Committee prior to organizing a national congress. However, these moves did nothing to calm the agitation of commanders at the front who felt that military reverses suffered during Portuguese offensives since 1968 could have been avoided through better organization of support and supplies by the leadership and through a policy of greater mobility. Hard-hitting Portuguese offensives in 1972 and 1973, during which napalm and defoliants were used against the MPLA, increased the dissatisfaction of the guerrillas, whose grievances were taken up by Chipenda. Chipenda himself appears to have disagreed with Neto's style of leadership, particularly his absence from Angola for extended periods, despite an MPLA policy of maintaining a high leadership profile in operational areas.

Chipenda and his supporters on the eastern front posed a serious threat to Neto's leadership and, at one stage during the split, reportedly succeeded in persuading the Soviet Union to support their faction rather than Neto's (Legum, 1975/6, p. A5; Burchett, 1978, p. 75; Anglin & Shaw, 1979, p. 317). At one stage, the Soviet Union suspended all aid to the MPLA because of doubts about the future of the movement. Worried about the effects of the MPLA divisions in the fight against Portuguese colonialism, Presidents Nyerere and Kaunda arranged talks between Neto and Chipenda. An attempt was made to hold an MPLA congress in Lusaka, but Neto and his supporters walked out, leaving a 'rump' of Chipenda followers who deposed Neto and elected Chipenda as President. The result of the congress went unrecognized. An MPLA reconciliation meeting was held in Brazzaville in September 1974. At the meeting it was agreed that Neto would remain in charge and that Chipenda and Mario Andrade would be

Vice Presidents. The agreement reached in Brazzaville did not last and the following month Chipenda opened an office in Kinshasa. As a result he was expelled from the movement in December 1974.

Prior to the conclusion of the Neto–Chipenda conflict, a far more important event had taken place—the Portuguese revolution of 25 April 1974. This not only brought about a complete change in the political regime in Portugal, it also offered the opportunity for the liberation movements in the colonies to press their case for independence and an end to the wars with Portugal. It was, after all, Portugal's colonial wars that had prompted the Armed Forces Movement to overthrow the Caetano regime in Portugal. In the aftermath of the military take-over it was unclear exactly what the new rulers had in mind for the colonies. One leader, General Spinola, favoured some form of federation, while younger, more radical officers supported the liberation movements' calls for total independence. Finally, in July 1974, Spinola announced that the new regime had conceded the right of the African territories to independence. The announcement came after a white backlash in Luanda against the revolution and African calls for independence. Portuguese troops had to be used to end white-settler attacks on defenceless African slum-dwellers in Luanda. The Portuguese coup was carried out by a movement made up of disillusioned captains, majors and colonels, many of whom had fought in the regime's African wars. The death toll in the colonial conflicts had reached 11,000 dead and 30,000 wounded on the Portuguese side. The Portuguese economy was suffering as a result of the expenditure on military campaigns: in the years preceding the revolution the trade deficit had reached $400 million per annum and inflation was around 23 per cent. In addition many hundreds of thousands of Portuguese had left the country to avoid conscription or to seek a better standard of living elsewhere. President Caetano had become more and more isolated and had abandoned very cautious moves towards reform in favour of repression and the creation of a police state (Marcum,1978, p. 241).

In the immediate aftermath of the coup, General Spinola's federal ideas for the colonies threatened more conflict in Africa, but these ideas were not implemented because of the more radical views of the majority of members of the Armed Forces' Movement. The post-

Spinola policy of the new order in Portugal led to the Portuguese government taking an active role in trying to bring together the three liberation movements in Angola to prevent a civil war. Thus the meetings first at Mombasa, Kenya, and then at Alvor, Portugal, between the MPLA, FNLA and UNITA were held with extensive Portuguese cooperation and encouragement. However, the attempts at mediation were doomed to failure.

In the wake of the coup there was still a massive split in the nationalist movement in Angola. MPLA–FNLA hostility had continued throughout the liberation struggle and there was a similar hostility between the two oldest movements and Jonas Savimbi's UNITA. Frequent attempts had been made during the years preceding the 1974 coup to bring the MPLA and the FNLA together, but these had failed despite strong efforts by Presidents Nyerere of Tanzania, Kaunda of Zambia, Ngouabi of Congo and, at times, Mobutu of Zaïre. Thus in 1974, far from there being a united nationalist stand on independence and the formation of an Angolan government, the three movements were ready to compete, on the battlefield if necessary, to assume control of the country.

The divisions were made plain when in June 1974, before a definitive Portuguese statement on independence, UNITA arranged contacts with the military authorites in Angola and on 14 June agreed on a suspension of hostilities. The FNLA under Roberto signed a ceasefire on 12 October, once it was clear that independence was to be granted and once Roberto felt that he had improved his chances of seizing power sufficiently to negotiate with the Portuguese. The MPLA, in the midst of the Neto–Chipenda conflict, signed a ceasefire accord on 21 October.

The differences between the three movements, which had led to fighting between them during the war against the Portuguese, resulted in extensive and political manœuvring in late 1974 and 1975. Within a month of the Lisbon coup the FNLA had received 450 tons of weapons and 125 military instructors from the Chinese, which they were to use in a bid to gain military supremacy, particularly in northern Angola. Roberto's forces also received military assistance from Romania. Soon after this, the MPLA began to receive arms supplies and other support from the Soviet Union once more, the Soviet leadership having decided either that the MPLA had healed its internal wounds or that the situation in Angola was such that aid had to be resumed regardless of the movement's apparent disunity. The MPLA received aid from Eastern European states and Cuba as well as from the Soviet Union, while the FNLA's Chinese and Romanian aid was complemented with extensive military help from President Mobutu of Zaïre and, according to a former CIA operative in Angola, growing amounts of American funding (Stockwell, 1978, p. 67).

FNLA and UNITA political activities after April were concerned with trying to exclude the MPLA from any independence deal with the Portuguese. In July 1974, representatives of both movements, along with Neto and Chipenda of the MPLA, had agreed at a meeting at Bukavu in Zaïre to form a joint front to negotiate with the Portuguese, but in September, Roberto, Chipenda and President Mobutu held a meeting at Sal in Cape Verde with General Spinola to discuss plans for independence that would exclude the MPLA. However, under pressure from the OAU and a number of African heads of state, the three liberation movements agreed to hold joint talks with the military authorities of Portugal, as a result of which the Alvor agreement on independence and a coalition government was signed on 15 January 1975. The plan was that a transitional coalition government involving all three groups would be formed prior to independence on 11 November 1975. The transitional government took office on 31 January. It was divided equally between the three movements and was headed by a Presidential Council consisting of Lopo do Nascimento (MPLA), Johnny Eduardo Pinock (FNLA), and José N'Dele (UNITA). Unfortunately, the government never really operated as a united body and its role was a very minor one as the animosity between its elements assumed more importance than African attempts to maintain the coalition.

Fighting broke out in Luanda in February between the MPLA and Daniel Chipenda's followers and was soon followed by a virtual invasion of northern Angola by FNLA forces supported by units of the Zaïrean army. Roberto's aim was to gain control of the north of the country and to expel the MPLA from its traditional stronghold in the capital before independence was formalized. The FNLA complemented this military strategy with a political offensive which involved the purchase of newspapers and other media outlets in Luanda. Neto charged that Angola was being subjected to a 'silent invasion from Zaïre, backed by the United States and South Africa' (*Africa Research Bulletin*, 1–30 April 1975). In March, the conflict escalated as Roberto strengthened his forces in their push for Luanda—at one stage he had nearly 1,500 Zaïrean regulars supporting his advance. The MPLA forces were very much on the defensive, though they were stockpiling Soviet- and Yugoslav-supplied arms ready to resist the FNLA.

In April, the South Africans began to get more closely involved. The *Star* newspaper of Johannesburg reported on 12 April that South African troops had been involved in an exchange of fire with Angolan forces (MPLA units) across the Namibian border. The following month, Chipenda went to Windhoek for talks on South African support (Savimbi and Roberto followed his example in subsequent months by arranging for South African military help in their fight against the MPLA.) The South African threat was so obvious that the Interior Minister of the transitional government, N'Gola Kabangu of the FNLA, was cited by the same South African newspaper as having said that the Pretoria government was making extensive preparations to take advantage of internal strife in Angola to annex Cunene Province to Namibia.

Fighting between the MPLA and UNITA in southern Angola started in May when Savimbi clearly plumped for the FNLA in the growing civil war. By early June, fighting was widespread in both the north and south of the country, with particularly heavy clashes in northern, eastern and Cabinda districts. Zaïrean troops were involved in the clashes. In yet another attempt to bring the opposing groups together and prevent open war, the OAU persuaded Neto, Roberto and Savimbi to attend a series of meetings in Kenya. These culminated in the signing of the Nakuru agreement on 21 June. The agreement was essentially a reaffirmation of the Alvor accord. The three signatories pledged their adherence to the transitional government and agreed to stop fighting.

As with Alvor, Nakuru was a failure and within two days of the signing fighting was under way in Luanda. By mid-July, MPLA forces had driven the FNLA and UNITA from the capital, although a major offensive by Roberto, again with Zaïrean support, threatened the

MPLA's positions in the north and around the capital. The fighting was growing in intensity and each side was arming itself more and more heavily. Increasing Soviet aid was being supplied to the MPLA, most of it via the Congo (Somerville, March 1984, p. 75), while the FNLA and UNITA were receiving extensive American financial and military help.

As the conflict intensified, external involvement increased. Zaïre was already intervening directly through the provision of troops but in May Cuba agreed to send military advisers to help the MPLA and in July South African forces became directly involved in clashes with MPLA units inside Angola, although the major South African offensive did not begin until 23 October (Somerville, winter 1984, pp. 295–6). It is hard to pinpoint the exact date of arrival of the first Cuban troops, but military advisers are thought to have arrived in May 1975, soon after a meeting in Brazzaville between Agostinho Neto and a Cuban delegation. The Cubans began training MPLA cadres at military bases inside Angola and became involved in clashes with the FNLA in northern Angola and UNITA in the south.

South African troops started operating in Angola in July and by mid-August there were 1,000 regular troops stationed at the Ruacana dam and at Caleque in southern Angola (Wolfers & Bergerol, 1982, p. 12; Hallet, 1978, pp. 347–86). In September, the South Africans captured the town of N'Giva and then began to give open assistance to both UNITA and the FNLA. On 23 October a major South African offensive was launched, in conjunction with UNITA, which was only stopped short of Luanda by a major MPLA counter-offensive supported by the Cubans.

The FNLA–Zaïrean offensive in northern Angola posed an equally dangerous threat to the MPLA as the South African–UNITA one in the south. On 17 September, the FNLA had captured Caxito and were advancing on Luanda. Roberto was determined to be in control of the capital on 11 November, the day set for independence. But the final push against the MPLA was a disaster for the FNLA forces—the MPLA forces used Soviet 122mm. rockets and artillery to smash the FNLA advance and to end Roberto's hopes of grabbing power in time for independence.

Immediately prior to the independence date the MPLA was in a beleagured position, with the South African forces advancing steadily towards the capital and the FNLA forces only just held off in the north. It was in this situation that a large airlift of Cuban troops began on 7 November; by independence day there were said to be 2,800 Cuban combat troops in Angola (Marquez, 1977, p. 128; Stockwell, 1978, pp. 231–2). The arrival of the Cuban troops, combined with massive arms shipments from the Soviet Union, turned the tide of the war. By January 1976, the FNLA had been smashed in northern Angola and by February the South Africans had withdrawn across the border into Namibia, leaving Savimbi's UNITA to fight a guerrilla war against the MPLA government. In Cabinda the MPLA was in control, although it was forced to fight periodically against Zaïrean-backed secessionists of the Front for the Liberation of Cabinda (FLEC).

the country but with the infrastructure of Angola shattered by the fighting and with FNLA guerrillas active in the north, UNITA preparing for a long, drawn-out insurgency campaign in the south and FLEC putting its spanner in the works in Cabinda. The MPLA government was supported by an estimated 10,000–12,000 Cuban troops and by huge supplies of arms from the Soviet Union ($200m. worth by January 1976, including MiG-21 aircraft, T-34 and T-54 tanks, SAM-7 anti-aircraft missile batteries and 122mm. rocket launchers).

The infrastructure of the country was not the only thing that had been damaged by the civil war and the preceding liberation war. The MPLA had lost large numbers of leading cadres through both the fighting and the results of the Chipenda split and the factionalism of a radical leftist group known as Active Revolt, led by Mario de Andrade. This meant that the MPLA had to take up the reins of government and the task of reconstructing the economy and building an independent nation when its own party organization was depleted, short of experienced cadres and barely recovered from the effects of factional conflict.

Independence: the Struggle for Survival and Socialism

The assumption of power by the MPLA on 11 November, in the midst of a civil war and extensive foreign intervention, was the culmination of nearly two decades of political and military efforts aimed at ending the colonial system and replacing it with an indigenous government basing its policies on socialism. As already noted, Neto had steered clear of a firm commitment to Marxist–Leninist policies during the years preceding the Portuguese coup. However, the movement was clearly moving in the direction of a strong commitment to development on Marxist–Leninist lines and had announced its intention of forming a vanguard party based on the workers and peasants—a course of action in accordance with orthodox Soviet thinking on socialist development in Africa (Somerville, winter 1984, pp. 293–4 and 300). Neto and the MPLA were far from being puppets or clients of the Soviet Union, however (despite frequent declarations that this was the case by leaders of Western governments and the Western media). Although the Soviet Union had supplied large quantities of arms and logistical aid during the vital period of the war against the FNLA and UNITA and had been a supporter of the MPLA since the late 1950s, the Angolan movement had received support from a wide variety of other sources, including China, Yugoslavia and the Scandinavian countries, and was committed to a foreign policy based on non-alignment.

Speaking at the independence celebrations in Luanda, Neto set out the general aims of the MPLA government:

the People's Republic of Angola will, under the guidance of the MPLA, gradually advance towards a people's democracy state, with an alliance between workers and peasants as its nucleus ... Having achieved independence, the MPLA and the Angolan people wish to express their heartfelt gratitude for the help rendered by all the friendly peoples and countries to our heroic national liberation struggle. Our gratitude goes to all the African peoples and countries which remained on our side, to the socialist countries, to the Portuguese revolutionary forces, and to the progressive organisations and governments of Western countries which understood and supported the Angolan people's struggle ... The foreign policy of the People's republic of Angola, based on the principle of total independence observed by the MPLA from the outset, will be one of non-alignment. [Lisbon radio, 11 November 1975.]

Neto added that 'the organs of the state will be under the supreme guidance of the MPLA, and the primacy of the movement's structures over those of the State will be ensured'. On economic issues, he promised that private enterprises, either domestic or foreign, would be protected if they benefited the country.

The government formed by the MPLA after independence was led by Neto as President, with Lopo do Nascimento as Prime Minister and Nito Alves as Minister of the Interior. Nascimento had been based on the northern Angolan front during the war and had been responsible for the MPLA Information and Propaganda Department. Alves had been a political officer on the northern front and had been involved in the attempts to provide assistance for the MPLA guerrillas isolated in the Dembos forest for much of the liberaton war. Iko Carreira, a veteran *mestico* MPLA militant and guerrilla leader, was Minister of Defence. The Planning and Finance Minister, Carlos Rocha, was also a *mestico*.

The tasks facing the MPLA government were immense. The country's economy was in tatters, as a result of the liberation and civil wars, and there was a desperate shortage of skilled and managerial manpower, resulting from the mass exodus of Portuguese settlers, who had monopolized all such skills during the colonial period. The destruction of bridges, roads and transport vehicles meant that many areas were cut off from food and other essential supplies, while the departure of the Portuguese had wrecked the distribution system, the wholesale and retail sectors being Portuguese preserves under colonialism.

The economic problems were compounded by the continuing guerrilla wars in the areas of Cabinda (FLEC), Zaïre Province (FNLA) and Moxico and parts of the southern and central districts (UNITA). Refugees and displaced persons complicated the economic and military situations. Many thousands of refugees who had fled to neighbouring Zaïre and Zambia began to return after independence and put a great strain on an already stretched administrative system.

In the midst of all the problems, the MPLA wanted to start its programme of socialist transformation. It had plans for the nationalization of vital industries, state control of foreign trade and greater control over foreign companies operating in Angola. However, before such programmes could be implemented the priority had to be economic reconstruction. With this in mind, the Neto government introduced a strict austerity programme and a productivity drive. In the first years of the new regime, the austerity measures and the

MPLA's increasingly Marxist stance led to conflicts between the administration and independent workers' groups and left-wing factions that had grown up, particularly in Luanda, towards the end of the liberation war and during the civil war.

Since security was a major problem for the MPLA as a result of the guerrilla conflicts in areas of the country, and because of the existence of a plethora of small armed groups, notably in the *musseques* (sand-slums) of the capital, among the first acts of the MPLA was the formation in September 1975 in liberated areas of the People's Defence Organization (ODP). This was designed to unite and bring under party control many of the self-defence groups formed by MPLA supporters in the aftermath of the white backlash that followed the Portuguese revolution. In November 1975, the MPLA government established the Angolan Directorate of Information and Security (DISA), basically the MPLA secret police. The task assigned to DISA was to combat anti-MPLA and 'anti-state' activities. At the neighbourhood or village level the MPLA set up the Department for the Organization of the Masses, whose work was to disseminate and explain MPLA policies. Mass organizations such as the Union of Angolan Workers (UNTA), MPLA-Youth (JMPLA) and the Organization of Angolan Women were also charged with 'agitprop' activities.

In February 1976, various ultra-left groups, led by the Active Revolt faction of the MPLA and by the Organization of Angolan Communists (a radical, left-wing group which had been formed in the *musseques*), demonstrated against the austerity measures and protested that a 'new bourgeoisie' was growing up in the form of government officials and civil servants. A focus for the protest was the shutting-down by the government of a radio programme which had strongly criticized the government and had called for rule by workers and peasants. Government reaction to the demonstration and the growing dissident voice of the leftists was to use DISA to crack down on dissent and to launch an offensive against Active Revolt and the Organization of Angolan Communists (OCA). In March 1976, Interior Minister Nito Alves, who had just returned from a visit to Moscow to attend the Congress of the CPSU, called on the People's Commissions (MPLA local groups which played a role in the security and agitprop fields) to exercise vigilance, particularly in the cases of Active Revolt and OCA members. As part of the anti-leftist campaign, Joaquim Pinto de Andrade of Active Revolt was detained along with other dissident organizers.

The People's Commissions came to play an important role in spreading MPLA control to the grassroots of the Angolan population. Although nominally independent of the party, they were bodies elected by the population on a neighbourhood basis from a list of MPLA candidates. This meant that the Commissions consisted of MPLA-approved cadres. The commissions were set up under Article 3 of the Constitution, which laid down 'that the masses shall be guaranteed broad, effective participation in the exercise of political power' (ACR, 1976–7, p. B452). Because of the security situation in the country, the only commissions elected during 1976 were those in Luanda. The plenum of MPLA Central Committee, held from 23 to 29 October, decreed that elections for the commissions should be held in the rest of the country.

In May 1976, the MPLA decided it was time to unify the workers' groups. Up until that time small workers' commissions had played the major role in organizing workers in Angolan industry. The commissions had been set up by generally pro-MPLA militants towards the end of the liberation war, but in the post-independence period they not only organized workers to support the MPLA but also played some role in the opposition protests against austerity measures. To unify the workers and bring them under MPLA control, the MPLA trade-union body, UNTA, took over responsibility for the commissions which effectively became part of the UNTA organization. In order to step up the productivity and reconstruction drive, UNTA took on the task of sending officials to factories to call for discipline, hard work and vigilance against economic sabotage. A strike by workers at a sugar factory in June was termed sabotage by the government and troops were sent to occupy the factory.

The first plenary meeting of the MPLA Central Committee took place in Luanda in late October. One of its principal decisions was the official adoption of Marxism–Leninism. A declaration by the party's Political Bureau stated, 'to defend and advance the Revolution, we must analyse and characterise the different phases and stages of our struggle, and clearly define socialism as the highest aim of our Revolution. We must arm all militants with the doctrine of scientific socialism—Marxism–Leninism' (MPLA, 1976, p. 4). The meeting also resolved to amend the constitution, to strengthen the Council of the Revolution and eventually to establish a People's Assembly. The Council of the Revolution was to act as 'the supreme organ of state power' until the setting-up of the People's Assembly. The Council was composed of the MPLA Central Committee, the Minister of Defence, Chief of the General Staff of FAPLA, the FAPLA National Political Commissar, three members of the government who were not members of the MPLA CC but who would be appointed by the MPLA Political Bureau, provincial commissars appointed by the President and the commanders and political commissars of the country's military regions. The Council had the job of implementing and guiding the domestic and foreign policies laid down by the MPLA CC. The Central Committee plenum vowed to move towards the building of socialism, although it stated very clearly that the transition could only be started following the success of national reconstruction.

The plenum also came out strongly against factionalism, a problem that had plagued the MPLA since birth. The particular problem in October 1976 was the growth of a strong group within the party centred around the Interior Minister, Nito Alves. Alves had been instrumental in crushing the Active Revolt faction and other dissident leftist groups, but following their demise had taken up many of their slogans, notably dissatisfaction with austerity, complaints about allegedly 'bourgeois' civil servants and, something the leftists had not taken up, the role of *mesticos* and whites within the MPLA and the government. Alves had strong support within the Luanda sections of the party and had allies in the armed forces, the trade unions and even the ruling government organs. His bid for greater power within the party was checked at the October plenum, but he continued to voice opposition to government and MPLA policies and to what he and his supporters considered the disproportionate number of *mesticos* in MPLA and government bodies.

Another problem at the time of the plenum was the growth of UNITA guerrilla operations in south–central Angola. With strong South African logistical support and with the use of rear bases in Namibia, Savimbi's movement launched attacks against economic and other government installations, notably the Benguela Railway. UNITA had some residual support among the Ovimbundu people of the central highlands and this was exploited to the full by Savimbi in his attempt to carve out a power base from which to fight the MPLA. South African support had kept UNITA going following its defeat in the civil war, and evidence of a continuing South African role in sponsoring and actively assisting the rebel movement came with the capture of a South African soldier during an FAPLA offensive against guerrillas in Cuando Cubango Province in August 1976. Members of SWAPO, allowed by the MPLA to use southern Angola as a base for operations in Namibia, said that UNITA forces were being trained by the South African Defence Force (SADF) at Grootfontein in Namibia.

In late 1976 and early 1977, MPLA activities were concentrated on entrenching the party's hold on power and on economic reconstruction. Aid for reconstruction was being received from the Soviet Union, Cuba and a number of Eastern European states. In May 1976, Premier do Nascimento had visited Moscow and signed a number of economic, cultural and scientific agreements, and in October President Neto paid an official visit to the Soviet Union. The discussions he held there resulted in the signing, by Neto and Soviet leader Leonid Brezhnev, of a Treaty of Friendship and Cooperation. The treaty included clauses dealing with economic and military relations and assistance from the Soviet Union. Agreements were also concluded with Cuba and Eastern European states in 1976, as a result of which 2,500 Cuban civilian advisers joined the 19,000 Cuban troops in Angola (for further details of assistance to Angola from the socialist countries, see the foreign relations section).

The first major threat to the Neto government came in May 1977 when Nito Alves and his supporters staged a coup attempt with the support of some sections of the armed forces. Alves had been removed as Minister of the Interior in October 1976 but had retained his position on the Central Committee and from there had continued his campaign of criticism against party policy and had built up a strong following.

The coup attempt took place against the background of food shortages, the collapse of the distribution system, and resentment among poor blacks in Luanda's slums of the role of *mesticos* in the government civil service. On 21 May, six days before the rebellion, Neto had told an

MPLA rally in Luanda that 'the problem of food supplies is serious. There is no cassava, no potatoes, no groundnuts, no palm oil. There is nothing on the market . . . this situation pleases no one' (ACR,1977–8, pp. B496–7). In this situation it was not surprising that the slum-dwellers came to resent the actions and authority of those responsible for implementing the MPLA austerity policy, the new layer of technocrats and administrators who had taken the place of the Portuguese civil servants. That many of the more educated and therefore more valuable civil servants and officials were *mesticos* did not help. It was among the discontented *musseque*-dwellers that Alves had much support for his attacks on the austerity programme and on the role of 'bourgeois' *mesticos* within both the MPLA and the government. The Alves line against the *mesticos* and bourgeois elements was in direct conflict with the MPLA policy of racial unity and of cooperation between the worker–peasant alliance and patriotic petit-bourgeois groups.

The attempted coup took place on 27 May, when dissident members of the armed forces tried to release Alves from prison; he had been arrested a few days previously following his removal from the Central Committee at a CC meeting on 20 May. José Van Dunen, FAPLA political commissar for southern Angola, had been removed from the CC along with Alves for factionalism. The coup was led by Ernesto Gomes da Silva (also known as Commander Bakalof), the national political commissar of FAPLA. The rebels seized the prison containing Alves and Van Dunen and then captured the main Luanda radio station and arrested a number of senior government ministers and MPLA leaders. The captives were killed prior to the crushing of the coup by loyal members of FAPLA (Cuban troops were also said to have actively supported Neto). Among those killed by the rebels were Major Saidy Vieira Das Mingas, the Minister of Finance and a member of both the MPLA Central Committee and the Council of the Revolution; Commander Dangereux (Paulo da Silva Mungongo), a member of the Central Committee, the Council of the Revolution and the FAPLA General Staff; Commander Bula Matadi (José Manuel Paiva), a member of the Council of the Revolution and Deputy Chief of Staff of FAPLA; Helder Ferreira Neto, a member of DISA; and Antonio Garcia Neto, Director of the International Cooperation section of the Ministry of Foreign Affairs.

Although Alves had potentially strong support, the plot was ill prepared and was easily put down by loyalist troops. The radio station and other buildings seized by the rebels were recaptured on the same day. Although it took several months for all the leaders of the coup to be rounded up, the reverberations were limited in the sense of the threat to the regime. Where the consequences were really felt was in the MPLA itself. A wide-ranging purge of suspected Alves supporters was carried out in MPLA organs and the People's Commissions. On 6 June, a special meeting of the MPLA CC suspended the party executive commissions in Luanda, Benguela and Malanje and the following day the Minister of Internal Trade, David Aires Machado, was dismissed— he was later arrested on the grounds that he had supported the coup attempt. The neighbourhood People's Commissions in Luanda were viewed by the Neto leadership as having been the breeding-grounds for anti-government feeling and centres of support for Alves; as a result, the party dismissed the leaders of seven commissions in Luanda. Provincial commissioners in a number of provinces were thought to have been in sympathy with the coup—the commissioners for Luanda, Benguela, Zaïre, Cuanza Norte, Cuanza Sul, Cuando Cubango and Malanje were all dismissed and replaced by Neto loyalists. The Secretary General of the trade-union body UNTA, Aristides Van Dunem, was also suspected of complicity. Suspicions about loyalty and efficiency led the MPLA leadership to form a National Committee for Restructuring UNTA.

The death of the Finance Minister and the dismissal of the Internal Trade Minister led to a Cabinet reshuffle with Premier Lopo do Nascimento taking over the portfolio of Internal Trade. Nascimento soon got to grips with the food problems, setting state-controlled prices for meat, milk, rice, sugar, flour and soap. A National Supplies Commission was established to control food resources.

Shortly after the coup, Western commentators began to suggest that Alves had received covert support for his attempt from the Soviet Union and other socialist states, basing their theories on Alves's attendance at the CPSU Congress in 1976 and his praise for the Soviet Union in speeches delivered on his return to Angola (Birmingham, 1978, p. 563; Klinghoffer 1980, p. 131; Marcum, 1979, p. 195). However, there is no evidence to suggest that Alves approached the Soviet

Union for assistance or at least acquiescence and it is unlikely that given Alves's views on race and his criticism of the MPLA programme of reconstruction, which the Soviet Union was assisting, the Soviet Union would have risked its good relations with Angola by supporting a poorly planned coup attempt (Somerville, winter 1984, pp. 298–300).

After the shake-up brought about by the coup, the MPLA demonstrated its continuing control of the country and its intention to go ahead with national reconstruction and then socialist transformation at the First Ordinary Congress of the MPLA, held in Luanda on 4–10 December 1977. The Congress was a landmark in the MPLA's development as a Marxist–Leninist party. The party renamed itself the MPLA-Workers' Party and stated its intention of transforming itself into a vanguard party. Congress documents emphasized that for the MPLA, the 'only road to development is socialism'. The party leadership stressed the importance of class struggle but also reaffirmed that the worker–peasant alliance, the basis for the party and for socialist development in Angola, would continue to cooperate with the petit bourgeois elements that supported MPLA policies. The Central Committee's report to the Congress set the party's main role and tasks as being the following:

The laying down of People's Democracy and Socialism as goals to be attained implies qualitative leaps in the politico–ideological and organisational sphere, so that the vanguard organisation may play its full role in the leadership of society. Indeed the class content of People's Democracy and Socialism and the consequent sharpening of class struggle internally and internationally requires that the working class as the leading force has an instrument capable of carrying out that task. That instrument, organised and structured in accordance with Marxist–Leninist principles, which will lead the revolutionary classes, will be the Vanguard Party of the Working Class. [MPLA,1977, p. 10.]

The Congress elected a fifty-four-member Central Committee, over half of them from FAPLA or the security forces, and an eleven-member (previously nine-member) Political Bureau. A party Control Commission was established and a Corrective Movement launched to purge the party of unsuitable members. The Central Committee report to the Congress emphasized in particular the need to combat factionalism and to prevent 'deviations from the revolutionary line' which would weaken the vanguard organization.

In early 1978, as the party began to exert greater control over society in the wake of the Congress, the Catholic Church began to object strongly to what it termed infringements of religious freedom by the MPLA government. The MPLA reacted by saying that the church's complaints were an 'attempt to put the honesty of the revolutionary process in question'. The ideology of the MPLA, with its open and firm commitment to materialistic Marxism–Leninism, was obviously in conflict with the teachings and position of the established churches in Angola, particularly the Catholic Church. The Neto leadership was unhappy about the power, in social terms, of the Catholic Church and the relatively privileged position it had enjoyed prior to the overthrow of colonialism. The new government was also suspicious of any large, independent organization that operated without MPLA control. Some sort of conflict was therefore inevitable between the church and party. In fact, the conflict has been limited in scale, partly because there is evidence that many MPLA members and supporters are Christians (there were certainly priests involved in MPLA work during the liberation war), but also because atheistic propaganda and efforts to combat the influence of religious groups come low on the list of government priorities at a time when defeating UNITA, fending off South African aggression, reconstructing the economy and rebuilding the party structure are the main tasks. One should also remember that the MPLA received moral support and possibly even financial support during the liberation struggle from progressive world religious bodies (such as the World Council of Churches) and so is aware that not all aspects of religion and the work of the churches stand in contradiction to its basic aims.

The MPLA government is unlikely to take an extreme line towards religion, as the Albanians have, for example, but it is more inclined towards allowing continued operations of religious organizations as long as these operations are limited to narrowly religious aspects of life. The MPLA has made it abundantly clear that religious involvement in political and social affairs will not be tolerated. A close eye will undoubtedly be kept on churches by the MPLA and they will be given little leeway for non-spiritual activity.

Throughout 1978, the party rectification campaign was in progress in tandem with efforts to reorganize and purge mass organizations such as UNTA, the MPLA youth wing and the Organization of Angolan Women (OMA). The restructuring of UNTA was carried out by the MPLA through UNTA's new chief, Pasocoal Luvualo, a senior member of the party and a loyal supporter of Neto. The youth wing was in need of reorganization following a far-reaching purge in the wake of the Alves coup. The reorganized youth wing held a congress in Luanda on 19 October 1978.

An indication of the confidence Neto felt in the party's position was given on 15 September when he announced a partial amnesty and called on Angolan exiles to return home. However, a Central Committee meeting in early December 1978 decided on a further purge of the MPLA and and government bodies. Speaking after the meeting, on 1 December, Neto announced that the post of Prime Minister had been abolished along with the posts of Deputy Prime Ministers. The aim, according to the President, was to enable the head of state to deal with ministers directly rather than through intermediaries. The measure greatly increased the powers of the President. The Deputy Prime Minister and Minister of Planning, Carlos Rocha, was dismissed by Neto and accused of being petit bourgeois. The Minister had been a close associate of Neto and was thought of as a gifted economist. In the same speech Neto announced that the government was willing to cooperate with private businessmen. At about this time the government gave permission for private companies to engage in construction and transport work.

By 1979, the MPLA had largely succeeded in uniting its ranks and in forming the organization into a cohesive vanguard of carefully selected cadres. Factionalism had been largely stamped out and the party was sufficiently stable to enable a smooth transfer of power to take place following President Neto's death in Moscow on 10 September 1979. A meeting of the MPLA's Central Committee appointed Eduardo dos Santos, the Minister of Planning, as President of the party. Under the Angolan constitution, the party leader was automatically Head of State and Commander-in-Chief of FAPLA. On taking office, on 21 September, Dos Santos pledged to adhere to the MPLA policies adopted under Neto's leadership.

By the time Dos Santos took over, the rectification or correction campaign was more or less over and the party had been drastically reduced in size, but its cohesion and ideological unity had been ensured. By the end of 1979, the MPLA-Workers' Party consisted of 16,583 members. The membership had been decided upon after countless rectification meetings at which the credentials of prospective members were scrutinized minutely. The aim was to admit only those who were sufficiently politically conscious and who had a record of loyal party work. Candidates applying for membership had to go through a period of probationary membership during which they had to prove their suitability. Purges were still being conducted in government bodies, however, to ensure that MPLA policies were implemented correctly and to weed out those who sought government positions for reasons of personal advancement rather than service to the country.

Shortly before his death, Neto signalled an end to the harshest phase of the purges by abolishing DISA and dismissing its head and his deputy. Neto explained the move against the security police by saying that the organization had indicated that it had strong reservations about the amnesty that was granted to certain detainees in 1978. The abolition of the security police led to a massive demonstration welcoming the move in Luanda on 2 August 1979. DISA was replaced by a new Ministry of the Interior. On 8 September another 130 political detainees were released by the government.

Throughout 1978 and 1979, UNITA guerrilla actions continued to be a thorn in the side of the government's afforts to administer the whole of the country and to implement its reconstruction programme. With extensive logistical support from South Africa, Savimbi's guerrillas launched hit-and-run attacks on government facilities and FAPLA units and frequently sabotaged the Benguela Railway. Although by the end of 1979 FAPLA and Cuban offensives had greatly reduced UNITA activities and effectiveness, the movement was able to cling to the last vestiges of support from the Ovimbundu people and to survive into the 1980s, when greater South African support and successive invasions by the Pretoria government's troops enabled UNITA to increase its military operations and to spread them into the northern provinces.

South African raids into Angola were launched sporadically in 1978 and 1979, purportedly against SWAPO targets but often against economic installations or refugee camps. Pretoria followed a clear policy of destabilization of the MPLA government and was intent on forcing Luanda, through UNITA attacks and SADF raids, into ending support for SWAPO and falling into line with South Africa's regional policies.

FNLA and FLEC activities in northern Angola and Cabinda, respectively, tailed off in 1979 following the agreement in mid-1978 between Neto and President Mobutu of Zaïre on improving relations and ending support for opposition groups from the neighbouring state. The *rapprochement* followed the March 1977 and May/June 1978 invasions of Shaba by former Katangan gendarmes and members of the Congolese National Liberation Front (FNLC). Mobutu had blamed the invasions on the MPLA government, which in turn had accused Mobutu of destabilizing its administration through support for Roberto's FNLA and the Cabindan separatists. The agreement signed between Neto and Mobutu at the end of the latter's visit to Angola in October 1978 led to a period of calm on the borders between the two countries and the commencement of greater cooperation over issues of joint concern, notably the operations of the Benguela Railway.

By 1980, the MPLA rectification campaign had progressed so far that party membership had not risen above the 20,000 mark, although cohesion and ideological unity were stronger than ever before. There had been no serious internal challenges since the Alves coup attempt. One problem, though, was the lack of Ovimbudu representation in the party and its leading bodies. The Ovimbundu made up at least a third of the total population but were not represented in the Political Bureau (all other ethnic groups were). One major reason for this was the geography of the liberation and civil wars. During the fight against the Portuguese, the MPLA had operated first from Zaïre (with guerrillas in northern Angola and near Luanda) and then from Congo (with the fighting front in Cabinda) and Zambia (concentrating on Moxico Province). The MPLA had not penetrated into the Ovimbundu heartland around Huambo and Bie or into Cuando Cubango or Cunene Provinces. Jonas Savimbi, on the other hand, had been forced to operate in those areas because they were where his initial support was concentrated. When the civil war came, the MPLA and Cuban forces had advanced into UNITA areas and defeated Savimbi, thus taking control of areas formerly monopolized by UNITA. Although the MPLA was not treated as an occupying force, the movement had no grassroots support there to begin with and so had its work cut out to create a political base in Ovimbundu areas. Food shortages and other economic problems, combined with the security measures necessary to combat South African raids and continuing UNITA insurgency, did not make it easy for the MPLA to win over as many Ovimbundu as they would have liked, and military priorities tended to take precedence over political activities. Although the MPLA entrenched itself in the bigger towns, such as Huambo, Bie and Menongue, it was harder for it to organize Ovimbundu people in the rural areas, given the scattered nature of settlements and the presence of UNITA guerrillas.

The unity of the MPLA was amply demonstrated at the extraordinary congress held in Luanda from 17 to 23 December 1980, when President dos Santos was confirmed unanimously as President of the party. The congress elected twelve new members of the Central Committee, bringing its numbers up to seventy. The party rectification campaign was reviewed and it was decided to extend it, giving greater emphasis to eliminating reactionary petit bourgeois elements. The congress condemned and pledged to fight the growing problems of black-marketeering and corruption in state institutions.

A major constitutional development during 1980 was the amendment of the constitution to allow for elections to Provincial Assemblies and the formation of a national People's Assembly. A meeting of the MPLA CC held in August approved an amendment replacing the Council of the Revolution, which up until then had exercised executive and legislative powers, with a People's Assembly. The constitution was amended to place the People's Assembly over the government and to vest in it the powers of supreme organ of state. Elections for the Provincial Assemblies started on 23 August. The electoral process involved voters (all Angolans over the age of 18 barring those who had been active members of UNITA, FNLA, FLEC or purged MPLA factions) casting their ballots to elect an electoral college, which in turn elected the Provincial Assembly. The members of the People's Assembly were elected by the Provincial Assemblies. Lists of candidates for the elections were drawn up by the MPLA, UNTA, the Union of Angolan Women, and the MPLA-Youth movement. The first session of the national People's Assembly took place on 11 November. On 13 November the Assembly elected a twenty-five member Permanent

Commission (whose members included the President and the entire Political Bureau) to conduct the Assembly's business between sessions.

Major problems were being experienced by the MPLA government at this stage with food production, distribution and housing. The latter was a particular problem in Luanda, whose population had reached 1.5 million by 1980, nearly double the 1975 figure, having been swollen by the return of 350,000 refugees from exile in Zaïre. Cuban and Angolan construction units were engaged in a frantic but generally unsuccessful race to keep up with demand for accommodation. Housing shortages, combined with the food problems and lack of improvements in living standards were major causes of discontent among the Angolan people, particularly those in Luanda's slums, which had at one time been the bedrock of support for the MPLA. Government concern over the economic problems was demonstrated in July when the Ministries of Industry and Energy, and Construction and Housing, were each divided in two to enable ministers to concentrate on the areas of particular need. At the same time, the Interior Ministry was divided in two, creating a Security Ministry. At the Ministry of Defence, Col. Maria Tonha Pedale was appointed as Minister, replacing Iko Carreira, who earlier in 1980 had gone to the Soviet Union for an advanced military training course (he later returned and took command of the air force). The MPLA campaign against incompetence, inefficiency and corruption in party and state organs was stepped up in 1981 with the formation of committees at municipal and provincial level to watch over the operation of the relevant bodies. In early 1982, people's vigilance groups were established on a local basis to assist the police and the ODP.

By June 1982, MPLA membership had risen to 30,000, but Ovimbundu representation was still low. The only Ovimbundu in a responsible position was the Transport Minister, Faustino Muteka. A session of the MPLA Central Committee held between 16 and 22 June 1982 approved the launching of a membership drive to increase party numbers to 60,000. The CC meeting also decided on an even stricter campaign against inefficiency. Food shortages and distribution problems were becoming more and more serious, as was discontent among the urban poor in particular. One major cause of resentment against government and party officials at a time of general shortages was the existence of special shops at which senior officials could obtain scarce goods. Another cause of dissatisfaction among many black slum-dwellers was the high proportion of whites, *mesticos* and formerly assimilated blacks among the state and party officials—they failed to see that massive shortages of skilled and educated cadres meant that the government and party could not pick and choose, but had to rely on what human resources were available.

In an attempt to improve the food and distribution situation, the June Central Committee session launched yet another efficiency and anti-corruption drive. The first major casualty was the Secretary for Agriculture of the Central Committee, Manuel Pedro Pacavira, who was dismissed from his post. Another government reshuffle took place following the CC session, in which the Foreign Trade portfolio was split from the Planning Ministry in order to give Planning Minister Lopo do Nascimento a chance to concentrate purely on economic planning.

The five years of internal unity within the MPLA was split in December 1982 when a play was staged in Luanda which appeared to attack various members of the government closely associated with President dos Santos. The play had been written by a prominent author and playwright, Costa de Andrade Ndunduna. Dos Santos reacted by purging from the party a group associated with Ndunduna and arresting him and a number of others. About thirty people were dismissed from party posts, notably in the Information and Propaganda Department of the Central Committee. Among those dismissed was the head of the department, Ambrosio Lukoki, and the wife of the party's organizing secretary (and *de facto* number two in the party), Alda Lara. Western analysts described the factional conflict as 'African nationalists against pro-Moscow Stalinists' (ACR, 1982-3, pp. B598). However, there seem to have been no hard-and-fast factions, but rather groups of discontented party members that came together as a faction over certain, but by no means all, issues. The criticism contained in the play, although said to have been aimed particularly at the Minister of Health, was just an indication of discontent within sections of the party at aspects of policy. If anything united the group involved in the play incident, it was a more hardline approach to cooperation with petit bourgeois elements than the party's programme laid down.

The internal disruption in the party had eased by February 1983, when most of those detained over the play were released (although the playwright was not set free for another year). By early 1983 it was clear that there were no definite pro-Moscow or hardline Stalinist factions within the MPLA and that any disunity resulted from coalitions of discontented cadres rather than organized groups reminiscent of Active Revolt or the Alves coup. Ironically, the man against whom the play had been ostensibly aimed, Health Minister Agostinho Mendes de Carvalho, was dismissed from his post in June 1983.

In October 1984, Western analysts again alleged that there was a split in the MPLA between 'nationalist and pro-Moscow' factions when President dos Santos dismissed the Foreign Minister, Paulo Jorge. It was said that Jorge was more pro-Soviet than the President and that his dismissal prepared the way for a downgrading of relations with Moscow and a new effort to reach an understanding with the United States and South Africa and perhaps even to open diplomatic relations with the United States (something the United States has consistently refused to consider since Angola's independence because of the presence of Cuban troops). In fact, Jorge was dismissed as Foreign Minister, though retained as a presidential adviser on foreign affairs, because of shortcomings of leadership and administration in the ministry. No downgrading of Soviet ties resulted and there was no change in the MPLA government's stand on the withdrawal of Cuban troops.

Throughout the first half of the 1980s, Angola continued to be beset by economic problems, notably food shortages, transport disruptions and economic dislocation caused by the war against UNITA. Guerrilla activity, combined with South African raids and sabotage activities, wrought havoc with agricultural production, transport and communications facilities and general development efforts in the southern and central regions of Angola. The main food-producing areas of the central plateau were frequently the battleground for UNITA guerrilla warfare and MPLA counter-offensives. Thousands of people were displaced by the fighting. The important Benguela Railway was consistently out of use as a result of sabotage attacks and the diamond industry in Lunda Norte, an important source of foreign exchange, was endangered by UNITA attacks on the mining site at Cafunfo (foreign workers being taken hostage during the raids, to be released later at Savimbi's headquarters at Jamba amid a blaze of publicity).

The course of the MPLA campaign to defeat UNITA military was marked by periods of near success, which were always followed by South African invasions of southern Angola and air attacks against the advancing FAPLA forces. During 1980, cross-border raids by South African forces drew enough FAPLA troops away from UNITA operational areas to enable the guerrillas to step up their guerrilla attacks and to spread their incursions into previously peaceful areas of the country. In early 1980, FAPLA sweeps in the Huambo–Bie highlands had reduced UNITA activity and restored MPLA rule to many areas: over 606 guerrillas were killed and 140 captured during the December 1979–April 1980 period (ACR, 1980–1, pp. B648–9). MPLA provincial leaders in the affected districts said that, following the counter-insurgency drive, 300,000 people who had fled into the bush in 1976 after the MPLA–Cuban advance had returned to MPLA-controlled districts in Huambo; 600,000 were said to have returned to MPLA areas in Bie. Partly as a result of FAPLA successes against guerrillas in rural areas, in the early 1980s UNITA launched a campaign of terrorist attacks in towns against MPLA officials and economic targets—the campaigns were aimed in particular at Huambo, Luanda, Benguela, Lubango and Mocamedes.

In early 1981, Western press reports revealed that since 1979 a South African force, known as 32 Battalion, had been engaged in military operations in southern Angola. Citing a former member of the battalion (a British mercenary named Edwards), the reports said that areas captured by the South African force were turned over to UNITA (ACR, 1980–1, p. B469).

In January 1981, the Geneva talks on the future of Namibia, which Angola hoped would lead to a solution of the Namibian independence problem and an end to South African raids and support for UNITA, concluded unsuccessfully. Within weeks of the breakdown of the Geneva talks, a South African force launched an invasion of Cunene Province. An SADF unit was flown into Angola by helicopter and used to attack the town of Cuamoto, 38 kilometres north of the border. But this attack was a minor affair compared with the invasion that took place in the last week of August 1981. Two South African armoured columns entered Cunene Province on 23 August, cutting the main N'Giva–Lubango road by blowing up the main road bridge at Xangongo. An advance on Lubango was stopped by the determined defence of Cahama by FAPLA forces. During the invasion, said by the South Africans to be a 'hot-pursuit' operation against SWAPO, several Soviet advisers were killed and one Soviet warrant officer was captured (*The Times*, 3 September 1981).

Following the invasion, South African forces remained in Cunene Province in some strength until mid-1985, although Pretoria periodically said it had withdrawn its troops. From the base in Cunene, the South Africans gave increased military, logistical and propaganda support to UNITA: the South Africans established a radio station on South African territory which purported to be a UNITA radio station broadcasting from UNITA-controlled territory. The station was called the Voice of the Resistance of the Black Cockerel. It carried UNITA battle claims, messages and speeches by Jonas Savimbi and warnings to foreign workers to leave Angola or suffer the consequences. Later the South Africans also set up a news agency, Kwacha UNITA Press (KUP), for Savimbi.

The South African occupation of southern Angola was a boon to UNITA as it not only gave them a safe rear base inside Angola and shorter communications and supply lines, but it also drew large numbers of FAPLA troops to the south and away from areas into which UNITA wished to spread its campaign of sabotage and guerrilla attacks. From 1982 to late 1984, UNITA increased its military activities and eventually spread the war north to Moxico, Huila, Lunda Sul, Lunda Norte, Cuanza Sul, Cuanza Norte, Malanje and Uige Provinces. Uige Province was an important target for Savimbi as he wanted to wreck the coffee industry there and so strike a blow against the economy's vital export sector. As UNITA activity spread, so did the UNITA tactic of seizing foreign hostages and using them to publicize the movement's fight against the government. In March 1983, eighty-four Czechoslovak and Portuguese construction workers were seized and marched to Savimbi's Jamba base, where they became the set piece of a large South African-orchestrated media show (foreign journalists being flown into Jamba by the South Africans). Western press coverage gave the movement a higher profile than its military position deserved and gave the impression that the MPLA government was on the point of defeat. In fact, although UNITA had some residual support among the Ovimbundu, the high level of military and political activity was only possible as a result of South African support and sometimes active assistance in the fighting from SADF regular troops and special forces units.

In April 1983, the South Africans launched a helicopter raid deep into Angola. The troops carried by air attacked Mulondo, 125 miles inside the border. The following month, South African aircraft bombed Cassinga and the railway terminal at Jamba (not the same place as Savimbi's base but further north). One aim of the bombing raid was to disrupt the iron-ore industry in the Cassinga area, yet another source of foreign exchange for the economy and an important part of the country's gradually developing mining industry. This attack and later ones, notably the abortive raid on oil installations in Cabinda in May 1985, indicated that the South African attacks were not, as the Pretoria government claimed, hot-pursuit or pre-emptive strikes against SWAPO, but calculated attempts to weaken the economy, aid UNITA and undermine the MPLA government.

In order to combat UNITA's growing insurgency campaign and South Africa's continued aggression, on 30 July 1983 President Dos Santos established regional military councils whose task it was to organize and control all military, political and economic activities in the areas affected by South African raids or UNITA insurgency. Speaking in Malanje on 5 September at the swearing-in of the Regional Military Council of the Ninth Region (Cuanza Norte and Malanje Provinces), President Dos Santos said:

The adoption of this measure is designed to improve, in the military field, the efficiency of the fight against the armed bandits and, on the other hand, to improve the operation of Party and State structures at all levels . . . The difficult situation we face constitutes the greatest challenge that imperialism, its agents and its lackeys have ever pitted against our capabilities . . . To implement its plans, racist South Africa, with the support of imperialism, established as a goal the destruction, by criminal actions, of our democratic and popular regime and the MPLA-Workers' Party . . . However, the links that have been forged between the people and the MPLA-Workers' Party in the unyielding defence of the overriding interests of our fatherland and in the application of our revolutionary principles both at home and abroad, are solid and indestructible . . . This is why, in view of the impossibility of the UNITA puppets' task of subversion in the field of military operations, assigned to them by South Africa, the regular army of this aggressor country finds itself increasingly compelled to intervene directly to create the false impression that the puppets control a vast area of Angola . . . [Luanda Radio, Home Service, 6 September 1983.]

An example of South Africa's direct intervention had immediately preceded the President's speech. In early August, a large UNITA force, possibly numbering 3,000, launched an attack on the FAPLA garrison at Cangamba. Initially the offensive was repelled with heavy casualties and UNITA looked set for a reverse. However, the South African air force launched a series of bombing raids against the town, which was reduced to rubble along with FAPLA's defences. This forced the Angolan forces to withdraw, something which was then claimed by UNITA as a major victory over the MPLA.

In October, FAPLA launched a major offensive against UNITA following the reported arrival of large shipments of sophisticated Soviet weaponry. It was aimed at UNITA bases and operational zones in Cuanza Sul, Benguela, Huambo and Moxico Provinces, while actions were also launched in Cuando–Cubango, Cunene and Huila. By early November, the military authorities in Luanda were claiming success and they reported that South African-made Ratel armoured vehicles had been destroyed during the fighting and that South African reconnaissance aircraft had been keeping an eye on the course of the offensive. In mid-November, a major government victory at Mussende in Cuanza Sul was claimed by the Defence Minister, Col. Tonha Pedale. He said that the whole Mussende area had been liberated and that 600 UNITA guerrillas had been killed. Soon after this, news agencies reported from Angola that counter-insurgency drives had achieved further success in Huambo, Bie and Cuanza Sul with UNITA's 'Second strategic front' being destroyed (Somerville, January 1984). Vague reports from UNITA officials seemed to bear out the government claims of victory, adding only that the MPLA forces had been backed by 8,000 Cubans, 3,000 SWAPO fighters and 1,000 members of the African National Congress of South Africa. UNITA also claimed that the whole offensive was organized by a Soviet general.

Revenge for FAPLA's evident success was swift. On 6 December, South African armoured units with artillery and air support launched an invasion of Huila Province from the occupied areas of Cunene. Fighting in the area continued into January with heavy engagements taking place at Cahama and Cuvelai in Cunene. On 29 December, South African aircraft bombed military installations at Lubango. Despite claims by the head of the SADF, General Constand Viljoen, and by government ministers, it was very clear that the attack was not just a strike against SWAPO guerrillas. The clear targets were FAPLA bases, economic installations and facilities such as airfields and radar stations. Although the SADF began to withdraw from the scenes of battle in early January, they continued their occupation of Cunene.

As a result of the fighting and of American pressure on both Angola and South Africa, talks started between Luanda and Pretoria, with American officials acting as intermediaries, to find a solution to the border fighting and continual South African raids. After several weeks of negotiations, South Africa and Angola signed the Lusaka accord. This provided for the disengagement of forces in southern Angola, the evacuation of all occupied territory in Angola by the SADF, the setting-up of a security commission to monitor the withdrawal, and the prevention of infiltration into Namibia by SWAPO forces in Angola. Through the accord the South Africans hoped to stop SWAPO activities in Namibia and Angola would regain control of its southern-most province and have a respite from South African military pressure. However, it soon became clear that the Pretoria government had no real intention of withdrawing its troops and every intention of gaining its benefits from the accord without fulfilling its side of the bargain. Far from withdrawing from southern Angola, the SADF dug in there and only moved out, prior to moving back again, in mid-1985.

Discussing the accord during a visit to Senegal in late February, Lucio Lara, the MPLA organizing secretary and a member of the Political Bureau, said that his government had discussed the situation in southern Angola with SWAPO before signing and had no intention of ending support for the movement. Lara made it clear that the MPLA had serious reservations about the sincerity of the South African and US governments but that a cessation of hostilities and a withdrawal of South African troops would be achieved through the accord (Luanda

Radio Home Service, 24 February 1984). The Angolan government also hoped that the accord would lead to a reduction in South African support for UNITA and would thus aid counter-insurgency operations aimed at wiping out Savimbi's forces.

However, South African aid to UNITA continued and periodic raids were carried out into Angola by the South Africans. Using the pretext that SWAPO forces were still active in Namibia, South African troops remained in southern Angola. After further Angolan complaints, the SADF forces moved out of Cunene. But despite an elaborate evacuation operation and a media campaign to create the impression of a complete withdrawal, some troops remained at the Ruacana and Caleque dam sites. Furthermore, periodic incursions into Angola continued.

A major event occurred in late May 1985 that confirmed statements by the Angolan government and suspicions of many international observers about South Africa's real role in Angola and its assistance for UNITA. On 21 May, a South African commando unit was discovered by Angolan troops near a major oil refinery in Cabinda. After a skirmish, some members of the commando group were killed and one, Captain Wynand Petrus du Toit, was captured. After his capture the South African officer admitted that his target had been a major oil refinery (run by the US Gulf Oil Company) and that he had taken part in other sabotage activities in Angola—the sabotage of an oil refinery in Luanda in 1981, the mining of Soviet and East European ships in Luanda harbour in 1984, and the destruction of a bridge over the Giraul river in 1982 (*Africa,* July 1985, pp. 26–7). The captured soldier said that responsibility for all these attacks had been claimed by UNITA and that if the attack on the Cabinda oil refinery had been successful, UNITA would have claimed that, too. Many of UNITA's operations thus seem to have been carried out by South African special forces.

Further evidence of the South African role in providing direct military help to Savimbi's movement emerged in September and October 1985 following the near success of a FAPLA counter-insurgency drive in Moxico, Cuando–Cubango, Huila and Benguela Provinces. A large FAPLA force drove UNITA from most of Moxico Province in August 1985, capturing the town of Cazombo. An offensive was then launched against UNITA forces around the Cuando–Cubango town of Mavinga, with the intention of pushing on towards Savimbi's 'capital' at Jamba, near the border with Namibia. FAPLA's success was such that the South Africans intervened with ground and air units to prevent UNITA's defeat. As usual Pretoria claimed that the action was 'a follow-up operation' against SWAPO. However, SADF aircraft bombed FAPLA units near Mavinga and heavy support for UNITA turned back the FAPLA advance. Pretoria was forced to admit that it was helping UNITA when the MPLA-Workers' Party government produced the body of a South African soldier who had been killed assisting UNITA in Moxico Province. The South African Defence Minister, General Magnus Malan, then admitted aiding UNITA and made it clear that his government was prepared to continue aid and military intervention to prevent the defeat of the rebel movement. The official Angolan news agency, ANGOP, described the admission as proof of Pretoria's continued campaign of destabilization against the MPLA. It added that South Africa 'has once again demonstrated its monstrosity and its hatred for the Angolan people and their revolution' (Luanda Radio, 22 September 1985).

By the end of 1985, it had become evident that the Angolan people would get no respite from South African raids and operations by Pretoria's allies, Jonas Savimbi and UNITA. There was every indication that until South Africa was forced to leave Namibia (Angola had been involved in numerous rounds of talks, all of them fruitless, with the United States and South Africa in an attempt to solve the Namibia problem according to UN Security Council resolution 435; Angolan proposals to effect a withdrawal of the South Africans from Namibia had been blocked by American and South African demands for a prior withdrawal of all Cuban forces from Angola, something refused by Angola and Cuba) there would be no peace in southern Angola, no end to UNITA activities and therefore no end to the main obstacles in the way of the MPLA-Workers' Party attempts to reconstruct the country's economy, start the transition to socialism and ensure government control over the whole of the national territory.

It is against this background of externally backed guerrilla war and destabilization by South Africa that one must view the MPLA's attempts to build a socialist state in Angola. One must also take into account the long history of factional struggle within the MPLA itself and the huge human, social and economic cost of the liberation war and the civil war. The struggle to build socialism has had to be joined with a struggle for party unity, national integrity, economic survival, and internal and external security.

2   Social Structure

The Colonial Inheritance

On independence, the MPLA government inherited a deeply divided society created by the Portuguese to maintain the supremacy of the political and economic interests of the imperial power and white settlers. Society was divided into privileged whites, poorer white peasant settlers, *mesticos*, assimilated Africans (*assimilados*), and the majority of Africans (*indigenas*). Within the African population, there were further divisions on ethnic lines. The Ovimbundu made up over a third of the population, with the Mbundu and Kongo as the next largest groups. Between them, the three groups made up around two-thirds of the whole population. Although there had been some mixing of African ethnic groups in Luanda and other major towns (also in the coffee-growing areas around Uige, as a result of migration of Ovimbundu workers), generally ethnic groups remained in specific areas: the Ovimbundu around the south-central highlands; the Mbundu in the Luanda region; and the Kongo in the north. The ethnic pattern within Angola was to have a profound effect on the make-up of the liberation movements. The MPLA grew up in Luanda and the Catete-Dembos areas, basing its movements on support from Mbundu peoples, *assimilados* and *mesticos*. The FNLA was based on and primarily interested in the Kongo peoples (more or less to the exclusion of other groups). For its part, UNITA was built up by Jonas Savimbi, following his split with the FNLA, in the Ovimbundu heartland, from where he originated. Only the MPLA made any real attempt to transcend ethnic barriers and appeal to the nation as a whole. The ethnic factor, combined with the geography of the guerrilla war, greatly determined the important role played by the Mbundu, *mesticos* and *assimilados* in the MPLA and, in particular, the under-representation of the Ovimbundu in the movement.

Although the Portuguese claimed that their colonial system was unique in being devoid of racism, in fact the whole system was based on implicit racism, reinforced by class distinctions based on Portuguese ownership of the means of production in industry, the best agricultural land and the distribution and productive sectors. As Gerald Bender contends:

... rigid educational standards and Draconian class barriers effectively precluded Africans in Angola from seriously threatening the white bastion of exclusivity ... whites in Angola rarely needed to resort to explicit or legalistic forms of racial discrimination because the virulent system of cultural or class discrimination effectively precluded Africans from participating as equals in Portuguese social, economic or political institutions. [Bender, 1978, pp. 200–1 and 213.]

Even *mesticos* and *assimilados* were barred from advancing beyond the lowest grades in colonial service. The only integration in Angolan society was caused by white downward mobility.

The division of the population into *assimilados* and *indigenas* and the continuation of the forced-labour system ended only in 1961 as a result of the Luanda and Kongo uprisings. The *assimilado* system had caused divisions between Africans, as was indicated by the high rate of attacks on *assimilados* (and *mesticos*) during the 1961 uprising in the north. The forced-labour system had exerted a destructive influence on African agriculture and on social life in rural areas, as able-bodied males were constantly being taken to work for the government or for Portuguese settlers. The administrative reforms of the Norton de Matos system destroyed the traditional authority systems through the establishment of controlled villages (a process heightened by the *aldeamento* systems during the guerrilla war) and fostered ethnic differences between Angola's population groups. Unassimilated Africans were effectively segregated from *assimilados, mesticos* and whites.

The destruction of traditional African systems, the inhibition of African economic advancement and the denial of education to all but a tiny minority of Africans meant that at independence Angolan society was in a state of fragmentation and enforced backwardness. Apart from those nationalists organized within the MPLA and some within the other movements, there was little sense of nationhood. Animosity and differences between *mesticos* and *assimilados*, on the one hand, and the majority of Africans, on the other, had been assiduously fostered by the

Portuguese. There were very few *assimilados*, only 30,000 in 1950 (Newitt, 1981, p. 138), but they were the most highly educated Africans and the only ones with experience of working within the administration of Angola. Many *assimilados*, and *mesticos*, too, were MPLA supporters or even leaders. It was clear that, with the exodus of the vast majority of the Portuguese settlers on independence, the government would be forced to rely heavily on former *assimilados* and *mesticos* to staff government institutions and managerial positions in the economy.

The other main social divisions that were inherited by the new Angolan state were those associated with the urban–rural dichtomy. The great majority of Angolans lived and worked in the rural areas— 1.2 million families based their whole lives on subsistence or very small-scale cash-crop farming. Their living and educational standards were extremely low and under the colonial system they had practically no access to health services or any form of social amenity. Africans involved in cash-crop production, particularly those on large plantations, were hardly better off. There was a small class of African cash-crop farmers and small traders in rural areas which was more prosperous, but this group made up only a minute fraction of the African population. African workers in mining, construction, transport, services, fishing and industry were hardly pampered by the Portuguese but generally they had a higher standard of living—in the early 1970s, there were around 100,000 Africans working in manufacturing and other industries, 35,000 employed in mining, 5,000–10,000 in fishing, 20,000–40,000 in the construction sector, 55,000 in the transport sector and 70,000 in the service sector (Ottaway, 1981, p. 110).

Social Problems and Policies After Independence

The core of the MPLA's socialist policies was the leading role of the working class and the worker–peasant alliance. While the party stressed the importance of peasant participation and the need to work to improve living standards and social welfare (i.e. health services and education) in rural areas, the party had as its political base the urban slum-dwellers, workers and intelligentsia rather than the peasants, although a fair-sized peasant following had been developed in the MPLA's liberated areas and operational sectors and it was certainly the case that many town-dwellers and workers had peasant origins and many retained close links with families in the countryside. The danger was that the party could serve the interests of the small urban pro-letariat while largely ignoring or at best relegating to second place the peasantry. There was also the danger that the high *mestico* and *as-similado* membership of the MPLA and its leading bodies could lead to the alienation of the poorer urbanites (a factor that was reflected in the Alves coup and surrounding events).

On assuming power, the MPLA made it clear that its primary aim was to forge national unity and to oppose all manifestations of tribal-ism, regionalism and racism and to combat the tendency of the small African bourgeois class in the towns (those with education who worked in the white-collar sector) to look down on the peasantry (Kaplan, 1979, pp. 96–7). The MPLA realized that it would have its work cut out to entrench itself in the FNLA heartland of the Kongo peoples in the north and among the Ovimbundu, many of whom had supported UNITA, in the south-central areas. Efforts to stamp out tribalism (particularly prominent in the FNLA policies but also evident in UNITA's Ovimbundu-based movement) would clearly have to be made at the same time as counter-insurgency operations were carried out against FNLA and UNITA guerrillas, a serious complicating factor in MPLA attempts to transcend tribal or regional loyalties and create national ones in their place.

Among the rural measures applied by the MPLA were the estab-lishment of state farms on land abandoned by the Portuguese and the encouragement of cooperatives and producers' associations. The party was keen to prevent the growth of a rural bourgeoisie, the necessary elements for which existed in the form of the more successful cash-crop farmers among the African population and the void left by the exodus of the Portuguese. The growth of such a class in the rural areas would be a serious obstacle to the MPLA's socialist agrarian policy, to the establishment of peasant cooperatives, and to the political penetra-tion of the peasantry by the MPLA and affiliated mass organizations.

Some success was made with the establishment of agricultural cooperatives in the first two years of indepenendence when the cooperative programme was under party control. However, by 1978, responsibility had been transferred to the government and the programme had lost its momentum. The result was that the cooperative movement regressed. Speaking in January 1985 to the First National Conference of the MPLA-Workers' Party, President dos Santos spoke of the need to put more effort into the rural cooperative drive. Noting its failure in recent years, he said, 'As a result, poor peasants dependent on a subsistence economy ceased to be organised and many were put at the mercy of exploitation by middlemen (small transporters and traders) and small farmers, encouraging the growth of the rural petty bourgeoisie and greatly harming the consolidation of the worker–peasant alliance' (dos Santos, 1985). The President also called for greater party recruitment efforts in the rural areas, obviously fearing that failures with key projects such as the cooperatives could endanger the MPLA's influence over the peasantry at a time when UNITA was still posing a serious threat in some of the main agricultural areas of the south-central plateau.

The party's opposition to the growth of a bourgeois or petit bourgeois class was not limited to the countryside alone. Although the MPLA adhered to a policy of cooperation between the worker–peasant alliance (which it saw as its fundamental base) and what it termed the 'patriotic petit bourgeoise', it was determined to prevent the enlargement of the bourgeois element in society and to curtail its influence in positions of importance within government structures and even the MPLA itself. At the Central Committee's plenary meeting in October 1976, President Neto had warned of the dangers of 'petit bourgeois opportunism'. By this he was referring to people who joined the party or obtained positions in the government or civil service with the sole objective of using the position for personal aggrandisement rather than to serve the country or implement party policy. The same plenary meeting approved a resolution on economic policy specifying that high salaries should be reduced and readjustment be made in cases where low wages for workers were flagrantly unjust. The resolution resolved to stick to the socialist dictum of 'from each according to his ability, to each according to his labour' (as opposed to the recipe for a fully communist society of 'from each according to his ability, to each according to his needs'). The Central Committee resolution made it clear that while the party was opposed to privileges for those in vital positions in the economy and administration and was against the formation of a bourgeois class composed of well-paid managers, technocrats and administrators, it saw the need in the national reconstruction period to reward the quality as well as quantity of work (MPLA, 1976, p. 11). The same meeting was told that the MPLA had inherited from the Portuguese the massive social, educational and economic problems of an illiteracy rate of 85 per cent. The party made a campaign for literacy the first priority of its educational programme.

The Central Committee's report to the First MPLA Congress in December 1977 also outlined the party's policies towards divisive trends and the bourgeoisie; the report spoke of the need to eliminate 'any manifestations of tribal, regional or racial nature'. It was also noted that 'certain sectors of the petty bourgeoisie in the state apparatus and even in the Movement, in an attempt to maintain their privileges, resumed feverish activity in scambling for leading posts' (MPLA, 1977, p. 9).

The MPLA's general social welfare policies and priorities were set out in a report delivered to the special congress of the MPLA in December 1980 by President dos Santos on behalf of the Central Committee. He said that the five areas of priority in the provision of services and assistance were: support for children and working mothers; support for ex-servicemen, war widows and orphans; support for returned exiles and displaced persons (something that assumed huge dimensions as UNITA expanded its guerrilla war and South Africa occupied parts of Cunene Province); help for the aged and the physically handicapped; and the re-education of juvenile delinquents. Unfortunately, no details were given of the scale of each of the problems or the resources that could be allocated to them. Given the almost constant state of war in Angola from the start of the liberation war in 1961 to the continuation of South African aggression and UNITA sabotage in 1985, it is likely that for many regions of the country no figures were available to shed light on the scale of the problems.

The few statistics available are general estimates, as South Africa's occupation of Cunene Province up until mid-1985 and UNITA guerrilla activity in rural areas hampers nation-wide statistical analysis. In

1983, the Angola National Institute of Statistics put the mid-year population at 8,339,000 (up 197,000 on 1982, an increase of 2.4 per cent). Angolan figures on the size of the different ethnic groups are not available, but the US Central Intelligence Agency has given the following estimate for the breakdown of population into ethnic groups: Ovimbundu, 37 per cent; Mbundu, 23 per cent; Kongo, 14 per cent; *mesticos*, 2–3 per cent; European, 1 per cent; others (Lunda–Chokwe, Ganguela, Herero, Ovambo and Bushmen), 23 per cent (CIA, 1983). Accurate figures on the economic activity of population are similarly scarce. The International Labour Organization has estimated that the statistics for employment in agriculture, industry and the service sector are as depicted in Table 2.1.

Table 2.1 Distribution of Angola's economic activity

	Males	Females	Total
Agriculture	939,000	57,000	995,000
Industry	215,000	6,000	221,000
Services	274,000	71,000	345,000
Total	1,428,000	134,000	1,562,000

Note: The figures are estimated for the mid-1970s and do not necessarily take account of the massive subsistence agriculture sector.

3   The Political System

Development of the Ruling Party

The MPLA-Workers' Party, as a Marxist–Leninist vanguard of the working class, is the leading force of all the country's economic, political and social forces. It is obvious that the party is neither an invisible nor an abstract force, but the result of the conscious selection of the best elements of the working class and other levels of our population who are loyal to the noblest aspirations of the Angolan proleteriat. Hence the need for all party members to be armed with a strong revolutionary awareness, to be honest, dedicated in work and to the unwavering defence of the socialist option of our people . . . The strength and leading role of the party depend on unity of thought and organisation based on the theory and practice of Marxism–Leninism . . . The party leads and organises the masses so that they can implement their class objectives, which are precisely the transformation of the current economic and social situation to build a socialist society . . . [Luanda Home Service, 3 February 1985.]

This statement, released by the party's Political Bureau on the twenty-fourth anniversary of the start of the armed struggle, clearly sets out the party's view of its position with regard to the Angolan struggle, social and economic situation and its major ideological and political tasks. There is a marked difference between this declaration and those made by the party leadership during the liberation struggle. Prior to independence the party was wary of making too strong and open a commitment to Marxism–Leninism. A major party policy document released in 1965 called for planned economic development, the establishment of agricultural cooperatives, state control of foreign trade and agrarian reform, but steered clear of calling for the construction of a socialist society. In 1968, the MPLA's Daniel Chipenda said that a vanguard party would be formed to lead the coalition of groups within the MPLA, but little mention was made of the Marxist–Leninist nature of the vanguard party. In 1971, the party denied an FNLA claim that the party had become a communist movement. Two leading observers of socialist movements within Africa said that prior to independence, the MPLA was 'a coalition of various socialist and nationalist factions strongly influenced by Marxists' (Ottaway & Ottaway, 1981, p. 103). In 1972, Agostinho Neto denied that the movement had a definite ideology. He said, 'for a single party it is possible but when a movement consists of people who are different politically and ideologically, it is not possible to say that this is, for example, a communist movement' (*Sunday News* (Tanzania), 20 August 1972).

Essentially, during the liberation struggle, the MPLA needed a broad, all-inclusive front that would unite the widest possible spectrum of Angolans in the struggle for independence from Portugal. What mattered was not a commitment to a particular ideology or concept of political organization in the event of victory, but rather a total commitment to fighting for liberation from colonial rule. The diversity of the movement's membership was demonstrated by the frequent factional and political struggles that plagued the MPLA from 1962 onwards—the Neto–Viriato da Cruz split, the Chipenda split and the problems with the Active Revolt faction.

During the civil war, pro-MPLA neighbourhood committees were formed in Luanda and other towns. They were established by MPLA supporters but were not directly controlled by them and incorporated a wide variety of political ideologies. In the immediate post-independence period the committees became the basis for the *poder popular* (people's power) form of representation (closely controlled by Nito Alves and later used by him as a weapon in the factional struggle). The committees complemented MPLA rule but also provided an alternative source of political power and local decision-making. Similarly, the MPLA itself was boosted in size soon after independence by the acceptance as members of many urban workers and civil servants who had not taken part in the party's liberation activities.

In his independence speech, Agostinho Neto made it pretty clear that the MPLA would be the supreme political body in the country and would take a leading role in all aspects of the running of the country. However, a broad movement lacking a well-defined ideology or set of objectives was not ideally suited to governing a country in need of economic reconstruction, the creation of a sense of national unity and firm leadership.

It was hardly surprising then that, given the Marxist beliefs of most of the leadership, a decision was made to transform the MPLA from a front organization into a more cohesive political party. The intention to create a vanguard party had been mooted throughout the liberation struggle, but it was made a reality at the plenary meeting of the MPLA Central Committee in October 1976. The meeting was a turning-point for the MPLA from the ideological point of view and also from the point of view of Neto and his supporters defeating Alves and his *poder popular*-based faction. The Central Committee removed Alves from the Ministry of the Interior and the Political Bureau (although he remained in the Central Committee). More importantly, in the long-term sense, it proclaimed the MPLA's intention to transform itself into a Marxist–Leninist vanguard party and to alter the Angolan constitution to ensure that the party could not be challenged as the supreme arbiter of political, economic and social affairs by state bodies or by those organizations set up by the *poder popular* movement.

At the plenary meeting, Neto told the Committee that it would have to draw up the guidelines for reshaping the government of the country in the light of developments since independence, though he warned that the task would be made difficult by the lack of cadres (MPLA, 1976, p. 7). Neto stated that the social transformation that Angola would have to go through during the period of reconstruction and the transition to socialism 'will necessarily lead to the formation of a Party guided by the ideology of the working-class, Marxism–Leninism, the leading force of the broad, national, anti-imperialist front, an historical imperative for our revolution because, as Lenin said, Socialism cannot be built without the leadership of the working-class party' (MPLA, 1976, p. 8). Speaking at the plenary meeting, the then Defence Minister and member of the Political Bureau, Iko Carreira, said, 'for the MPLA, the only socialism that exists is the socialism of Marx, of Engels and of Lenin—scientific socialism'. Carreira warned that true socialist construction would have to await the reconstruction of the country (ACR, 1976–7, p. B453).

The MPLA had clearly nailed its colours to the mast of Marxism–Leninism, eschewing African socialism or other forms of socialist theory that fell short of a full commitment to Marxism–Leninism. Neto spoke at the meeting of the commencement of a 'struggle for transition to People's Democracy, where the working class, the peasantry, the patriotic bourgeoisie, united in struggle will exercise revolutionary democratic dictatorship' (MPLA, 1976, po. 7). The MPLA had no intention of sharing power with other political forces or of comprising its ideological position. The vanguard party, to be formed from the most ideologically and politically reliable cadres of the liberation movement, would, on behalf of the worker–peasant alliance, exercise power and preside over a 'revolutionary democratic dictatorship'.

The terminology used to describe the nature of the state to be established under the guidance of the MPLA followed closely the language used by Lenin to describe the form of government that would be necessary to destroy the tsarist system in Russia. In his work entitled *Two Tactics of Social Democracy in the Democractic Revolution*, Lenin said that the revolution could only be achieved after the creation of a 'revolutionary democratic dictatorship of the proletariat and the peasantry' (cited by Hough & Fainsod, 1979, p. 74). The MPLA was also following Leninist guidelines when it came to the formation of a vanguard party consisting of ideologically sound activists. As Hough and Fainsod have pointed out, Lenin believed that party membership should 'be limited to those who were willing to submit themselves to party discipline . . . a second distinctive characteristic of Lenin's conception of a party was his insistence that its members should be active. His formal requirement for entry into the party was not only support of the party program and payment of dues but also "personal participation in one of the party organizations"' (Hough & Fainsod, 1979, p. 21). When the MPLA launched its rectification campaign to streamline the membership down to those who were genuine party supporters and activists, Lenin's dictums on participation and discipline were very much to the fore. The MPLA's belief that only a vanguard party of the working class could carry through the revolution was modelled on Lenin's 'Preliminary Draft Resolution of the Tenth Congress', written by Lenin for the Communist Party Congress of 1921. Lenin wrote that 'only the political party of the working class . . . is capable of uniting, training and organising a vanguard of the proletariat and of the whole mass of the working people that alone will be capable of withstanding the inevitable petit-bourgeois vascillations of this mass' (Lenin, 1960–70, vol. 32, p. 244).

The MPLA was also very much concerned with the role of the petty bourgeoisie in party and government bodies. Neto said in his opening speech to the Central Committee plenum that the patriotic bourgeoisie was a component of the revolutionary democratic dictatorship. But the Central Committee resolution on the organization and functioning of the Committee warned against 'petit bourgeois opportunism'. The Central Committee documents on the plenum stated that the workers were the leading force of the revolution, the peasants the principal force, the worker–peasant alliance the motive force. Members of the petit bourgeoisie and the intellectuals would be admitted to the party if they passed through the rectification process and could demonstrate their ideological commitment, their adherence to the party line and discipline, and a record of revolutionary activity.

The major organizational developments at the October plenum were: the decision to create a party secretariat (which would include members of the Central Committee under the direction of the President of the MPLA), the creation of a commission to direct and control the Department of Political Orientation and the Department of Information and Propaganda, and the formation of a National Control Commission and a National Organization Commission (to be appointed by the Political Bureau). The plenum also resolved to hold the first MPLA congress, which would 'decide upon the creation of a party guided by Marxism–Leninism' (MPLA, 1976, p. 28). In connection with the congress, a National Party School and a Congress Organizing Commission would be established and a political education and mobilization campaign launched.

The National Party School opened in Luanda on 12 February 1977. Its task was to train the leading cadres of the party to fill national and provincial party positions and to raise the educational and ideological level of leading cadres. Three months after the opening of the school and amid the preparations for the congress, the Alves coup took place (following the expulsion of Alves and some of his supporters from the Central Committee). During the coup (and also prior to his expulsion from the leading party bodies), Alves and his supporters adopted an anti-white and anti-*mestico* position, referring to these two groups as bourgeois opportunists. Alves aimed at eliciting the support of poor urban workers, particularly those organized in the people's committees, by playing on the discontent among the poor with relatively privileged positions held by many whites and *mesticos* in the party and government hierarchy. Although labelled 'leftist' by many observers, Alves and his supporters were essentially opportunists using bourgeois slogans based on racism rather than leftist, anti-bourgeois terminology. Avles based his faction on support in the people's committees, but the committees were far less revolutionary than the party and, prior to their downgrading in importance at the October 1976 plenum, were centres of factional opposition to the increasingly Marxist–Leninist leadership of the MPLA. The committees did not represent an ideologically more left-wing faction, but rather the politically uneducated slum-dwellers who were recruited to the organizations during the civil war.

In the wake of the coup, the MPLA continued with preparations for the congress. In August 1977, a plenary meeting of the Central Committee selected twenty-two candidates (one per vacancy) to fill the gaps left on the Committee by the coup. The Committee also criticized strongly 'the opportunist race by certain sectors of the petit bourgeoisie for official posts'. This referred to attempts by non-Marxists, some of them inside the MPLA, to take advantage of the chronic shortage of party cadres and loyal, educated civil servants (which had been exacerbated by the killings during, and dismissals following, the Alves coup) (Wolfers & Bergerol, 1983, p. 164).

At the time of the plenum, a seminar was conducted by the party Organization Secretary, Lucio Lara, and two other Political Bureau members, Dino Matross and Bernardo de Sousa, to carry out organizational work ready for the congress. In November, meetings were in progress across the country to select delegates for the congress. According to Wolfers and Bergerol, opportunists took advantage of the meetings to try to enhance their positions for reasons of personal advancement. Shortly before the congress, Lucio Lara warned party officials and civil servants against adopting superior, bourgeois attitudes towards poorly-educated workers and peasants. The party was setting the stage for a congress that would lead to the establishment of a united and ideologically cohesive party purged of those elements whose political views and activities were not in accordance with the orthodox Marxist–Leninist line set at the October 1976 plenum. To ensure the smooth running of the congress, commissions were set up to prepare the party reports to the congress; Lucio Lara chaired the political and ideological commission, Iko Carreira the defence and security one, and Carlos Rocha the economic and social one (the three men chosen were all *mesticos*, an indication that the racist undertones of the Alves coup had led to no dilution of the MPLA commitment to anti-racism).

The congress opened on 4 December 1977 in Luanda and lasted until 11 December. Its major achievement was the approval of the Central Committee document declaring the formal adherence to Marxism–Leninism, the adoption of the name MPLA-Workers' Party and the start of the party rectification campaign. The congress reaffirmed the importance of the class struggle, but emphasized that the worker–peasant alliance should cooperate with reliable sections of the petit bourgeoisie. The congress also created the National Control Commission and elected new members of the Central Committee.

Presenting the Central Committee report to the Congress, Agostinho Neto explained why it had become necessary to transform the MPLA into a vanguard party.

The MPLA, after heroically leading two national liberation wars and having started the process of laying the material foundations for building socialism, has now fulfilled its historic mission as a national liberation movement. The laying down of People's Democracy and Socialism as goals to be attained implies qualitative leaps in the politico-ideological and organisational sphere, so that the vanguard organisation may play its full role in the leadership of society. Indeed, the class content of People's Democracy and Socialism and the consequent sharpening of class struggle internally and internationally requires that the working class, as the leading force, has an instrument capable of carrying out that task. That instrument, organised and structured in accordance with Marxist–Leninist principles, which will lead the revolutionary classes, will be the Vanguard Party of the Working Class. [MPLA, 1977, p. 10.]

Neto went on to say that the new party would unite 'in a solid alliance' the workers, peasants revolutionary intellectuals and other working people 'dedicated to the cause of the proleteriat'. The Central Committee report stressed the socialist goals of the party and the need to step up the class struggle. The leading role of the party in society and the role of the state as the instrument of the party and the working class in 'carrying out revolutionary change' and achieving the political domination of the working class were stressed in the report to the congress. In orthodox Leninist fashion, the Central Committee stated that the worker–peasant alliance, through the vanguard party, would 'exercise a Revolutionary Democratic Dictatorship over internal and external reaction, creating the conditions for the establishment of the Dictatorship of the Proleteriat in the stage of building socialism'.

The Central Committee report reminded party members that the leading role of the party was enshrined in the Angolan constitution 'and therefore has force of law'. The report said that 'all social activities and all political and social bodies came under its [the party's] supreme leadership', but that the party did not take the place of the state institutions in the implementation of policy. In defining the role of the party, Neto said that the Central Committee had established the following five principles:

1. The MPLA congress lays down the party's political line, defines final and middle-term objectives, and identifies allies and enemies.
2. The congress, the Central Committee and the Political Bureau draw up general directives for the basic spheres of social activity and define 'the role and principal tasks of the State and mass organisations'.
3. The party leads state and mass organizations, while the Secretariat of the Central Committee and intermediate and basic party organizations exercise control over the work of the state bodies and mass organizations—by monitoring the implementation of party decisions; the party must support state bodies and mass organizations to ensure the correct implementation of party policy.
4. The party leads state and mass organizations by selecting, educating and appointing the leading cadres.
5. The party plays its leading role through members, whatever the posts they hold, who are obliged to fulfil party decisions and ensure their implementation (MPLA, 1977, pp. 35–6).

The congress was told that these principles had not always been respected or correctly applied and that there had been shortcomings in higher party bodies and structural deficiencies in the Secretariat—state bodies had frequently ignored party supervision. No details of the incorrect applications of principles or the party shortcomings were given in the open sessions of the congress's work. One obvious problem was the shortage of cadres, which led to the holding of senior positions in both party and state institutions by individuals and to the employment of former colonial civil servants in important positions in state bodies. It was clear from the report to the congress that in some areas party officials had interfered too directly in the implementation of policies and that, conversely, some civil servants and state bodies ignored the guidance of the party.

Elections were held at the congress for the vacant positions on the Central Committee. Although the Central Committee was to have seventy members (both full and alternate), the congress elected only forty-five full and ten alternate members, leaving fifteen vacancies, which the congress (on Neto's wishes) left vacant in order for a special congress to be held in 1980 to appoint working-class cadres to the Committee following the completion of the rectification campaign that the 1977 congress launched at the suggestion of the Central Committee. Of the Committee members elected, thirteen full members and three alternate ones were from the list of twenty-two presented to the congress by the Central Committee to fill the twenty-two vacancies left by the Alves coup and its aftermath. Six of those put forward as candidates by the Committee were rejected by the congress and other cadres were elected to fill the positions.

According to Wolfers and Bergerol (1983, p. 167), there was criticism at the congress of a 'small regional lobby' known as the Catete group. The group reportedly aimed at obtaining as many Central Committee seats as possible and at gaining a place in the Political Bureau. In the charged atmosphere of the post-Alves coup period, there was immense hostility at the congress to such obvious factionalism, and the group got little support in the elections to the Committee.

The congress established a new organizational structure for basic party units (Figure 3.1). The new structures would be peopled by those cadres selected for membership of the MPLA-Workers' Party during the rectification campaign. The basic unit of the party was to be the cell, which would have between three and thirty members and be set up in work-places rather than on a geographical basis; cells would elect a Party Sector Committee, which would in turn elect a Party Area (or in rural areas a Village) Committee in conjunction with other sector committees. The next layer would be the Party Rural/Urban District Committee and above that the Party Province Committee. At the national level, the Central Committee and the Political Bureau would be the leading bodies, with the congresses as the supreme decision-making organ. Between the sittings of the congresses, the Central Committee would be the locus of power, with power delegated to the Political Bureau between the meetings of the Committee. The decisions of the higher bodies would be binding on lower bodies, in line with the principle of democratic centralism, which the MPLA adopted as its guiding organizational doctrine. The Central Committee would be elected by the congress and would in turn appoint top government leaders and elect the Political Bureau. The Secretariat, elected by the Central Committee, would direct day-to-day party work under the guidance of the Political Bureau. Party organizations were to follow the administrative divisions of the country.

At the provincial, district and communal levels, the supreme party body would be the conference (meeting every two years) which would elect an executive committee and a committee coordinator. All national and provincial bodies would base their work on the decisions and directives of the party congress and of the Central Committee (which would hold a plenary meeting every six months). Party control commissions would be elected on a national, provincial and district level to eradicate all signs of factionalism. Members of the control commissions would be elected by the respective party committees but would have to be approved by the party committee one higher in the party hierarchy (MPLA, 1977; Wolfers & Bergerol, 1983; Kaplan, 1979).

At the time of the First Congress in 1977 there were 110,000 members of the MPLA. Many of these had been recruited without any great degree of rigour in checking the members' backgrounds or their political and ideological consciousness or willingness to submit to party discipline. The frequent factional struggles gave evidence of the

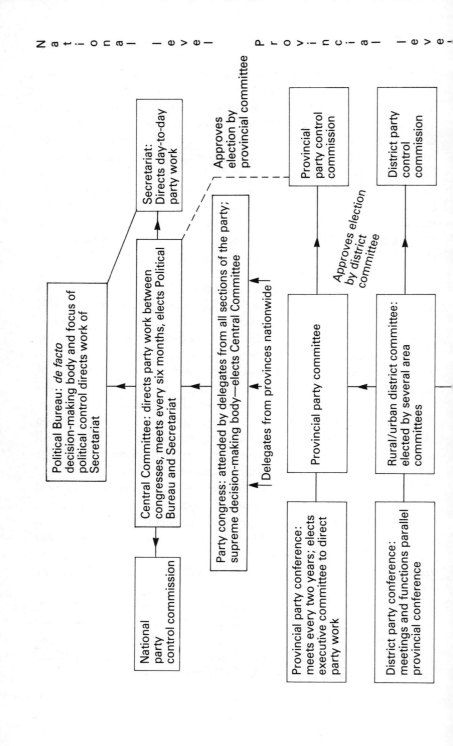

National level

Provincial level

Political Bureau: *de facto* decision-making body and focus of political control directs work of Secretariat

Secretariat: Directs day-to-day party work

Central Committee: directs party work between congresses, meets every six months, elects Political Bureau and Secretariat

Party congress: attended by delegates from all sections of the party—elects Central Committee

Delegates from provinces nationwide

National party control commission

Approves election by provincial committee

Provincial party control commission

District party control commission

Approves election by district committee

Provincial party committee

Rural/urban district committee: elected by several area committees

Provincial party conference: meets every two years; elects executive committee to direct party work

District party conference: meetings and functions parallel provincial conference

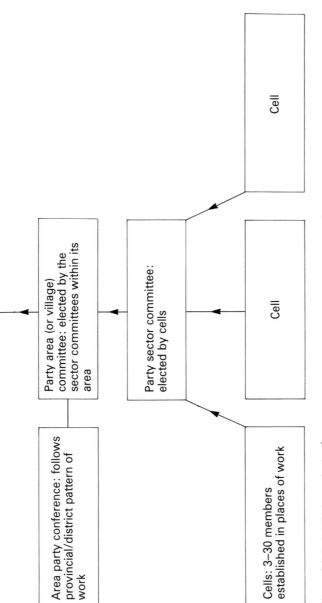

Figure 3.1 Basic MPLA organizational structure

Note: Higher bodies are elected by lower ones; decisions of higher bodies are binding on lower ones according to the principle of democratic centralism.

lack of unity and ideological cohesion. These factors, combined with the Marxist–Leninist vanguard party doctrine, were instrumental in convincing the MPLA leadership of the need for a thorough purge of party members to weed out those who indulged in factionalism, those who had joined the party with the intention of using membership for personal material advancement, and those who were not adherents of Marxism–Leninism or active supporters of party policies. The purge took the form of the party rectification movement.

The Central Committee report stated that

a vast rectification movement will be launched at all levels in order to correct errors, improve methods of work, cleanse the organisations of harmful elements and unite all militants behind the party's goal. The rectification movement will be the guarantee of unity within the party and of the ideological firmness of its militants . . . [MPLA, 1977, p. 12.]

The report added that unity did not mean the absence of ideological debate within the party

. . . on the contrary, frank debate on ideas by all members of the party . . . is the guarantee of the organisation's vitality. Applying the principles of democratic centralism, the party will demand of and guarantee its members free discussion of all questions which affect the organisation and conscious participation in its decision-making . . . democratic centralism excludes all forms of authoritarianism, arbitrariness and unity not based on the revolutionary principles of Marxism–Leninism. [MPLA, 1977, p. 12.]

The party's declaration of strict adherence to democratic centralism mirrored the adoption of the principle by the Russian Social Democratic Labour Party (the precursor to the CPSU) at the Fifth Congress in 1907 at Lenin's prompting. The MPLA-Workers' Party's (henceforth to be referred to by the Portuguese abbreviation—MPLA-PT) conception of democratic centralism and its role in party work was identical to that of Lenin in pre-revolutionary Russia. The principle has been succinctly encapsulated as follows by E. H. Carr:

The system of organisation has long been described in party circles as 'democratic centralism', a term intended to denote that double process by which authority flowed upwards from party cells in town or factory or village through intermediate local or regional committees till it reached its apex in the cental committee which was the organ of the sovereign congress, and discipline flowed downwards through the same channels, every party organ being subordinated to the organ above it and ultimately to the central committee. [Carr, 1966, volume 1, p. 195.]

The Central Committee report to the congress made a point of re-affirming the party's opposition to 'any manifestation of a tribal, regional or racial nature' (MPLA, 1977, p. 9). The party was determined to establish itself as a national organization, eschewing divisive or non-revolutionary ideologies. The anti-tribal and anti-regional declarations were also intended to signal the MPLA's intention to defeat the remnants of UNITA and the FNLA, which were still active in their respective areas of the country, basing their guerrilla campaigns and propaganda on ethnic differences (Ovimbundu tribalism on the part of UNITA and Bakongo nationalism and separatism on the part of the FNLA).

Related to the party's attempts to forge national unity and destroy anachronistic tribal or regional loyalties and the rectification movement was the great stress placed on educational work by the congress. Neto said in his report that one of the MPLA-PT's essential tasks was to raise the 'politico-ideological level of elements' through educational work and the through dissemination of party directives. Party schools would be established to train cadres for the party, state and the armed forces: 'those cadres will be the guarantee of the structuring of the party and the defence of the purity of Marxism–Leninism against all distortions' (MPLA, 1977, pp. 134–14). The party President also stated that radio, television and the press, 'under the leadership of the party', would have the task of mobilizing and educating the people in the objectives of the socialist revolution. The party and the state were also faced with the awesome task of combating illiteracy, which exceeded 80 per cent. The rectification campaign was launched soon after the congress and very quickly became a major factor in Angolan political life, with seminars and rectification meetings being held across the country.

On 14 December, following the end of the congress, the new Central Committee met and elected a Political Bureau with eleven full and three alternate members—nine of the eleven full members had been on the previous bureau. The congress and the Central Committee meeting confirmed Neto's position and power. His pre-eminent position introduced the 'presidential' factor into party and national politics. Although decision-making was the prerogative of the congress, the Central Committee and the Political Bureau, Neto was clearly the dominant force and guided the work of leading party and state organs. He had to have the support of his colleagues, but he was very much the first among equals on the Political Bureau. The other leading members were Lucio Lara, the veteran ideologist, Lopo do Nascimento, who had particular responsibilities in the economic field, and Iko Carreira, the Minister of Defence.

In the wake of the congress the party rectification campaign was launched along with identical campaigns in the mass organizations (notably the trade-union body, UNTA, and the youth wing of the party, the JMPLA, both of which had been implicated in the Alves coup). In December 1978, Neto and the party leadership decided on a reorganization of the government structure and a purge of senior party and state officials. The moves were intended not only to ensure ideological cohesion among leading post-holders but also to increase the power of the President. In the state sector, the posts of Deputy Prime Minister and Prime Minister were abolished. The justification given was that the removal of the posts would enable the President to deal directly with ministers rather than through the premier and his three daughters—the axeing of the jobs meant the dismissal of Lopo do Nascimento.

The Central Committee session held from 6 to 9 December instituted the purge of those party and government officials thought to be following divisive policies. On 10 December, Neto announced the dismissal of the former Second Deputy Prime Minister and Minister of Planning, Carlos Rocha Dilolwa, who was denounced as petit bourgeois. Dilolwa had been a close associate of Neto for many years and was considered to be a gifted economist. It is possible that he had disagreed with Neto and other leaders over the Central Committee decision to allow Angolan capitalists to continue to play a role in economic activity—the meeting of the Central Committee had decided to permit private businesses to set up construction and trading companies (this had been necessitated by the serious shortage of housing and the problems with the distributive system which had resulted from the exodus of the Portuguese). Another former Deputy Prime Minister, José Eduardo dos Santos, a leading supporter of Neto and a member of the Political Bureau, was appointed as Minister of Planning (ACR, 1978–9, p. B487).

Serious problems with party rectification were encountered in Benguela, formerly a stronghold of the MPLA. The problems resulted from the strength of support there for Alves and the shortage of cadres resulting from the coup and the subsequent purge of Alves supporters. Petit-bourgeois elements (notably small traders, owners of small fishing businesses and employees of government departments) used the shortage of cadres to gain admission to local party bodies. In 1979, Neto and a group of leading party officials visited the town with the intention of restructuring the party organizations. The communiqué on their work said that a 'rightist' group had infiltrated government bodies and party units, endangering working-class control of the decision-making process. A number of leading party officials in the town and province were dismissed and Dino Matross, the National Political Commisar of the Armed Forces, was appointed as party political leader of the province to oversee party restructuring and rectification there (Wolfers & Bergerol, 1983, p. 174).

Structural changes were introduced on a national basis during rectification. Chief among them was the increase in the number of Central Committee departments in December 1978, 'in order to exercise better control of government activity, (MPLA, 1980, p. 5). But measures such as these were not as successful or efficient as intended because there was still a massive shortage of educated and politically reliable (in terms of understanding of, and adherence to, Marxism–Leninism) cadres. The Special Congress of the MPLA-PT in 1980 noted that leading party bodies suffered from a shortage of cadres and that there were more of them in government rather than party institutions.

By early 1979, 2,734 rectification meetings and 4,952 sensitizing assemblies had been held around the country and 2,572 work-place meetings had been organized and attended by over 500,000 Angolans. The credentials of prospective party members had been discussed and subjected to comment and criticism by their fellow workers (whether party members or not). The result of the work had been the formation of 654 cells with over 8,750 militants, 6,338 aspiring members and 3,386 sympathizers. The MPLA youth organization had been rectified and had 4,000 members (Ottaway & Ottaway, 1981, p. 122).

The campaign greatly reduced the size of the membership, but was successful in forging a more united and ideologically uniform organization. The restructuring meant that when on 10 September 1979 Agostinho Neto died while undergoing medical treatment in the Soviet Union there was a smooth hand-over of power to the new President, José Eduardo dos Santos. There was no evidence of factionalism or internal dissension at the time of Dos Santos's appointment. He was appointed by the Central Committee as head of state and of the party; his appointment was approved by the party congress in 1980. By the end of 1979, with Dos Santos at the helm, the MPLA-PT had 16,583 cadres. The Luanda party bodies, which had been swollen by new members immediately after independence, had been reduced in size to 1,074 militants and 308 aspiring members; 488 rectification meetings had been held to select members. Luanda had seventy cells, twenty-eight nuclei bodies and a party committee.

The process of rectification and the role of workers in checking the credentials of prospective members was set out by Lucio Lara, the party organizing secretary and leading ideologist, as follows:

We have a list of members in a certain factory according to the census taken by the MPLA liberation movement. This list will be put to the workers of the factory . . . all workers will be asked for their opinions, not just militants. A workers' assembly will give its opinion on the comrades whom we consider to be militants of the party . . . [the workers' assemblies] will indicate to us which of the factory workers are really exemplary and have a worthy attitude towards production and who for one reason or another have not been linked to [the] MPLA when the liberation movement set up its structures inside the factory.

The exemplary workers would then be contacted by the party to sign up as militants, aspirants and sympathizers. As is obvious from Lara's stress on worker involvement, priority was being given to the recruitment of industrial workers. Under party regulations, industrial workers had only to serve one rather than two years' probation (Wolfers & Bergerol, 1983, pp. 167–8). According to Wolfers and

Bergerol, the party found it necessary to have militants from outside the area at rectification meetings in order to prevent undue influence or intimidation being exercised by local party officials or by members of the petit bourgeoisie. They also noted that rectification was less sharp and penetrative among office workers, media employees and civil servants than in factories and the armed forces.

The results of the rectification campaign and of party restructuring were the leading topics discussed at the Special Congress of the MPLA in December 1980. In the Central Committee report, presented to the congress by José Eduardo dos Santos, it was stated that the size of the party in 1977 and the lack of cohesion had necessitated a revision of organizational principles and the rigorous selection of members. Rectification started with the dissolution of the old structures—the MPLA Action Groups, Action Committees and Provincial Executive Committees—and their replacement by cells, party committees, provincial committees and conferences at various levels. The report said that initially selection of those to be rectified was carried out on the basis of those who had appeared on membership lists prior to the First Congress; this had been followed by direct consultations at workers' meetings. The Political Bureau had appointed provincial party committees to oversee party building in the provinces, while a National Rectification Committee had been established to view the process on a country-wide basis.

Four phases of rectification had been instituted before completion of the campaign:

1. Appointment of the National and Provincial Rectifiction Committees and the approval of guiding documents; the launching of pilot schemes (in the ports, public departments and the armed forces).
2. Analysis and correction of shortcomings in the initial application of guidelines and of the first phase of national rectification—launched after the pilot schemes; preparation of rectification meetings; discussion of membership registration; role of party youth bodies in rectification discussed.
3. Launching of rectification in rural areas; organization of 'rectified' people into cells; analysis of the 'age profile' of the membership;

establishment of the first neighbourhood sector committees; establishment of the party in defence and security bodies; the founding of a party newspaper, *A Célula*, which would be the medium of communication with party base organizations to ensure that they 'act in a uniform way'; drawing-up of regulations on party base organizations and the running of party committees at work-places.

4. Checking on the progress of rectifiction; removal of wrongly rectified people, establishment, through the National Rectification Committee and DORGAN, of various party echelons and issuing of directives on the running of party cells.

During the four phases of rectification, the Central Committee report said, nine rectification seminars were held by the party to analyse and guide the whole process (MPLA, 1980, pp. 12–13). The report said that during the process of party base organization formation, an inquiry was held into party activities in production units, as a result of which a national meeting of party cell coordinators was held to strengthen party organization and 'to make cells more conscious of their duty to control and follow the economic and social situations at work places' (MPLA, 1980, p. 14).

Dos Santos reported to the congress that as a result of rectification and the surveys of membership that had accompanied it, it had been possible to draw up statistics on the social backgrounds of party members. He said that 51 per cent of members were from worker or peasant backgrounds and that of those working as party or government employees a large number came from worker or peasant backgrounds. The party President said that an analysis of the origins of 15,471 of the membership of 31,098 had given the following breakdown (based on a sample of 49 per cent of party militants): 1.9 per cent peasants, 6.0 per cent intellectuals and technicians, 16.8 per cent employees, 22.5 per cent office-holders, 3.4 per cent others. The survey had revealed that 8.6 per cent of members were women (MPLA, 1980, p. 15) (Table 3.1).

One thing that the survey revealed was that, despite Dos Santos's comment that many office-holders and employees were of peasant origin, peasants were unrepresented in comparison with other groups. Given that 60 per cent of the labour force was engaged in agriculture, most of them as peasant farmers, and that about 79 per cent of the

Table 3.1 Party membership and composition as set out by the Central Committee reports to MPLA congresses

	1980	1985
Total membership	31,098	34,732
Militants	15,294	18,901
Aspirants	15,804	15,831
Number of cells	2,765	3,510
Party work-place committees	65	62
Number of women militants	974	1,775
Number of women aspirants	1,694	1,879
Composition of the party (%)		
Workers	49.1	35.0
Peasants	1.9	23.0
Office-holders	22.5	21.9
Employees	16.8	12.9
Intellectuals and technicians	6.0	6.0
Others	3.4	1.2

Note: The 1980 figures for party composition were based on a study of 49 per cent of members and the percentages add up to 99.7 per cent rather than 100 per cent. In addition, the report to the congress stated that many officials were of worker and peasant origin. The figure for peasants seems unnaturally low in 1980: according to the Central Committee report, workers and peasants made up 51 per cent of party membership in 1980, but a separate figure gave peasant representation at only 1.9 per cent.

Sources: MPLA, 1980, pp. 17–18; Luanda Radio, 6 December 1986.

population lived in rural areas, the figure of 1.9 per cent party membership for peasants plus others designated as office-holders showed that few peasants had been rectified and accepted as party members or that few peasants were interested in party membership. Either way it was not a positive outcome of rectification if one considered the MPLA-PT's oft-repeated principle that while the working class was the leading force of the revolution, the peasantry was the principal force. The danger for the MPLA-PT in failing to mobilize and recruit the peasants was that the party could become identified by those in rural areas as an organization run by and for the urban workers, intellectuals and office-holders.

The Central Committee report dwelt not only on the results of rectification, but also on the tasks of the party, the role of class struggle in the process of reconstruction and transition to socialism, and short-comings in party and state work. An important section of the report covered analysis of the revolutionary phase through which the leader-ship believed the country was passing. In orthodox Leninist termino-logy, the report said that Angola was in the phase of people's democratic dictatorship,

> . . . that is the initial period of transition from colonial capitalism to socialism, without going through the phase of building national capitalism . . . In keep-ing with this period of transition, the nature of the State is a reflection of the political rule of the working class, in alliance with the peasantry and other workers dedicated to the revolutionary cause of the proletariat. [MPLA, 1980, p. 31.]

The congress was told, as the 1977 congress had been told, that the political system in Angola was a revolutionary democratic dictatorship which was itself 'an embryonic form of the dictatorship of the pro-letariat', one of whose roles was the suppression of the enemies of the revolution. The report said that the revolutionary democratic dictator-ship 'makes it possible to unite all social forces of the nation to fulfil the tasks of the revolution'. However, the report then went on to stress that the current stage of the revolution involved a sharpening of the class struggle and an intensification of the fight against bourgeois tendencies and reactionaries.

The importance of the class struggle was emphasized very strongly at the Special Congress, even though the social and class make-up of the country meant that the concept was being imposed from above as a means of preventing the formation of a bourgeois ruling class rather than being a struggle against an existing, exploitative bourgeoisie. Although party leaders and documents spoke of the unity of the work-ing class and the peasantry, much of the stress on class struggle appeared to be aimed at the peasantry. This comes across very clearly in the following extract from the Central Committee report to the congress:

> The working class, although numerically small, is in the most favourable position to absorb Marxist–Leninism . . . The working peasantry, owing to its

living and working conditions and the concepts derived from them, is not in a position to assume the leading role in the struggle. This is so because the working peasant, in the words of the late Comrade President Agostinho Neto, has 'the seeds of capitalism', since he owns a small plot of land, means of production and hopes to expand them more and more. Therefore the transformation of society, whether capitalist or socialist, tends to lead to the disappearance of this class, either by joining the petit bourgeois, joining the working class or forming a new social group—the cooperative peasantry. In view of these tendencies to change, its size, the importance it assumes in the national economy and the role it played during the liberation struggle, the working peasantry is the basic ally of the working class and the principal force of the revolution. [MPLA, 1980, pp. 31–2.]

Although the extract ends on the theme of worker–peasant alliance, the message of the report and its reference to class struggle could have easily been interpreted by peasants wary of the government, and deliberately misinterpreted by UNITA and its supporters, as meaning that the MPLA–PT was intent on combating the peasantry because of its potential capitalist leanings or at the very least was planning to merge the peasants into the working class, this having the implication that land could be appropriated. In fact, the intention was that cooperatives should be formed by peasants which would wean them away from the petit bourgeoisie and make them more amenable to the socialist–collectivist aims of the ruling party. Dos Santos and his colleagues certainly did not have in mind the single-minded elimination of bourgeois-inclined peasants that was carried out in the Soviet Union under Stalin under the slogan 'Eliminate the kulaks (rich peasants) as a class' (Hill, 1985, p. 20).

The anti-bourgeois struggle was aimed at stamping out the economic and political influence of the few large-scale farmers, small tradesmen and industrialists who had been able to take advantage of the exodus of the Portuguese to increase their economic role and, in some cases, were able to gain admission to the MPLA–PT. The party was also determined to prevent the rise of a bourgeois-orientated bureaucratic elite. One result of the party's anti-bourgeois policies was the nationalization of private businesses in the early years of independence. Nationalization even affected very small-scale traders in rural areas, who had their shops and transport businesses taken over by the government. Because of a shortage of experienced cadres and the problems of economic dislocation caused by the liberation and civil wars, nationalization did not work and instead created immense problems in the countryside at a time when the party was trying to win over the peasants in their cooperativization campaign. In the end, many of the small distribution, transport and retail businesses were returned to private ownership—a move reminiscent of the Leninist New Economic Policy adopted in the wake of War Communism in post-revolutionary Russia at a time when economic reconstruction was the most vital task.

Unlike post-revolutionary Russia (which was only renamed the Soviet Union in December 1922), Angola had no history of class struggle or the social base for such a struggle. Thus the use of the term was very much a symbolic one, with the exception of the fight against the small numbers of petit-bourgeois public servants and businessmen, but it had applications, as David and Marina Ottaway have indicated, 'as a theory of hierarchical organisation and engineered change' in the absence of significant social conflict and class consciousness. The only real form of class struggle in Angola was the ideological struggle, in which the leadership of the MPLA-PT was striving to ensure the primacy of their form of Marxism–Leninism. They had to fight against factions within the party that held different views on socialism and the path to development and, on a nation-wide basis, they had to fight illiteracy, political apathy and the legacy of a century of colonial oppression and exclusion of Africans from political activity. Finally, the struggle was to prevent the formation of a bourgeois class that could exercise political and economic power and divert resources away from the productive sector and assume the role left vacant by the departing Portuguese. To some extent, as the Ottaways have argued, class struggle is an artificial concept in Angola (Ottaway & Ottaway, 1981, pp. 199–200) in that it does not derive from antagonistic classes; rather it has been imposed from above by the ruling party. Nevertheless, it has some validity in the sense of ideological struggle and the protection of what the MPLA-PT would term the gains of the national liberation struggle and the revolution, that is, control by a Marxist–Leninist party and the adoption of a socialist path of development, from the attacks on the MPLA-PT by UNITA and its external backers.

Class struggle certainly has validity for Angola in terms of external aggression. The active role played by ultra-capitalist South Africa in supporting the anti-Marxist UNITA movement and in conducting an undeclared war against the country's southern provinces undoubtedly derived from Pretoria's fear of the rise of socialism in a neighbouring state and from Angola's forthright stand in support of SWAPO and the ANC. American opposition to the MPLA-PT resulted from the latter's adherence to Marxism–Leninism and from Angola's close, cooperative relations with the Soviet Union, Cuba and other socialist countries.

The ruling party's emphasis on class struggle was, therefore, a symbolic move derived from adherence to orthodox Marxism–Leninism, but one did have definite ends in terms of ideological conflict, social engineering and highlighting the background to the externally inspired and supported guerrilla struggle being conducted by UNITA. This contention is supported by the stress placed by the Central Committee report on the role played in the class struggle by 'imperialism and its agents' (MPLA, 1980, p. 33). The congress made it clear that the MPLA-PT saw party unity and ideological cohesion as the chief weapons in the fight for political and ideological supremacy. The Central Committee report stated that 'working class ideology and democratic centralism will thus become as natural as breathing for every member of the party, which will become more cohesive and even achieve the monolithic unity required for the battles to be waged against imperialism and against petit-bourgeois ideology'.

Problems in achieving such unity and adhering to democratic centralism were discussed at length by the report and by the congress delegates. It was said that frequently decisions and directives passed by leading party bodies were not promptly or efficiently passed on to the base organziations and so were reduced 'to mere documents on file'. This implied a failure of the Central Committee Secretariat and of lower party control bodies to ensure that the party line was communicated to party cells and that directives were implemented fully and correctly. Other party shortcomings pointed out by the report were interference in cell activity by high-level officials 'destroying the spirit of initiative and creativity of base organizations'; improper interference by cells in the operation of enterprises 'to the detriment of . . .

authority and workplace discipline'; and the absence of dynamism in cell activity (MPLA, 1980, p. 19).

As with many of the other problems affecting party and state activity, the above shortcomings in party work were directly attributable to the shortage of trained, educated and experienced cadres and to the generally low educational level of the population.

One important task performed by the congress was the election of party members to the posts left vacant on the Central Committee at the 1977 congress. The membership of the Committee was brought up to seventy with the election of new representatives. The congress also decided to continue with the rectification campaign, giving particular emphasis to the rectification of bourgeois elements remaining in party and state bodies.

A potential problem that haunted the party leadership throughout the late 1970s and early 1980s was factionalism. Lucio Lara described the problem as 'part of the logic of revolutionary movements' and as a factor that could easily re-emerge within the party. In an interview with the magazine *Afrique-Asie*, he said that class conflict in the country was inevitable and that the party was ready to make it 'even more active, more biting and more conscious'. However, he cautioned against conducting a struggle incorrectly and, perhaps with the delicate position of the peasantry in mind, said that 'we cannot at the same time want national unity and arouse false divisions and contradictions poorly understood by the people'. He went on to say that the class struggle would therefore be limited to the party (Ottaway & Ottaway, 1981, p. 123).

By the beginning of the 1980s, the MPLA-PT had moved away from the Mbundu–*mestico* preponderance that had characterized it at the time of independence. It had become more representative of Angolan people as a whole, though it lacked high-level representation for the Ovimbundu peoples—by the mid-1980s, there was still no Ovimbundu representation on the Political Bureau. Although the MPLA-PT would argue that the Bureau was not chosen on ethnic lines, most of the other major groups were represented. The only senior official who was Ovimbundu was the Minister of Transport, Faustinho Muteka.

By June 1982, party membership was around 30,000, but the Central Committee plenum held that in that month launched a recruitment drive to push the numbers up to 60,000. The meeting also launched a drive against corruption and inefficiency in party and state organizations. The first casualty was the Central Committee Secretary responsible for agricultural production, Manuel Pedro Pacavira, who was dismissed for failing to effect significant improvements in agricultural performance. A government reshuffle took place in which Internal Trade was made into a separate department under its own minister, allowing Lopo do Nascimento, who had been Minister of Planning and Internal Trade, to concentrate on economic planning.

According to some reports, a factional struggle developed in 1982 between supporters of President dos Santos and 'a faction of Stalinist hardliners'. The conflict developed around a play written and presented by the allegedly Stalinist group which was critical of government policies. A major purge followed the performance of the play in which the head of the Information and Propaganda Department of the Central Committee, Ambrosio Lukoki, was dismissed by a meeting of the Central Committee held between 30 November and 8 December. Western observers said that a number of the 'Stalinists' were arrested and thirty-two MPLA-PT officials, including Lucio Lara's wife, were dismissed from party posts (ACR, 1982-3). The general Western interpretation of events was of conflict within the party between a 'nationalist' and a pro-Soviet faction. This fitted in with the generally uninformed Western picture of Angola as a Soviet client-state. In fact, the factional conflict developed between groups with differing ideas on the pace of socialist transition and over specific economic and political issues. By 1984, the factional struggle had died down, though, as Lara warned (see above), it is likely that factional disagreements will continue to arise periodically.

Speaking at the First National Conference of the MPLA-PT in Luanda in January 1985, President dos Santos said that although the rectification movement had provided the party with the right structure and improvements had been effected through the operation of the Political Bureau, the Central Committee and the Secretariat, 'there are still shortcomings in the liaison and information mechanisms at various levels, particularly between central and provincial structures and between them and the base organizations'. The party leader went on to state that 'it is a matter for concern that most of the grassroots bodies and organisations are not yet capable of exercising their leading role at workplaces, thus rendering more difficult the Party's leadership of society and the state' (MPLA, 19895, p. 3). It was clear from the deliberations of the conference that cadre shortages remained a serious obstacle to the coordination of party activity and that the low level of political consciousness of the majority of the population impeded optimal functioning of basic party units.

In his address to the conference, Dos Santos made plain what many observers had suspected—that the MPLA was still very weak in the countryside and had a low peasant content. He told the conference that 'the rectification movement ended its mandate without fully achieving the goals advocated for structuring the party in the countryside'. He went on to list some of the problems of party work in rural areas:

The criteria established for the selection of party members provided no margin for the recruitment of party members in the countryside, either . . . because the state farms were not organised or the majority of peasants were not organised in cooperatives or production associations . . . the virtual abandonment of the countryside . . . prevented us from organising the peasants to consolidate and expand socialist production and achieve the worker–peasant alliance. [MPLA, 1985, p. 4–5.]

Dos Santos warned that if socialism triumphed only in the factories and urban areas, 'the bourgeoisie will take the countryside'. He went on to say that

. . . our own experience has already shown that armed counter-revolution makes the countryside the starting point . . . the peasants are the victims and the main targets of the terrorist attacks . . . It seems to me more than evident that there is an imperative need for the party effectively to reassume the promotion of revolutionary activity in the rural areas . . . to establish mass organisations and increase the number of the party's base organisations in the countryside.

He added that priority should be given to training activists for political work in the countryside.

The President also dealt at length at the conference with the question of the educational level of party members. He said that attention should be given to 'the overcoming of theoretical shortcomings and education' and he noted that many members had been admitted to the party who, although politically conscious and active, had never had the opportunity to study Marxist–Leninist theory. He stressed the importance of party study groups and of the better dissemination of party documents and guidelines.

The major message of the conference, along with the special requirement of party work in the countryside, was the need to increase party membership in order to ensure a party presence in 'the most vital priority sectors'. It was noted that too many members were drawn from administrative workers and that party workers favoured work in the party apparatus rather than work as activists and organizers. An estimate published in 1985 put party membership at around 31,000 (Staar, 1985, p. xii).

The Second MPLA–PT Congress was held in Luanda at the beginning of December 1985. Again, shortcomings in party work and problems in the rural areas were high on the agenda. The low peasant representation at the congress (only twelve out of 600 delegates were peasants) showed that the party was far from solving the question of party work in the countryside. This could also be deduced from President dos Santos's litany of failings in agricultural production contained in his report to the congress. The other key problem for the party, education, was also examined in the Central Committee report, where it was stated that 14 per cent of party members were illiterate (*Guardian*, 9 December 1985). Party membership was announced to be around the 35,000 mark, still well below the target of 60,000. The congress elected a new ninety-member Central Committee from over 100 candidates, all of whom had to undergo rigorous questioning at cell, local, regional and provincial level meetings to assess their adherence to the party line and their understanding of party policy.

In his report to the congress, Dos Santos said that the membership was organized in 3,150 cells, with sixty-two party committees at workplaces. Total party membership was 34,372 with 15,831 candidate members. Women members only accounted for 3,644, just under 10 per cent. The President said that industrial workers made up 26.4 per cent of the party; agricultural workers, 8.6 per cent; peasants, 23 per cent; intellectuals and experts, 6 per cent; state employees, 12.9 per cent; and officials, 21.9 per cent. According to those figures, worker–peasant membership of the party was 58 per cent of total membership (compared to 51 per cent in 1980). If the figure for peasant membership was correct, it was inexplicable why there were only twelve peasant delegates at the congress. One possible reason is that party members with peasant backgrounds but who were no longer making their living through peasant agriculture may still have been counted as peasants (Luanda Home Service, 2 December 1985).

Although the congress dealt at length with shortcomings in party work, shortages of cadres, problems with the countryside, and many of the other obstacles raised at previous meetings, the party reaffirmed in no uncertain terms its continuing commitment to Marxism–Leninism. As one Western reporter who attended the conference put it, 'the debate here ... is how, not whether, to build a Socialist state' (*Guardian*, 9 December 1985).

The State Structure

Given the primacy of the MPLA-PT in the Angolan political system, the government structures play a less crucial role than the political party. Their function is to implement rather than formulate policy and they carry out this function under the close scrutiny of the party— though, as outlined above, party control is not always exercised as efficiently as party regulations require and as the leadership of the MPLA-PT would like.

In the period immediately after independence, the situation in Angola did not allow the holding of elections or the formation of representative local or national government bodies. In the period between independence and the establishment of the National People's Assembly and of local government institutions, the executive function was fulfilled by the Council of the Revolution, which was made up of members of the MPLA Central Committee and leading members of the armed forces. Above the Council was the Council of Ministers.

The Council of the Revolution was presided over by the President, who also directed the work of the Council of Ministers. MPLA control over the Council of the Revolution was ensured by the massive majority of senior MPLA cadres on the Council. The composition of the Council was as follows: the Central Committee of the MPLA, the

Minister of Defence, the Chief of the General Staff, the national political commissioners, members of the Council of Ministers appointed by the MPLA Political Bureau (up to three non-members of the MPLA Central Committee), provincial commissioners and military commanders and political commissars of the military regions.

The October 1976 plenum of the MPLA Central Committee ratified the Angolan constitution and decreed that under its terms the Council of the Revolution would discharge legislative functions, 'conduct the country's domestic and foreign policy, defined by the Central Committee of the MPLA', approve the general state budget and national plan drawn up by the government, appoint the Prime Minister and other members of the government 'on the recommendation of the MPLA', and authorize the President to declare war and make peace (MPLA, 1976, p. 24). The plenum decreed that the government should consist of the President, the Prime Minister, the Deputy Prime Ministers, the Ministers, Deputy Ministers, Secretaries of State and any other office-holders authorized under the constitution.

The constitution established that, on a provincial level, the representative of the government would be the provincial commissioner. At the district level the chief government official would be the local commissioner, at the commune level the commune commissioner, all of whom would be appointed on the recommendation of the MPLA. Below national level, the administrative divisions were established as the province, the district, the commune, the neighbourhood and the village—each would have a commission as its administrative body. It was intended that eventually the commissions, also known as *poder popular*, would be elected. However, at the time of the plenum in October 1976 there had been problems with the commissions that had grown up in Luanda during the civil war. These had come under the influence of the Nito Alves group and had, for a while, functioned as a parallel or alternative source of power to the party. The Central Committee stated in its report to the plenum that elections to the commissions would only be held 'where MPLA structures are sufficiently strong, organizationally stable and mature, from the political and ideological point of view'. The party leadership had no intention of allowing a repetition of the Luanda people's commission affair to challenge party supremacy.

One problem that hindered the MPLA in setting up a new government structure was the massive shortage of educated people to fill administrative posts and the fact that many of those who had received education under the Portuguese had gone on to work for the colonial administration—hardly the best qualification for a public official in a revolutionary administration. As already noted, the education shortage also deprived the party of sufficient cadres, thereby making the party's aim of guiding and monitoring the work of government organs more difficult. The October 1976 plenum of the party resolved that in building the new state machinery the MPLA would have to make use of 'functionaries who were least compromised with colonial policy'. This meant employing in senior administrative positions former employees of the Portuguese whose political complexion was very different to that of the ruling party and whose willingness to implement socialist policies was very much in question.

The First MPLA Congress in December 1977 reaffirmed the party's approach to the government institutions and, coming as it did after the Alves coup attempt, emphasized that the *poder popular* idea was being remodelled to give total control over the administrative bodies to the ruling party. The Central Committee report to the congress stated that the exercise of state power by the people could not be achieved without the leading role of the MPLA. The report added that 'the state apparatus is the principal instrument in the hands of the working class, under the leadership of the party, to achieve its political domination and exercise People's Power' (MPLA. 1977, p. 15). The report restated the intention of the party to destroy the old state machinery and replace it with the organs of revolutionary democratic dictatorship. The congress decided to pass statutes on control of the work of the people's commissions that had been created in Luanda and that had provided a power base for the supporters of Nito Alves. The law on the setting-up of the *poder popular* movement was severely criticized in the Central Committee report. The law was castigated for expressing

. . . a petit-bourgeois and hardly correct concept of State Power, with illusory ideas about democracy and about the way the working masses should ensure and consolidate their political power. The principles on which the law is founded are unrelated to the MPLA's leading force . . . People's Power is presented as an expression of spontaneous mass struggle which could be used against the party. [MPLA, 1977, p. 16.]

The report added that as a result of conceptual errors in the drafting of the law, it had been possible for factionalists to use it in a confrontation with the party. The result of the congress's deliberations on the future of *poder popular* was that the formation of the local government bodies was to be delayed until the party could be certain of complete control over the election and operations of the people's commissions.

Up until December 1978, the Council of Ministers, which stood at the head of the government structure, consisted of the President, the Prime Minister, the deputy Prime Ministers, Ministers, State Secretaries, and the Deputy Minister of Defence. The Prime Minister exercised control over the work of the ministries, with the assistance of his three deputies, and over the provincial commissioners. In December 1978, President Neto decided that he wanted more immediate control for the presidency without the Prime Minister and Deputy Prime Ministers as intermediaries. The result was that the posts of Prime Minister and Deputy Prime Minister were abolished and the President assumed direct control over the ministries. This not only enhanced the power of the President over day-to-day government operations; it also freed four very senior cadres for work in particular ministries or within the party machine. In 1979, Neto carried out a reorganization of the state security services, scrapping the unpopular Directorate of State Security (DISA) and sacking its commander, Ludy Kissassunda, and his deputy, Henriqué de Carvalho Santos.

By 1980, President dos Santos and the MPLA-PT leadership felt confident enough about the power of the party to start the process of establishing elected assemblies on a national, provincial and district basis. The party drew up lists of candidates from which Provincial People's Assemblies were elected. The members of the provincial assemblies in turn elected the deputies to the National People's Assembly. A meeting of the party Central Committee on 8–12 August approved changes to the constitution which replaced the Council of the Revolution with the People's Assembly, which became the supreme organ of state. The amendments to the constitution laid down that the government was now subordinate to the guidelines passed by the People's Assembly (which was itself subject to party guidance). The constitution stated that the Provincial People's Assemblies and the National People's Assembly would be elected every three years on the basis of universal adult suffrage—the right to vote was denied those who had been active in purged MPLA factions, UNITA, the FNLA or FLEC. Provincial Assemblies would have between fifty-five and eighty-four members according to the size of the province and the National Assembly would have 206 members. Elections for the provincial bodies took place at mass meetings with the vote being conducted on a show of hands. Those elected formed electoral colleges which then elected the Assemblies (6,750 delegates were elected at mass meetings held on 23 August 1980). The electoral colleges met on 12 October and elected the Provincial Assemblies from lists drawn up by the MPLA-PT, UNTA, the Organization of Angolan Women and the MPLA-Youth.

The National People's Assembly was inaugurated on 11 November 1980 and on 13 November it elected a twenty-five member Permanent Commission to carry out its business between sittings—the President and the whole of the Politburo were members of the Commission. The People's Assembly meets twice a year and has as its main tasks the approval and implementation of the budget and the national plan. According to the Central Committee report to the Special Congress of the MPLA-PT in December 1980, the first People's Assembly had the following social profile: political and administrative leaders, 31.5 per cent; workers, 28.6 per cent; peasants, 23.6 per cent; members of the defence and security forces, 9.9 per cent; intellectuals, 3.4 per cent; and state employees, 3.0 per cent. Again, peasants were under-represented given their numerical predominance. The report also said that it was the party's intention to extend the process of establishing people's assemblies right down to municipality, neighbourhood, commune and village level.

With regard to the judicial system, on 24 February 1978 a National Court Administation was established within the Ministry of Justice with the task of reorganizing the court system. On 30 March 1978, a law was promulgated instituting a new legal system based on People's Courts. These were set up throughout the country. The new courts had a professional judge with two lay judges, who were nominated by the MPLA and its mass organizations. The three judges had equal powers and standing and deliberated over criminal and civil cases without a jury.

Party-State Relations

Presenting the Central Committee report to the Special Congress of the MPLA-PT in December 1980, President dos Santos stated that one of the fundamental principles of Marxism–Leninism was 'the leading role of the party in society as a whole'. He went on to remind delegates that this concept had been affirmed by the late Agostinho Neto at independence and had been rigorously defined by the First MPLA Congress. Dos Santos said that the 1977 congress had stressed 'the Subordination of the State and all economic and social life to the leadership of the vanguard party of the working class' (MPLA, 1980, p. 43).

The leadership role of the MPLA was clearly set out in the constitutional amendment decreed in January 1980, which said that, 'all sovereignty shall be vested in the Angolan people. The MPLA-Workers' Party is the organised vanguard of the working class and, as a Marxist-Leninist Party, it shall exercise political, economic and social leadership over the State in efforts to build a socialist society.'

The MPLA-PT was careful to define its role and that of the state machinery. The 1980 congress report emphasized that the party had no intention of taking the place of the state, of mass organizations or of other social organizations. Rather, 'the party guides their activity and supports their work, strengthening their authority' (MPLA, 1980, p. 44). The relationship between party and state was defined as follows in the Central Committee report to the 1977 party congress:

The working class achieves its political domination through the party. It is the guiding, rectifying and organising force, the nucleus of power. There can be no working class political power or socialist state power without the leadership of a Marxist–Leninist party. Therefore, the party is the leading force in the revolution and the state apparatus is the principal instrument in the hands of the working class, under the leadership of the party, to achieve its political domination and exercise people's power ... the revolutionary democratic state apparatus is the principal instrument for carrying out revolutionary change. Hence, the state apparatus represents the power of the people, which means, in other words, that the organs of people's power cannot exist outside it, separate from state power. [MPLA, 1977, pp. 15–16.]

But despite these clear definitions of party–state relations and roles, the relationship between the two and between them and other social organizations was not trouble-free. In the early years of independence, the growth of the people's commissions in and around Luanda had taken place more or less beyond the control of party and state organs. The commissions, under the influence of Alves, had become alternative sources of political power. Following the abortive coup, these developments had resulted in the downgrading of the people's commissions in political importance and a stronger reaffirmation and constitutional enshrinement of the leading role of the party over all state and other organizations. In a way, the strengthening of party control was a victory for Leninist-style centralism over 'leftist', decentralized and populist forms of administration. It was also a victory of the orthodox Marxists in the MPLA over the more opportunistic elements, such as Alves, which shifted their ideological position to suit the state of the factional struggle (hence Alves's support for Neto's suppression of leftist factions and his subsequent adoption of leftist slogans as a means of fighting Neto).

The other problems that affected party–state relations were connected chiefly to the shortage of cadres and the lack of experience of the many cadres that did exist. This was compounded by the need to employ in senior public positions those colonial public servants regarded as 'least compromised' with colonialism. These obstacles meant that not all party and state cadres understood the exact role of party and state bodies and that some state functionaries deliberately ignored party guidelines and directives or only implemented them half-heartedly. This situation was recognized by President dos Santos when he told the 1980 Special Congress that:

Analysing the experience of party leadership of the state over these years it must be said that in some cases there has been a certain lack of understanding of its significance and of the manner in which the leading role of the party is exercised, both by state bodies and at some levels of the party structures themselves, giving rise to some lack of definition, dúplication and reciprocal interferences in both spheres of action. Party structures have frequently been improperly used for executive tasks, forgetting or misrepresenting their leading role. At the same time, state bodies have not always accepted or fulfilled the party guidelines and directives. [MPLA, 1980, p. 44.]

There seemed no quick or easy solution to this problem. Its basic cause was, as already noted, the shortage of and inexperience of existing cadres. This could only be overcome by expanding the membership of the party and stepping up training of cadres to ensure complete understanding of the party's tasks. Similarly, increased public education would help provide a greater pool of possible employees for state organizations, thus lessening dependence on those who had served the Portuguese.

One factor that, paradoxically, served both to increase party control over the state and to blur the differences beween the party and the state was the dual role of many senior party and government leaders. President dos Santos, for example, was head of state, head of the state apparatus, commander-in-chief of the armed forces and leader of the MPLA-PT. Other senior party leaders also exercised control over government ministries. At the highest level of overlap the responsibilities did serve to ensure close party supervision of government work, but it also meant that leaders had to play the dual role of formulating and implementing policy. Ordinary Angolans and inexperienced party and state officials must have been in a state of confusion over party–state relations as a result. When the Defence Minister made a speech, was he speaking as a member of the MPLA-PT Political Bureau or as a government minister implementing party directives? Table 3.2 demonstrates the overlap of party and state responsibilities.

The Political Bureau outlined in Table 3.2 was elected on 12 December 1985 by the new Central Committee which had been appointed by the December 1985 party congress. Absent from the Bureau was the former number two in the party and chief ideologue, Lucio Lara. Others dropped from the Political Bureau were Agriculture and Forestry Minister, Evaristo Domingos Kimba, Joao Luis Neto, and former head of DISA (the scrapped security directorate), Ludy Kissassunda. At the party congress, former Defence Minister and Political

Table 3.2 The overlap of party and state responsibilities

	Political Bureau	Council of Ministers
José Eduardo dos Santos	Member	President
Afonso Pedro Van Dunem Mbinda	Member	Foreign Affairs
Antonio dos Santos	Member	
Francisco Magalhaes Paiva	Member	
Juliao Mateus Paulo Dino Matross	Member	State Security
Kundi Payama	Member	
Manuel Alexandre Rodrigues Kito	Member	The Interior
Pascoal Luvualo	Member	
Pedro de Castro dos Santos Van Dunem Loy	Member	Energy and Petroleum
Pedro Maria Tonha Pedale	Member	Defence
Roberto Antonio de Almeida	Member	
Antonia Jacinto do Amaral Moutinho	Candidate member	
Maria Mambo Café	Candidate member	

Note: The Ministers of Agriculture, Provincial Coordination, Construction, Education and Culture, Finance, Fisheries, Foreign Trade, Industry, Internal Trade, Health, Labour and Social Security, Justice, Planning, and Transport and Communications and the Deputy Minister of Defence were all members of the Council of Ministers but not the Political Bureau. (All posts as of 12 December 1985.)

Bureau member Iko Carreira had been relegated to candidate member of the Central Committee, a fate also meted out to the former Foreign Minister, Paulo Jorgé.

The party changes did not imply any drastic alteration in ideological position or socialist policy. Rather, the dropping of Lara and Kissassunda from the Political Bureau and the demotion of Carreira and Jorgé seemed linked to the entrenchment of dos Santos's power and the gradual replacement of the old guard in the party who, although loyal to the party and its leader, were more associated with Neto and the struggle for independence than dos Santos and the tasks of national reconstruction and socialist transition. Although many Western journalists immediately termed Lara's political demise as a victory of the pro-Western over the pro-Soviet elements in the MPLA, there was no evidence of a change in direction in foreign policy. In fact, Dos Santos's speech to the December 1985 congress exhibited a strong anti-US line—particularly condemning over the repeal of the Clark Amendment and the debate over resuming military and financial assistance to UNITA.

Mass Organizations

A number of organizations affiliated to the MPLA grew up during the liberation struggle and played a supportive role in the fight against colonialism. In the post-independence period these movements have become important instruments in the MPLA's political, economic and social strategies. Chief among the organizations are the National Union of Angolan Workers (UNTA), the Organization of Angolan Women (OMA) and the MPLA-Youth (JMPLA). As Marcum points out, 'the services and organisational activities of these groups were important to the process of mobilising political support among thousands of Angolan refugees and *émigrés* in the Congo' during the war against Portugal (Marcum, 1978, p. 32). Following independence, the MPLA looked to the organizations to mobilize support for government and party policies and to pass up to the party leadership the views and feelings of the mass of the population.

Other mass organizations that came into being at the end of the liberation war were the people's neighbourhood commissions and self-defence groups, particularly strong in the slum areas of Luanda. They were an important factor in the MPLA's expulsion of the FNLA and UNITA from the capital during the civil war. After independence they became the basis for the *poder popular* movement, but fell into disfavour and were more or less destroyed after the Alves coup attempt.

During the liberation war and the civil war, the MPLA sought to control and direct the activities of the mass organizations through the Mass Organizations Department (DOM). One of DOM's major tasks was to mobilize people in liberated areas to maintain agricultural and other economic production. Cadres from DOM played an important role in organizing the first cooperatives in rural aeas. UNTA, the pro-MPLA trade-union organization, fulfilled a similar role in urban areas, organizing workers in factories and offices and trying to keep the economy going in the wake of the exodus of the Portuguese.

In the first years of independence, although the mass organizations were theoretically subject to party directives, they operated far more independently than the party leadership would have liked. The result of this was that the Alves group was able to gain a strong position in the JMPLA and UNTA and to use these groups along with the *poder popular* movement, as a counterweight to party authority. In his address to the nation on 1 June, following the crushing of the coup bid, Agostinho Neto said that there was evidence that the rebels had followers in the JMPLA, the OMA and UNTA. A purge of the organizations followed, as a result of which they became firmly subordinated to the party (Kaplan, 1979, pp. 139–40). The party rectification campaign had its counterparts in the mass organizations.

The creation of the vanguard party at the 1977 congress had immediate repercussions for the mass organizations. Not only were they brought under strict control, but they were given the role of intermediaries between the vanguard party and the population. The report to the congress set out their role as follows:

The mass organisations are unity bodies which, leading and organising the broad masses of the people, constitute the main vehicle for the transmission of Party policies to the whole people, and they are the guarantee of the participation of the masses in the study, discussion and implementation of Party policy in all sectors of activity in the country. The task of the mass organisations is to ensure that the masses participate in the life of the state in an organised way, to guide their work, contribute to the formation of a new mentality which makes a definitive break with the ideas of colonial and capitalist society. [MPLA, 1977, p. 13.]

The approach was identical to that taken by Lenin in the years immediately after the Russian revolution. He specifically stated that the trade unions should act as 'transmission belts' between the party and the workers. This was exactly what the MPLA had in mind. Mass organizations were to encourage political participation, disseminate and explain party policies, and assist with the implementation of state tasks. The danger was, as has happened to a great extent in the Soviet Union and Eastern Europe, that the mass organizations could just become tools for party control of the masses rather than vehicles for mass participation in decision-making.

Potentially, the most important of the organizations is UNTA. Given the tasks of national economic reconstruction and the transition to a socialist economy, it is vital for the MPLA-PT to have an organized and disciplined work-force in tune with party aims. Thus the Central Committee report to the 1977 congress stated that UNTA 'must cultivate in the working people socialist consciousness, developing in them a new attitude towards work, raising their technical level, their work productivity and their degree of discipline'.

A major shake-up in UNTA had been initiated by the MPLA leadership in the wake of the coup. The Secretary General of UNTA, Aristides Van Dunem, was dismissed on suspicion of complicity with the rebels. A National Commission for Restructuring of UNTA was formed under the leadership of a veteren Neto supporter, Pascoal Luvualo. He was given the task of rehabilitating UNTA and of looking into UNTA's future role in a system of worker participation in economic management.

It was a hard task to rebuild UNTA into a viable trade union, partly because of the debilitating effects of the coup but also because there was little experience of effective union activity inside Angola under Portuguese rule—UNTA had been more or less totally an exile movement prior to the April 1974 revolution. Wolfers and Bergerol have pointed out that under colonial rule the only workers' organizations were powerless *sindicatos*, which were not empowered to negotiate wages or working conditions and could not exert pressure on management. In these circumstances UNTA had an uphill task as it had to create a viable union system while at the same time helping to maintain labour discipline and productivity (Wolfers & Bergerol, 1983, p. 118).

At first, UNTA was far from successful. There was little working-class consciousness among the small industrial work-force and little political experience—the peasants had borne the brunt of the guerrilla war against the Portuguese. The situation improved under Luvualo and he gained extensive help from Cuban shop stewards and union administrators who went to Angola to assist with the restructuring programme. By the early 1980s, UNTA had achieved some success in building unions in various economic sectors (Table 3.3).

Table 3.3 Membership of the National Union of Angolan Workers (UNTA)

Name of union	Number of members
Coffee Workers' Union	112,000
Agriculture and Livestock Workers' Union	43,000
Heavy Industrial Workers' Union	49,000
Transport and Communicatons Workers' Union	30,000
Construction and Housing Workers' Union	35,000
Light Industrial Workers' Union	12,500
Health and Public Administration Workers' Union	50,000
Food and Hotel Workers' Union	42,000

Despite the improvement in membership levels, all was still not well with UNTA as far as the MPLA-PT was concerned. The Central Committee report to the 1980 congress stated that

... it has not yet been possible to structure a dynamic nationwide trade union movement to mobilise the working people effectively with a view to fulfilling the major economic tasks. This is partly due to the lack of a legal framework permitting the effective participation of the working masses in the solution of labour questions ... and to the shortage of trade union cadres who combine political preparation with managerial and administrative experience, basic technical know-how and understanding of economic matters [MPLA, 1980, p. 46.]

The congress set out the union's task over the next five years as follows:

... trade union organisation, trade union participation in the planning projects of enterprises, active participation in complying with labour legislation and establishing the system of labour justice, mobilising workers throughout the country for socialist emulation campaigns, setting up brigades to carry out tasks in the most varied sectors of our economy—all this will enable UNTA and its trade unions to establish themselves over the next five years as a broad organisation of the Angolan working people which, under the leadership of the Party, will play a decisive role in laying the material and technical foundations for socialism.

The clear stress in the congress's plan was on the leading role of the party and on the role of UNTA in increasing production (through productivity-emulation campaigns and through the organization of workers' brigades to help with basic tasks such as coffee-picking and infrastructural work).

In the year prior to the congress there had been evidence of dissatisfaction within UNTA over the running of some industrial enterprises and over the failure to implement worker participation in economic decision-making. In its May Day message, UNTA said that genuine worker participation had not been established and that enterprise managements and the state were too keen to blame all problems of productivity and plant breakdown on poor labour discipline and alleged UNTA failures. The messsage went on,

... in no way can our workers be held responsible for widespread breakdowns in stocks of raw materials and spare parts, for the lack of planning and economic coordination between different organisations, for damage to equipment and other goods in our ports and airports, and for the shortcomings in the proper use of our foreign technical assistants. [Wolfers & Bergerol, 1983, p. 120.]

But despite this broadside, in 1982 party and UNTA leaders were still calling on the government to institute MPLA policies on worker participation in the running of the economy.

Although its problems were by no means solved and there remained much to be done in terms of organizing effective industrial and agricultural unions and gaining a direct say in management, UNTA had by mid-1984 been able to boost overall union membership to around 600,000 (out of an estimated work-force of 2,000,000—the majority of whom were engaged in small-scale agriculture). A national congress of the body was held in mid-April 1984 and it was addressed by the Minister of Planning, Lopo do Nascimento, who told the delegates that all union members should understand their responsibilities in the process of economic reconstruction. The tenor of the meeting and the exhortations to discipline and increased productivity indicate the extent to which UNTA had developed into a Soviet-style union pre-occupied with fulfilling party instructions on economic reconstruction (the level of party control over UNTA is shown by the appointment of Pascal Luvualo, a leading member of the Political Bureau, as Secretary General).

The JMPLA (MPLA-Youth) has a crucial role to play in the political process in Angola as it is the sole path to party membership for people under the age of 25. The youth wing of the party is for those aged between 17 and 25. Members of the youth organization progress to party membership at the age of 25 if they can prove that they have been active party youth workers and have accepted party guidance and discipline. Members of the youth movement also take part in the Popular Defence Organization (ODP—for further details of this organization see the military affairs section in Chapter 5). As with UNTA, The JMPLA was restructured following the Alves coup. A major rectification campaign was carried out within the organization to ensure loyalty to the party. Following the campaign, which ended shortly before the party congress in 1980, youth organization membership was said to have reached 70,000. However, the 1980 congress pointed out a number of shortcomings in the JMPLA, notably inefficiency in administration and insufficient work in the field of political education and mobilization. But the Central Committee report to the congress pointed out that 'the poor response to the need to coordinate efforts with state bodies, in some cases, and lack of sufficient dynamism in agitation and propagandising revolutionary ideas, in others, means that it has not yet been possible to overcome the situation of apparent apathy among our youth'.

The Central Committee admitted, though, that it, too, had made mistakes in dealing with the youth question, not giving sufficient attention to analysing the needs of the party youth wing. The Committee added that ultimately it was the responsibility of the JMPLA to organize young people, educate them in Marxism–Leninism and prepare them for joining the party. It added that the JMPLA should play a leading role in establishing and redirecting youth brigades, whose task would be to assist in the task of national reconstruction and increasing productivity. Among the youth problems which the congress identified as needing urgent attention from the JMPLA were corruption among young people in urban areas, apathy, the flow of young people to the towns from the countryside, and the struggle for equal rights for young women.

The Organization of Angolan Women (OMA) has been assigned by the party the role of ensuring the emancipation and equality of women. The Central Committee report to the 1980 congress noted that Angola had inherited certain ideas about women from traditional and colonial society that were not in line with the concept of women and their role held by the MPLA-PT. The report stated that 'women can no longer be instruments of labour, decorative figures or sexual objects. We must see women as companions in struggle and work who take an active and enthusiastic part in all tasks of national life' (MPLA, 1980, p. 47). The OMA was instructed to give particular attention to literacy work (as the rate of illiteracy is higher for women than for men) and to improving political and professional education for women. Wolfers and Bergerol have pointed out that the OMA has been relatively quiet on womens' rights *per se*, partly because MPLA decrees have legally abolished sex discrimination at work and in payment of wages. The First National Congress of the OMA was held in 1983. The OMA is led by Ruth Neto, sister of the late President, who is also a member of the Central Committee (as is her sister Irene). Women are represented on the Political Bureau by Maria Mambo Café, the Central Committee Secretary for the economic sector.

Other leading mass organizations which play an important role in mobilizing the population to follow party policies and educating people politically include the peasants' unions, which group together cooperatives in the rural areas. The 1980 MPLA congress was told that unions had been set up in Uige, Malanje, Kwanza Sul, and Huila, grouping together 16,894 cooperatives. This is a minute fraction of the peasant population—another indication of the failure of the MPLA to pay sufficient attention to the political education of the peasants and their mobilization in support of the party. Given that peasants made up the bulk of guerrilla fighters during the war and constitute the majority of the population, it is a major shortcoming in political work and is undoubtedly an important factor in UNITA's relative success in infiltrating those rural areas which were not MPLA operational areas during the liberation war or which have not been paid sufficient attention during the party and mass organization rectification and restructuring campaigns.

Political Dissent

Political dissent has taken three basic forms in post-independence Angola: factionalism within the party; petit-bourgeois opposition to government policy within the party and state apparatus and peasant resistance to political organization by the MPLA in rural areas; and the guerrilla war and international propaganda campaign waged by UNITA (with massive South African support). The first two of these forms of dissent have been dealt with, but the third and by far the most serious has only been noted in passing.

UNITA was formed on 13 March 1966 at Muangai in eastern Angola by a group of dissidents from Holden Roberto's FNLA. Its leader was Jonas Savimbi, the former Foreign Minister in Roberto's government-in-exile. Although Savimbi claims to have spent extensive periods leading UNITA military operations inside Angola during the struggle against the Portuguese, his movement was relatively insignificant as a threat to the Portuguese, but it was a major irritant to users of the Benguela Railway, which he attacked periodically, to the consternation of President Kuanda of Zambia. Kuanda expelled Savimbi from

Zambia in February 1967 for sabotaging the railway, one of Zambia's major trade routes for its vital copper exports. Despite his expulsion, Savimbi was able to slip back into Zambia and then Angola with help from the South West African People's Organization (SWAPO).

In the late 1960s and early 1970s, Savimbi claimed to have built up 2,900 UNITA branches within Angola and to have sixty-six military units operating against the Portuguese—US State Department documents estimated in 1970 that UNITA had only 2,000 members and at most 200 guerrillas. Nevertheless, UNITA claimed in 1972 to have 4,000 fighters and to be militarily active in Bie and Huia Provinces (Wolfers & Bergerol, 1983, p. 197). UNITA received a little support from China during the guerrilla struggle, and immediately after the Portuguese revolution contacts were made with Savimbi by the CIA.

UNITA was the first of the Angolan liberation movements to sign a ceasefire with the Portuguese—on 14 June 1974. During 1974 and 1975, UNITA manœuvered to try to prevent the MPLA from taking power. In order to achieve this, Savimbi allied himself with the FNLA, the CIA and South Africa (it was said that President Kuanda supported this coalition against the MPLA through the provision of moral and material support for UNITA (Anglin & Shaw, 1979, pp. 330–1 and 337). UNITA was heavily involved in the fighting which took place in the run-up to independence in 1975. A joint UNITA–South African force was very nearly successful in its advance on Luanda in October and November 1975, prior to being defeated by an MPLA–Cuban force and then pushed out of Angola in February 1976.

Following its defeat in the civil war, UNITA launched a guerrilla war in the traditionally Ovimbundu areas of southern-central Angola (Savimbi is Ovimbundu and he used tribalism as a major tool in inciting rural dwellers against the MPLA government). UNITA continued to receive South African support and was able to use occupied Namibia as a secure rearguard base. South Africa supplied Savimbi with arms, financial support and, perhaps most importantly of all, logistical support in the form of road and air transport to enable Savimbi's guerrillas to operate in widely dispersed areas without having to worry unduly about extended lines of communications. Combat support was also provided by South Africa. Special commando groups of the South African Defence Force (SADF) carried out raids against bridges, roads and other major economic and infrastructural targets. These raids were then claimed by UNITA. For many years, MPLA claims that South African troops were posing as UNITA guerrillas were not generally believed, until a South African army captain, Wynand du Toit, was captured in the Cabinda enclave in May 1985 while on a mission to destroy oil installations.

A main target of UNITA guerrillas, and their South African sponsors, in the late 1970s and early 1980s was the Benguela Railway. The line was frequently put out of action by UNITA. The guerrillas also attacked isolated rural settlements, frequently forcing the inhabitants to move to UNITA-controlled areas adjacent to the Namibian border. Savimbi's 'capital' of Jamba is situated in a sparsely populated part of southern Cuando Cubango Province. UNITA claims to have large liberated areas in central and southern Angola in which it has administrative control. This is disputed by the Luanda government, which does admit however, to UNITA activity in most of the provinces in the country. From 1979 onwards, Savimbi claimed that UNITA controlled about one-third of Angola. What is probably true is that UNITA has scattered areas of total control in southern and central Angola and that its forces are a serious problem for FAPLA in a third of the country.

By 1980, it appeared as though the MPLA was bringing the UNITA problem under control. A FAPLA offensive in September 1979 pushed the rebels out of many of the areas which they had occupied along the Namibian border. However, in 1980 and 1981, the South Africans commenced a series of cross-border raids from Namibia and stepped up military support for UNITA. This not only enabled UNITA to resume extensive guerrilla activity; it also drew Angolan troops away from areas of rebel activity by forcing them to confront the South African threat. The South Africans consistently claimed that their raids were not aimed at Angolan troops or installations but at SWAPO guerrilla concentrations (until the signing of the Lusaka accord in February 1984, the MPLA government allowed SWAPO to use southern Angola as a base for operations against the South African occupying forces in Namibia). However, the size and the geographical location of the raids made it pretty clear that they were also aimed, if not primarily aimed, at destroying MPLA control along the border area and enabling

UNITA to operate in relative safety. Between December 1979 and April 1980, FAPLA sweeps in Bie and Huambo had reduced UNITA activity there. Over 300,000 people in Bie and 800,000 in Huambo were said to have returned to government-controlled areas from the bush following the counter-insurgency drives. To counter FAPLA successes in some rural areas, UNITA stepped up bombing campaigns in the towns of Huambo, Luanda, Benguela, Lubango and Mocamedes.

In early 1981, details began to emerge, as a result of desertion by Western mercenaries, of long-term South African military operations in southern Angola. A British mercenary who had served with the South Africans in that area said that the SADF's 32nd Battalion had been constantly involved in combat activities inside Angola since 1979. He also gave details of atrocities committed against Angolan civilians by the South Africans. His testimony gave increased weight to the reports issued by the Angolan government outlining continued South African aggression and military aid for UNITA (ACR, 1980-1, p. B649).

In August 1981, the SADF launched a major invasion of southern Angola code-named Operation Protea. The Angolan Defence Ministry reported in late August that SADF aircraft had carried out over 100 bombing missions during the invasion and preceding raids. The South African attacks, although again justified by Pretoria as hot-pursuit raids or pre-emptive strikes against SWAPO, involved the cutting of the N'Giva-Lubango road, the destruction of the main road bridge over the Cunene at Xangongo and an advance by ground units to within 80 kilometres of Lubango. A major battle took place between the SADF and FAPLA at Cahama, but FAPLA was unable to prevent the South Africans from creating an occupied buffer zone along the border in Cunene Province. This zone was more or less cleared of Angolan civilians—over 130,000 fled north into FAPLA-controlled areas. The SADF used the zone to support UNITA operations further north and to draw off large numbers of Angolan troops who had been engaged in an increasingly successful offensive against UNITA in Cuando Cubango. The South African occupation continued until mid-1985, though even after that intermittent raiding meant that Angola's Cunene Province was rarely free of South African troops and FAPLA had to split its forces to deal with the rebels and with the South

African threat. On 29 November 1981, once the South Africans had dug well in in Cunene, a commando raid was launched by them against the Petrangol oil refinery in Luanda. The raid was claimed by UNITA, but all the indications are that it was carried out by the SADF (*West Africa*, 7 December 1981).

The South African presence in Cunene and its raids into Namibe and Huila Provinces during 1982 took pressure off UNITA and enabled it to spread into provinces further north, such as Malanje and Cuanza Sul. On one occasion in 1982, UNITA guerrillas launched raids within 130 kilometres of Luanda. In December 1982 a major FAPLA offensive was launched in Cuando Cubango and heavy fighting took place between FAPLA and UNITA forces at Mavinga. Although the offensive pushed UNITA back into southern areas of the province, raids and sabotage in other provinces did not abate. In March 1983, UNITA achieved a major propaganda victory when it seized eighty-four Czechoslovak and Portuguese workers from a construction project in central Angola.

In July 1982, UNITA had held its Fifth Congress at Mavinga. The congress confirmed Savimbi's leadership and called on the MPLA to send home all Cuban troops and to start negotiations on the formation of a government of national unity that would include members of UNITA. The dos Santos government refused to negotiate with UNITA. By late 1983 and early 1984, UNITA had spread its area of guerrilla activity into Moxico, Huila, Lunda Sul, Lunda Norte, Cuanza Sul, Cuanza Norte and Malanje Provinces. In a new year's broadcast to the Angolan people, carried by the South African-run radio station broadcasting in Savimbi's name, Jonas Savimbi said 1984 would be the year of the anti-Cuban patriotic front. He claimed that UNITA had been able to infiltrate Luanda Province and that during the coming year UNITA would launch campaigns in Uige (the main coffee-growing area), Zaïre Province, Luanda town and Cabinda (the centre of oil production). The UNITA leader called on the MPLA to start negotiations and demanded the withdrawal of Cuban troops and Soviet advisers from Angola. It was hard to pinpoint any definite ideological content in the speech other than anti-communism and anti-Sovietism. Savimbi denied being a South African puppet but said that Angola had to live in peace with its southern neighbour. The rebel leader referred to the capture of foreign workers during 1983 and warned that such operations would continue in 1984 (Voice of the Resistance of the Black Cockerel, 7 January, 1984).

In late 1983, the South Africans had come to Savimbi's aid during the height of a FAPLA offensive. The offensive had started during August, when there was a major battle at Cangamba in Moxico Province. Angolan government forces had pushed UNITA out of the town, which had then been reduced to rubble by SADF aircraft. In October, reportedly after the arrival of a major Soviet arms shipment, the FAPLA offensive continued. On 6 December 1983, the South Africans launched a major offensive from their buffer zone in Cunene. At one stage the South Africans pushed right up into Huila Province. Extensive fighting took place between the SADF and FAPLA at Cahama and Cuvelai. On 29 December, South African aircraft bombed Lubango. The fighting died down in early January, once the offensive against UNITA had been frustrated, and the SADF returned to its buffer zone. In January, South Africa used the threat of further military action to force Angola into talks on the disengagement of forces in southern Angola (Somerville, February 1984, pp. 26-7). The talks, with American mediation, ended in mid-February with the signing of the Lusaka accord, which provided for South African withdrawal from Angola in return for the prevention by the MPLA of SWAPO infiltration of Namibia from southern Angola. South Africa refused to negotiate on its relations with UNITA.

Although Luanda stuck to its side of the bargain, Pretoria did not and aid continued to be given to UNITA by the South African forces which continued to occupy parts of Cunene Province until the middle of 1985, even though withdrawal was supposed to be completed by the end of March 1984. When the South Africans withdrew from the town of N'Giva, they left behind nothing but rubble and flattened buildings. But partial withdrawal still left troops inside Angola and necessitated the detachment of substantial military forces from the FAPLA units fighting Savimbi.

During 1984 and 1985, UNITA continued to operate over a wide area of Angola and continued to get substantial press coverage in South Africa and the West as a result of South African help and the tactic of seizing foreign workers and then releasing them at elaborate media ceremonies at Savimbi's Jamba headquarters. UNITA was at its peak as far as press coverage and guerrilla attacks were concerned in 1984. The following year saw more concerted FAPLA campaigns. In the closing months of the year, UNITA was defeated at Cazombo and then Mavinga, and it looked as though FAPLA was on the point of pushing Savimbi out of Jamba and back into Namibia. Once again, South Africa came to the rescue. Air and ground attacks were launched against the victorious FAPLA units at Mavinga and victory was turned into defeat once more. The major South African role was revealed when a South African army medical orderly was killed in Moxico Province. Until then, the South African Defence Minister, General Magnus Malan, had claimed that his troops were operating against SWAPO in Cunene Province. The death of the soldier forced him to admit that South Africa was giving UNITA 'humanitarian aid'. He later said that South Africa would not permit the MPLA government to defeat UNITA.

In early 1986, UNITA was continuing its guerrilla warfare in much of the rural zone of southern and central Angola and periodically attacking targets further north. FAPLA was continuing its counter-insurgency drives, but with little hope of finally defeating UNITA because of the South African factor. At the end of 1985, it was estimated that UNITA's military wing (FALA—the Armed Forces for the Liberation of Angola) was nearly 60,000 strong, with 26,000 in what a FALA officer described as the regular forces and the other 34,000 in the guerrilla forces. Lt.-Col. Jardo of FALA said the regular forces were used in conventional operations on the edges of UNITA's 'liberated areas', while the guerrilla forces carried out the fight into FAPLA-controlled areas. The UNITA arsenal is said to contain 122mm. howitzers, 76mm. and 57mm. field guns, recoilless rifles, mortars, surface-to-surface and surface-to-air missiles, anti-aircraft guns and various infantry weapons (many of them Soviet and Eastern European weapons captured by the South Africans and supplied to UNITA). Fuel for UNITA's logistical vehicles is supplied by South Africa (*Jane's Defence Weekly*, 16 November 1985, pp. 1086–7). It must be borne in mind that these estimates of military strength are based on reports supplied by UNITA, which in the past has been guilty of vastly inflating its claims of support and military activity.

It is hard to pin a definite ideological or political label on Savimbi. At times during the liberation struggle, he veered towards socialism and Maoism, presumably as a means of obtaining Chinese assistance. His style has always been populist and his support based on peasants in chiefly Ovimbundu areas (although the founders of UNITA, along with Savimbi, were chiefly Angolan students studying in Western Europe and the United States): the Ovimbundu base of the party explains the use of tribalism as a means of inciting people against the government. UNITA claims that the MPLA is not only dominated by the Soviets and the Cubans; it adds that the movement is run by *mesticos*, whites and Mbundus and that other tribal groups are excluded. Although there is only one Ovimbundu in leading party and state positions, one chief reason for the absence of members of this ethnic group from leadership bodies is that UNITA guerrilla activity has prevented or hindered MPLA efforts to mobilize and recruit people in Ovimbundu areas where UNITA is present as a political and military force.

The main components of Savimbi's speeches and broadcasts are demands for the withdrawal of Cuban troops and Soviet advisers, the need for better relations with South Africa, and calls for a government of national unity in which UNITA would be represented. Savimbi has support from right-wing and official circles in the United States (at the time of writing a decision on the resumption of aid to UNITA by the Reagan administration was keenly awaited by Savimbi, who visited Washington in January 1986 and was received by President Reagan) and conservative and multinational business circles in Western Europe. His blueprint for government would be a populist one, though also an autocratic one—Savimbi has allowed no other UNITA leaders to achieve prominence. UNITA would favour the cessation of extensive cooperation with the Soviet Union, Cuba and Eastern European states and the building of closer political and economic links with the West and South Africa. In the past Savimbi had close links with SWAPO and cordial relations with other liberation movements, but his pro-South African stance makes him fairly isolated in Africa, although he may well receive covert support and encouragement from conservative, pro-Western leaders such as President Mobutu of Zaïre. Despite his habit of kidnapping foreign workers in Angola, Savimbi has made it clear that he would welcome the expansion of foreign investment in a UNITA-run Angola.

But whatever Savimbi's political plans, the movement has become almost completely dependent on South African military, logistical, financial and propaganda support. His ten-year guerrilla war would have crumbled, as did the attempts by Holden Roberto's FNLA, without the sponsorship given by Pretoria. UNITA is unlikely to defeat the MPLA government militarily unless the South Africans decide on a full-scale invasion, and even then the 20,000 Cuban troops in Angola would be brought into play. The most likely scenario for the next few years is that Pretoria will provide Savimbi with sufficient assistance to enable him to maintain the military conflict at the present level, stepping in only to bale him out when FAPLA offensives threaten to swamp UNITA. For South Africa, UNITA is an ideal tool for destabilizing Angola. It is conceivable that Pretoria does not intend to bring about the complete destruction of the MPLA. Without the Marxist MPLA in control in Angola, South Africa would be without one of its major arguments for limiting Western pressure for the abolition of apartheid—the need for a conservative, white-ruled South Africa capable of keeping at bay the Marxist 'threat' to southern Africa's mineral resources and to the allegedly vital Cape sea-lanes. The presence of Soviet advisers and Cuban troops is another card in South Africa's propaganda pack.

Overall, UNITA is likely to remain a running sore in the side of Angola for years to come. Only the withdrawal of South African troops from Namibia and the cessation of direct military support for the movement would enable the MPLA to wipe it out militarily and politically.

Although in the years of independence the FNLA and FLEC (Front for the Liberation of Cabinda Enclave) were active in northern Angola and Cabinda, the partial *rapprochement* between Angola and Zaïre following the two Shaba crises meant that from 1978 onwards they declined in importance and are now either inactive or lingering on but peripheral to the future of the security of Angola. In late 1984, there were reports of mass desertions by former FNLA fighters in northern Angola.

4 The Economy

On independence, the MPLA inherited an economy with massive long-term potential but huge short-term problems. The country had extensive oil reserves, commercially viable diamond and iron-ore deposits, significant hydroelectric power production and potential, a thriving coffee industry, a reasonably large manufacturing sector geared towards internal consumer needs, a stable food-production sector, and more or less adequate road and rail systems. One writer said that the economy 'offered considerable promise for the future . . . under almost any circumstance' (Kaplan, 1979, p. 203). The country was generally able to feed itself, supply its basic consumer needs and produce enough oil, diamonds and coffee to bring in hard currency with which to purchase necessary imports and contribute towards development.

The fly in the economic ointment was the departure of the Portuguese in the wake of the Portuguese revolution and the civil war. The vast majority of settlers and government and economic administrators left the country, taking with them capital, transport vehicles and much of the country's fishing fleet. What they also took with them was managerial experience and the majority of the skilled workers and technicians who had run the economy. Under colonial rule, the Portuguese had monopolized all managerial and technical jobs and most skilled occupations right down to the level of truck and taxi drivers and small shopkeepers. The exodus in 1975 left the economy devastated. The potential and the material resources were there, but colonialism had denied the Angolan people training and experience to enable them to take on the role of running the economy unaided. The transport system fell to pieces, as over two-thirds of the vehicles were taken out of the country by the Portuguese, and the retail and distribution set-up all but collapsed, particularly in rural areas.

In financial terms, the MPLA government was in a strange situation, as the currency in use was the colonial one, the Portuguese escudo, and the main banks were owned by the Portuguese (some with other foreign countries owning shares). The national bank, the Banco de Angola, was controlled by the Banco de Portugal, while the five commercial banks were either Portuguese-owned or of mixed Portuguese–Western European ownership.

The basic approach of the MPLA to the economy was extremely cautious. The movement was committed to the creation of a socialist economy but it was pragmatic enough to realize that considerable reconstruction efforts had to be made before any serious attempts could be made to transform the nature of the system. The MPLA programme of 1962 had set out the objectives of abandoning the one-crop system in agriculture (which created over-reliance on the export crop, coffee), achieving state control over foreign trade, instituting price controls, nationalizing land, and implementing some form of national economic planning. Between 1962 and independence, the movement's commitment to Marxism–Leninism had deepened, as had the intention of establishing a fully socialist economy. However, these plans were very much in the long term, and after independence the MPLA set about the task of reconstruction and the replacement of the 300,000 managers, technicians and skilled personnel who had fled the country.

The Neto government took an extremely careful line in dealing with the agricultural sector and made no immediate moves to nationalize or collectivize land. Some large plantations and farms abandoned by their Portuguese owners were taken into state hands, but peasant farmers were not rigidly organized. Addressing a conference of the trade union movement, UNTA, in October 1976, Agostinho Neto said that collectivization was a long-term goal, but he added that the process of achieving it would have to be gradual, warning that 'if now in the name of socialism we were to begin to expropriate the peasants, our people would at once feel they were being sacrificed to our socialist option' (Ottaway & Ottaway, 1981, p. 121). In the short term, he emphasized, ideology was going to have to give way to production. This principle was put into practice not long after independence, when coffee plantations which had been made into state farms were given over to the Ovimbundu agricultural labourers who worked the farms when it became obvious that the large state farms were inefficient—the Ovimbundu grew coffee for export on a small-scale farm basis following the breakup of the state farms.

The overall economic programme of the MPLA was set out in the Resolution on Economic Policy approved by the Central Committee plenum in October 1976. The resolution made it clear that a planned, socialist economy 'with agriculture as its basis, and industry as the decisive factor' was a strategic goal rather than an immediate one. The resolution outlined eighteen short-term tactical aims. They included: achievement of the production levels of 1973 in the shortest possible time (GNP had declined by 20 per cent during 1976 as a result of the post-1974 dislocation); continuation along the road of nationalization and confiscation; institution of a rigorous system of control over the economy through a national plan, control of financial resources and banking; combating corruption and diamond smuggling; preparation of new customs policies, ending Portugal's preferential tariff; working towards a state monopoly of foreign trade; fighting inflation; establishment of a wage policy, involving the reduction of high salaries and the freezing of other salaries, allowing for readjustments in cases of flagrant injustice; combining moral and material incentives; institution of a universal 44-hour week; defining the oil, construction, fisheries and mining sectors as the key sectors of the economy in the short and medium term; and giving increasing importance to the roles of the MPLA and UNTA within industrial enterprises to assist in the drive for greater productivity and work discipline (MPLA, 1976, pp. 10–11).

The resolution sounded strongly socialist. However, the resolution on planning passed at the plenum made it clear that planning for socialism would be adopted gradually. A National Plan would be drawn up, though, to direct economic and social development. It was announced at the plenum that a National Planning Commission would be created as an organ of the Council of Ministers and charged with supervising the implementation of the National Plan. The members of the Planning Commission would be chosen by the MPLA Political Bureau and the head of the Commission would be Minister of Planning (when the post of Prime Minister was abolished, the Minister of Planning became the overall coordinator of economic policy implementation). The Commission was given the task of directing activities in the following sectors: agriculture, cattle-breeding and forestry; extraction and processing industries; fisheries; subsoil resources and mining; energy; construction industry; finance and credit; trade and services; transport; communications; labour and training; education, culture and sport; health; social affairs; and international economic relations.

The plenum decided that economic planning should take place on four levels: national, regional, ministerial and production–unit level. The National Planning Commission was given the role of coordinating planning at all levels and supplying statistics and forecasts of production and growth. The Commission would also have a major role in drawing up national plans and presenting them to the MPLA Political Bureau and the Council of Ministers. Planning groups were set up in each ministry to draw up sectoral plans. In addition, Regional Planning Commissions were to be created at regional level.

Prior to the plenum, in February 1976, the MPLA government had promulgated the Law of State Intervention, which contained the guidelines for nationalization. One clause of the law declared that the state would acquire a 70 per cent share in the capital of all banks. The law basically legalized the nationalization of enterprises of strategic importance to the economy and of those abandoned by their former owners. However, the law did not lead to wholesale nationalization and the MPLA made it clear that it would not expropriate the enterprises of foreign companies which were willing to work with the government.

In early 1976, there were fundamentally two types of enterprise in Angola, according to Basil Davidson: those abandoned by their owners and managers but which had been kept in production on the initiative of the workers, and those which were completely idle. A few multinational companies were still operating their factories in Angola (Davidson, 1977, p. 142). Gulf Oil, the major multinational involved in oil production in Cabinda, suspended operations in December 1975 as a result of the continuing fighting. Payments owed to Angola were paid to an escrow account because of the conflicting claims by the MPLA, UNITA and the FNLA to the funds. Once the MPLA had crushed its rivals' conventional military opposition, Gulf resumed payments, and in April 1976 restarted oil production in Cabinda.

Shortly after the October 1976 MPLA plenum, the government in Luanda nationalized the main bank, the Banco de Angola, and confiscated the leading commercial bank, Banco Comercial de Angola, which was renamed Banco Popular de Angola. This gave the government control of 85 per cent of banking operations in the country. In early February 1978, Premier Lopo do Nascimento announced that the government intended nationalizing all banking: the intention was made fact on 25 February when the government promulgated a decree instituting state control over banking. On 31 May of that year, all private insurance companies were abolished—the state-run National Insurance and Reinsurance Company had been established in April 1978. In November 1976, the old colonial currency, the escudo, had been replaced by the kwanza. During the currency change-over, a maximum of 20,000 kwanza notes was permitted to be exchanged and 200,000 in bank deposits.

By mid-1977, more than 85 per cent of the enterprises (agricultural, industrial, mining and trading) which had been abandoned by their former Portuguese owners had been taken under state control, although all non-Portuguese foreign concerns and capital were untouched. Most of the nationalized enterprises were medium- or small-scale ones. By the end of 1978, the government owned 51 per cent of the oil industry (through the State Oil Company, Sonangol), 61 per cent of the diamond-mining industry (through Diamang, which had been nationalized), 100 per cent of the sugar-processing sector, 100 per cent of textile-manufacturing, 100 per cent of bicycle and motorcycle factors, 100 per cent of paper-, pulp- and plywood-manufacturing, 100 per cent of the production facilities for ironwork for the construction industry, 100 per cent of ship repair and maintenance facilities, 100 per cent of motor-vehicle assembly works, and 85 per cent of the brewing concerns (Bhagavan, 1980, p. 190).

One problem that arose for the MPLA as a result of nationalization and of the restarting of industries which had been halted by the fighting was that of the role of workers and the trade-union body, UNTA, in economic decision-making and the running of enterprises. In the immediate aftermath of the MPLA victory, many workers, with encouragement from neighbourhood commissions and the Alves faction in the MPLA, tried to take over control of the day-to-day running of enterprises. This led to conflicts between workers and managers/technicians and between workers and the workers' commissions set up by the MPLA. The Neto leadership felt that the assertiveness of some of the

workers and the disruptions in production caused by strikes and conflicts with enterprise management were too harmful to the economy.
Thus, at the October 1976 plenum it was decided to end the system of
collective management involving enterprise directors and the workers'
commissions and to replace it with more conventional forms of
management, although the decrees adopted by the Central Committee
laid down that enterprise directors should be picked from party ranks
and be approved by the Political Bureau. The UNTA workers' commi-
sions were abolished. Following the Alves coup, UNTA was thoroughly
reorganized.

In October 1977, the MPLA decreed a new regulation controlling
the working of enterprises and the role of workers in economic
decision-making. The regulation decreed that workers should discuss
and comment on plans for their enterprises and suggest alternatives
through the medium of the party or the restructured trade-union
centre. Overall, this measure has ensured greater control of economic
production by managers and government departments. Only in a few
small- or medium-scale enterprises have workers been permitted to
take control of the day-to-day running of production operations.

In December 1977, the First Congress of the MPLA reviewed
economic reconstruction work since independence and set new
targets. In its review the Central Committee told the congress that on
independence Angolans had an average life expectancy of 35–40 years,
more than 90 per cent of the population was illiterate, over 130 road
and rail bridges had been destroyed, over 80 per cent of transport
vehicles had been taken out of the country by the Portuguese, much of
the country's livestock had been abandoned or slaughtered, the iron
and diamond mines and oil wells had ceased work, most of the fishing
fleet had been stolen or destroyed, the internal trade and distribution
system had collapsed, and the country did not have a single expert in
foreign trade.

The Committee report said that in the first two years of independence, abandoned and confiscated enterprises were being reorganized
as state production units, a new currency had been created, a national
bank had been set up, planning organs had been established, thirty-
eight bridges had been rebuilt, 12,000 transport vehicles had been
imported, ten medium- and long-distance aircraft had been acquired

and much work had been carried out to rehabilitate ports and airports. However, major problems still remained and agricultural, mining and industrial production had not made significant progress towards the goal of reaching 1973 levels. The Committee report said that agricultural production had fallen in 1976 and it was vital that attention be given to restoring full food supplies and production of raw materials for industry and export. In the fishing sector, much effort had been put into reviving production and boats and expertise had been obtained from the socialist countries (particularly the Soviet Union). But the total catch for 1977 was only 22 per cent of the 1973 total—the congress set the target of 107 per cent of 1973's catch for 1980.

The conclusion reached by the Central Committee about the economy was that the situation 'is still serious and is characterised by low production and productivity, a great lack of skilled manpower, a shortage of raw materials and spare parts, the poor management of economic units and the big budget deficit' (MPLA 1977, pp. 30–1).

The 1977 congress established the following guidelines: the centralized supervision and planning of the economy should be improved by creating and invigorating mechanisms of direction and management; socialist production relations and the socialist sector of the economy should be expanded and the material base for revolutionary political and economic transformation created; the policy of nationalization and confiscation should be continued; in the countryside priority should be given to establishing agricultural and livestock cooperatives; the 1973 production levels should be restored; the oil, fisheries and construction sectors should be made priority areas for the short-term take-off of reconstruction; the programme of bridge and road repairs should be continued; every effort should be made to improve people's living standards and to redistribute national income; the training of politically, technically and scientific capable cadres should be pursued and illiteracy should be eradicated.

The congress laid down specific guidelines emphasizing the need to develop the production of maize, wheat, potatoes, rice, cassava, oil-bearing plants, vegetables, meat for canning, and cotton for the textile industry. The guidelines for agriculture called for a diversification of crop production and the creation of agricultural 'belts' around major centres of population (necessitated by the parlous state of the food-marketing and distribution system). In the industrial sector, the congress called for maximum effort to exploit existing capacity and to ensure steady supplies of raw materials. Priority had to be given to improving management and organizaton of state-run enterprises. The guidelines for the fishery sector said that there were good prospects for rapid short-term growth even though the fishing fleet was only 30 per cent of the size of the pre-independence fleet. Guidelines were also laid down for the construction, trade, transport, education, health and labour sectors.

The MPLA Special Congress in 1980 noted that some progress had been made in implementing past guidelines and in creating structures for socialist transformation. However, the Central Committee report noted continuing problems with the execution of plans and coordination at different levels of the party and state machinery. The most serious problems were outlined as follows:

The delay in drawing up a single national plan with force of law, ensuring the proportional and balanced development of the economy as a whole and of the various sectors, and defining the scale of priorities in carrying out State tasks, was to a great extent the cause of failure to achieve some important objectives, such as establishing the exchange of goods between town and countryside and industry and agriculture, reducing the exodus of the rural population to the towns, ensuring balanced income and expenditure of the State, of enterprises and the population, introducing the socialist principle of remuneration for work done and for proper correlation between increased productivity and higher wages . . . [MPLA, 1980, p. 65.]

The report did point out, however, that some progress had been made in achieving the centralized direction of economic development—the central planning body had been set up and planning offices had started to operate in the ministries. Work was still underway, according to the report, to establish provincial planning offices. One of the major problems in national planning was the failure to implement 'the basic principle of socialist leadership which means unified guidance, execution and supervision'.

Among the other achievements in socialist economic construction since the 1977 congress, the report said, were the laying of the foundations for a centralized price-control system through the setting-up of a

Commission for Fixing and Controlling Prices. With regard to prices, the Central Committee noted that there was no direct relationship between wages and the volume of goods in circulation—total wages were far higher than their production equivalent. The most serious result of this, and one that still had not been solved in 1986, was the existence of a black market for scarce goods. Austerity programmes in the early 1980s were aimed at bringing wages and production closer in line and thereby undercutting the factor supporting the black market. But problems with agriculture and commodity production meant that speculation was still a problem a decade after the MPLA assumed power.

The Central Committee report outlined some of the increases in production achieved since 1977: in 1979–80, 25,000 hectares of land were planted with maize; 10,000 hectares of cotton were cultivated (with plans to increase this to 30,000 by the mid-1980s); 2,414 tractors and 203,400 tons of fertilizers were provided for the agricultural sector; 1,500 animals were imported to help bring the numbers of cattle, pigs and poultry back to pre-independence levels; foreign technicians and specialists were hired to help in restoring production of cotton, maize, sunflowers, potatoes, fruit, vegetables and milk; and aid was obtained from the socialist countries' Council for Mutual Economic Assistance in conducting vaccination campaigns. However, production problems in agriculture had not been solved. The congress was told that commercial agricultural units under state control were producing only 12 per cent of the food needs of the urban population and agricultural workers and only 15 per cent of the raw-material requirements of the country's industries. In addition, bottlenecks in collecting produce were still a serious check to development and expansion of production.

Success had been achieved, though, in the mining sector: production had increased by 450 per cent and the processing side of the industry had stepped up output by 60 per cent. Significant increases in production were also registered for maize-meal, margarine, dried and semi-cured fish, canned fish, soft drinks, leather shoes, textiles and clothing, bicycle, motorcycles, machetes, fibre bags and the assembly of motor vehicles. Diamond production was said to have increased fourfold.

The Central Committee report noted that a monopoly over foreign trade had been established and that as a whole foreign trade had increased by 47 per cent between 1977 and 1979.

The 1980 congress was followed by a series of austerity budgets and concerted drives to increase production in all spheres. Successes were registered in the vital oil sector and in diamond production, although smuggling and attacks by UNITA guerrillas were a serious obstacle to yet greater output by Diamang. Agriculture remained a serious problem. Although increased areas were cultivated, state farms did not prove a great success overall: Soviet-backed state farms on the central plateau around Bie and Huambo turned out to be a failure. Cooperatives were not 100 per cent successful and there was some evidence of peasant opposition to the introduction of cooperatives and state farms; some observers reported 'subtle opposition' by managerial staff in agricultural and industrial enterprises to the introduction of socialist methods.

Agriculture

Over 80 per cent of Angola's population lives in the countryside and the total agricultural labour force numbered 995,000 out of an estimated total national labour force of 1,562,000 in the 1970s, according to International Labour Organization figures. The staple foods produced and eaten in the rural areas are cassava and maize, while the staple foods of town-dwellers are cassava and wheat. Because of the importance of these crops, and of rice as a subsidiary to them, strict price controls are applied to them. Collection and distribution of all food crops is controlled by the state-run National Company for Purchase and Distribution of Agricultural Products (Encodipa). Because of distribution problems in rural areas, private traders were initially allowed to operate on a limited basis (in a move reminiscent of the New Economic Policy adopted in Soviet Russia in the early 1920s as a means of stimulating production and trade).

As a result of disruptions to the agricultural sector caused by the war and UNITA insurgency, imports are necessary to cover some food requirements. In the 1976–8 period, when food production was at its lowest level, annual cereal imports amounted to 153,700 metric tons on average (US Dept of Agriculture, 1981, p. 177). Between 1970 and 1979, agricultural production fell by 10.2 per cent (World Bank, 1981,

p. 144). Reliable statistics are not available for overall production in recent years. In December 1984, the Angolan Finance Minister, Augusto Teixera de Matos, said that food production was falling and imports of basic foods rising as a result of the increased UNITA and South African military activity in important agricultural areas. De Matos said of the origin of the production decline, which also hit industry badly, that it could be traced to Pretoria's war against the MPLA (*African Business*, April 1985, p. 15). Some food rationing was introduced to overcome the shortages and combat speculation.

In 1977, prior to the major livestock campaigns, Angola had an estimated 920,000 goats, 21,000 sheep, 3,050,000 cattle, 510,000 poultry, and 53,000 horses and mules (SADCC, 1981, p. 142). Efforts were made in the late 1970s and early 1980s to increase the livestock herd through importing breeding stock. The Food and Agriculture Organization (FAO) of the UN has estimated that 23.3 per cent (29m. ha) of Angola's land area is permanent pastureland, while 6.4 per cent of land area (8m. ha) is arable land; 1.8m. ha, 1.5 per cent of land area, is under cultivation (Kaplan, 1979, pp. 208–9). These figures show that the country has great and so far unused potential for cultivation and livestock-raising.

In the 1960s and early 1970s, agriculture provided the majority of exports—60 per cent in the 1960s, falling to 45 per cent in the early 1970s and down to 34 per cent in 1973. The fall was not a result of declining production but of the massive increase in oil output. The major agricultural export crops were coffee, cotton, tobacco and sisal. In 1973, sisal production totalled 60,000 tons; tobacco 4,000 tons; and coffee, 192,000 tons. After independence production fell sharply. Guerrilla activity in the 1980s inhibited attempts to increase production and exports. The 1984 coffee crop was a mere 24,000 tons, down even on 1983's low of 26,000 tons (Somerville, 1985, p. 44). Other export and food crops were drastically reduced. In the agriculturally important southern and central districts farming was devastated by military activity. In mid-1985, the Red Cross estimated that over 200,000 people had been displaced from their homes by the fighting, mostly in the southern and central plateau areas. Drought in the early-to-mid 1980s also hit food and cash-crop production in Angola.

Manufacturing

At independence Angola had a reasonably broad range of manufacturing plants—geared mainly towards the domestic market and structured so as to complement Portuguese industries and to avoid competition with the colonizing country's industries. In 1973, industrial production accounted for 18–20 per cent of GDP. Industrial production was concentrated in Luanda, Huambo and Lubango. Food processing made up 36 per cent of manufacturing: major products were sugar, animal oils and fats, canned fish, canned and preserved foods and bread. Textiles were next in importance (12 per cent of manufacturing); brewing and beverage production made up 10.8 per cent of production. Other manufactured products included cigarettes, paint, pesticides, paper, metal furniture, containers, cutlery, footwear, soap, rubber tyres, leather goods and cement. Most industries were on a small scale and, prior to independence, were owned and operated by Portuguese settlers. In 1972 there were 5,561 manufacturing plants in Angola and total investment in the sector came to 7,336 million escudos.

After independence manufacturing suffered from the withdrawal of the Portuguese, shortages of raw materials and spare parts, and the effects of civil strife and insurgency. Of these obstacles to development the most serious was the dearth of trained managers and skilled workers. Although Cuba, the Soviet Union, East Germany and other socialist countries came to Angola's aid and oil revenues enabled the government to hire technicians and advisers from Western states, this still could not make up for the absence of indigenous expertise. The cost of foreign assistance was also a drain on resources that could be put into development and expansion. Addressing the MPLA congress in December 1985, President dos Santos said that, in 1982, 7.5 billion kwanzas had been paid out for foreign technical and managerial assistance. Although the figure spent fell to 5.4 billion kwanzas in 1983 and was reported to have fallen further in 1984 as a result of strict austerity measures, dos Santos said that it was still eating up 10 per cent of hard-currency earnings every year.

The decline in manufacturing production was catastrophic: output was down to 40 per cent of 1973 levels in 1977. Although output then levelled out, the problems in the agricultural sector in the 1980s, combined with the increasing cost of fighting UNITA and South Africa, meant that less money was available to buy spare parts from abroad or to import the raw materials that farmers were failing to produce in sufficient volume. Agreements on technical, managerial and scientific cooperation with the Soviet Union, Cuba, East Germany, Brazil and Italy helped to alleviate some of the manufacturing sector's problems, but provided no permanent solution. Between 1970 and 1979, industrial production fell by 3.9 per cent and service industries' output by 10.9 per cent (World Bank, 1981, p. 144). Although most industrial products were aimed at the domestic market, some processed foods and canned goods were exported—these accounted for 7 per cent of exports in 1978.

There was extensive nationalization in the manufacturing sector, mainly as a result of the exodus of Portuguese businessmen. By the end of 1978, when there was a slow-down in nationalization and the announcement by President Neto that private ownership of small enterprises would be allowed, 100 per cent of textile production, 100 per cent of bicycle and motorcycle manufacturing had been nationalized, 58 per cent of cement output, 100 per cent of paper, pulp and plywood production, 100 per cent of motor-vehicle assembly and ship repairs and maintenance, and 98 per cent of metal sheet production were in state hands.

Following Neto's announcement in 1978, greater leeway for business activity was given to small private manufacturers. The MPLA government also maintained a relatively open policy on cooperation with capitalist companies and major multinationals. A law was passed in 1979 permitting foreign investment in Angola provided that the country's independence and interests were resepected. Foreign firms active in Angola in manufacturing, mining and oil extraction and exploration were required to train and employ as many Angolans as possible. The law on investment prohibited investment in defence-related industries, banking, insurance, telecommunications and water supplies. There were no such restrictions on involvement of experts and enterprises from socialist countries in Angolan industry; however José Eduardo dos Santos speaking on the eighth anniversary of independence, said that although economic cooperation with the Soviet

Union and the other socialist states was 'cheap and safe', it should be 'properly controlled in order to help build the material and technical bases for the new society' (Somerville, March 1984, p. 84).

Apart from being a drain on resources available for investment, South African and UNITA attacks also directly damaged manufacturing capacity. In 1979, South African aircraft bombed Lubango, destroying a furniture factory and killing twenty-nine of its 100 skilled workers.

The management system in Angola's manufacturing system has developed along Soviet lines since the failure of the Alves coup in 1977 and the subsequent reorganization of the trade-union movement. Control by state-appointed enterprise directors has superseded earlier experiments involving high-level participation by workers' committees in decision-making. A small number of cooperatives have been set up in the small-scale manufacturing sector, but cooperatives have not played a major role in the management of major factories.

Although the MPLA has given a high priority to industrial production, naming it the decisive factor in the building of socialism, since independence the sector has been prevented from developing significantly as a result of managerial and skilled labour shortages, raw materials and spare parts problems, the effects of South African destabilization and inexperience and inefficiency among government and party officials responsible for planning and management. Angola has yet to make any great steps forward in manufacturing large quantities of capital goods. The majority of machines for the manufacturing sector are imported from West Germany, Britain, France, other Western countries (which were the major sources of industrial goods under Portuguese rule, given the backward state of the Portuguese industrial sector) and increasingly from the Soviet Union and other socialist countries.

Mining and Hydrocarbons

Mineral deposits in Angola offer great potential for future development of the mining sector, in addition to the current exploitation of iron ore and diamonds. Viable reserves of tobernite, a copper–uranium phosphate, have been discovered along the Benguela Railway, although exploitation has been prevented largely by UNITA activity.

Diamonds are a vital export commodity for Angola. They are mined by the state-owned company Diamang, with significant foreign assistance. About three-quarters of the diamonds mined in Lunda Norte Province, the main diamond-mining centre, are of gem quality. In 1973, production stood at 2.1 million carats. The civil war led to a serious decline in output, which was compounded by the departure of the Portuguese. In 1975, production had fallen to 750,000 carats and Diamang, then owned by Portuguese and foreign interests, was making a loss. By 1977, output had fallen catastrophically to 353,000 carats and illicit mining and smuggling had become a serious problem. By the end of 1977, the MPLA government had taken control of 61 per cent of Diamang's shares. In a bid to cut smuggling and provide better security for the mines, Lunda Province was divided in two in mid-1978. This created the Provinces of Lunda Norte and Lunda Sul. Mining was concentrated in the northern province, and this became a restricted zone in which movements were closely controlled. For a while the sector began to improve its performance and production rose to over the million-carat level. Diamonds regained their position as the country's second most important export commodity—oil is the most important and coffee comes third.

The prospects of expanding mining and increasing revenue were hit badly by the expansion of UNITA activity to Lunda Norte in 1983 and 1984. Production fell in 1983 to 1 million carats and is expected to continue dropping as the war continues. Foreign workers at diamond mines were a particular target for UNITA. Raids against a major mining complex at Cafunfo led to the kidnapping and eventual release of a large group of British and Portuguese workers. Apart from disrupting production, UNITA's attacks reduced foreign interest in investment and provision of skilled personnel.

Major iron-ore deposits are found in Huambo, Bie and Malanje Provinces. The most important mining centre is Cassinga in southern Angola. Prior to independence, the mines were owned by the Portuguese state-run Companhia Mineira do Lobito and production of ore at Cassinga in 1973 totalled 5.7 million tons (national output amounted to 6.1 million tons). Most of the iron was exported to Japan and West Germany. The Angolan government nationalized the mines in 1977 and now runs them with Yugoslav assistance.

The oil sector is now the mainstay of the economy and it is no exaggeration to say that without oil exports the economy would have been hard put to survive South African–UNITA destabilization and the slump in diamond and coffee exports. Oil earnings have enabled the MPLA to keep up the fight against sabotage and insurgency without ignoring reconstruction and preparations for socialist development. It is paradoxical that the factor that has enabled the MPLA to keep the socialist option alive has been extensive cooperation with the paragons of American and Western capitalism, the multinational oil companies.

The major areas of oil production are Cabinda and areas off the northern sector of the Angolan coast. Gulf Oil of America started operations in Cabinda in 1957 and is still Angola's most important partner in the oil sector. Oil was first discoverd in the Cuanza basin in 1955 and a major commercial deposit was found at Tobias on the coast 120 kilometres south of Luanda, in 1961. By 1962, production had reached 471,000 tons. By 1974, production was around 7.5 million tons a year (about 150,000 barrels per day (b/d). In mid-1976, the MPLA created the state oil company Sonangol (Sociedaded Nacional de Combustiveis de Angola) to supervise the exploitation of all hydro–carbon resources, including refining (the Luanda refinery was set up in 1958 by the Portuguese). In Cabinda, Sonangol shares production with Gulf and runs major petroleum installations at Malongo (the target of an unsuccessful South African commando raid in 1985).

By the end of 1985, it was estimated that Angola was producing 250,000 b/d from the Cabinda and offshore oilfields. The government had set a target of 500,000 b/d by 1987 and with assistance from a number of foreign oil companies had launched a multimillion–dollar project to achieve this aim. Cabinda was producing 170,000 b/d in 1985 (49 per cent of which went to Gulf and the rest to Sonangol). To reach its target of doubling production in two years, Sonangol has opened up offshore oil deposits for exploitation by foreign companies. Elf–Aquitaine of France and Braspetro of Brazil are assisting Sonangol with the Palanca offshore deposits. Palanca is expected to be producing 30,000 b/d by the end of 1986. Naftagas of Yugoslavia has also been signed up to help with lifting oil from the Atlantic, in return for which

Angola will supply Yugoslavia with 70,000 tons of Palanca oil per annum. In 1984, the total contribution of oil to the Angolan economy was $2 billion in taxes and royalties. Cooperation with foreign oil multinationals has been very successful in the oil sector and the MPLA shows no signs of ending the arrangement in the near future. More than any other sector of the economy, the oil industry needs foreign assistance because of the skill dearth in Angola.

Angola also has natural gas deposits which are expected to be exploited in the near future.

Foreign Aid and Trade

Since independence, the MPLA has developed close and cooperative relations with the Soviet Union, Cuba, the German Democratic Republic, and other countries of the socialist community, in addition to Yugoslavia, the Nordic states and Brazil. Economic relations with the United States and EEC countries are important in the trade sphere, and since it joined the Lomé Convention in 1985 Angola has been eligible for aid from the EEC (in addition to EEC and other Western aid to the Southern African Development Coordination Conference, SADCC, of which Angola is a member).

Exact statistics on foreign aid to Angola are hard to obtain. Angola itself puts out few reliable statistics on aid or trade and is still in the process of developing efficient statistical services. Aid from socialist states is hard to gauge as the donors release few details of disbursements. However, it is known that the Soviet Union pledged $2 billion worth of aid for the 1984–90 period and that in 1983 Angola received $30.5 million in aid from Belgium, Denmark, France, West Germany, Italy, the Netherlands and Britain (Somerville, July 1985, p. 45). Membership of the Lomé Convention, which will not affect Angola's economic or political relations with the Soviet bloc, will enable Angola to take advantage of compensation funds in the event of shortfalls in commodity export earnings and also preferential trade tariffs for exports to the EEC.

Soviet aid for the 1976–8 period, when reconstruction work was getting under way, has been put at $17 million and it is estimated that

Table 4.1(a) Trade with industrialized countries, Africa and Asia (US $m.)

	Exports				Imports			
	1978	1980	1982	1984	1978	1980	1982	1984
World total	889.3	1,903.3	1,743.8	2,257.7	665.7	1,352.8	1,000.5	1,003.1
USA	398.5	709.1	658.1	957.7	34.7	122.4	174.4	113.4
Belgium	5.7	8.5	132.8	55.0	42.4	30.6	34.5	25.3
Japan	5.6	94.5	1.4	.8	40.2	91.8	57.1	23.4
France	4.5	1.2	12.5	1.4	30.9	102.0	127.9	108.5
W. Germany	5.3	2.6	1.0	8.5	87.5	112.6	65.1	58.9
Holland	40.3	41.9	154.8	157.5	54.9	82.5	32.7	74.6
UK	77.8	175.6	12.0	192.6	43.4	71.1	48.8	51.4
Portugal	6.5	13.6	20.7	31.7	72.1	194.5	93.3	168.6
Brazil	–	102.6	95.2	122.8	24.9	130.5	93.9	99.0
Africa	3.5	73.4	14.1	12.8	9.8	1.9	7.8	2.3
Asia	.6	1.7	.1	–	9.5	39.9	22.0	15.4

Source: IMF, 1985, p. 80.

between 1975 and 1982 the Soviet Union offered Angola aid amounting to $40 million, of which only about half was disbursed (Somerville, winter, 1984). Other Soviet aid includes agreement to cooperate with a Brazilian company in the construction of a 450 megawatt hydro-electric dam at Capanda on the Kwanza river—the scheme will provide electricity for rural electrification and help irrigate 400,000 hectares of farmland. In January 1984, Planning Minister Lopo do Nascimento visited Moscow and there signed a protocol on Soviet aid for the fishing industry. Under the agreement the Soviet Union will supply Angola with fishing vessels, materials for the construction of a fishing complex and will send experts to carry out design work. The complex will include a processing factory, wharves, repair facilities and will employ 6,000 Angolans. Angola has observer status with the CMEA.

One of the most valuable, but hard to quantify, forms of assistance given by the socialist states has been the provision of skilled personnel and training for Angolan cadres. Thousands of Cuban teachers, medical staff and technicians have been sent to Angola to help with construction efforts, and hundreds of Soviet, East German and Bulgarian advisers have helped in a broad spectrum of economic activities.

Although Angola has extensive economic and aid ties with the socialist countries, and trade has been gradually increasing between Angola and CMEA states, the country's external trade is still geared strongly towards the Western states with which trade was originally initiated by the Portuguese colonial regime (Tables 4.1(a), (b)). The absence of diplomatic relations with the United States has not prevented an expansion of trade, particularly sales of coffee and oil and imports such as sophisticated machinery (including aircraft and aviation equipment). Trade and Western capitalist states made up over

Table 4.1(b) Trade with the Soviet Union (millions of roubles)

Exports				Imports			
1978	1980	1982	1983	1978	1980	1982	1983
9.6	15.8	3.4	2.8	47.8	69.1	61.0	170.3

Source: *Vneshnaya Torgovlya*, 1980, 1982, 1983, 1984.

Table 4.2 Composition of external trade (kwanzas m.)

Commodities	Imports		Commodities	Exports	
	1978	1979		1978	1979
Foodstuffs	5,382.7	7,326.5	Crude oil	16,507.1	26,746.0
Textiles	1,447.0	2,341.5	Oil products	1,102.7	2,497.1
Machinery	3,940.2	11,015.9	Coffee	6,732.1	5,699.9
Consumer goods	2,209.2	1,292.6	Diamonds	2,996.6	4,219.0
Chemicals	563.0	800.7	Cement	89.7	59.1
Raw materials	4,098.7	3,050.9	Sisal	82.4	164.6
Tools	478.4	1,191.1	Fish meal	59.6	39.7
Medical goods	1,039.9	716.0			
Total (incl. other goods)	19,158.9	28,093.1	Total (incl. others)	27,739.0	39,530.8

70 per cent of Angola's trade even after ten years of independence. In the 1980s, efforts were made to increase trade with neighbouring African states through the South African Development Coordination Conference (of which Angola was a founder-member and which had as its objective the ending of trade with, and other economic dependence on, South Africa) and through relations with the other Portuguese-speaking countries in Africa.

Despite the apparent trade surplus, invisible imports and services pushed the current account into deficit every year. A debit of 5,564 million kwanzas on services in 1978 led to a deficit of 330 million kwanzas, this rose to a deficit of over 1 billion kwanzas in 1980 and 6.2 billion in 1982. Austerity measures reduced the figure to 2.3 billion in 1984 and 1985's was expected to be just 200 million kwanzas.

5   The Regime's Policies

Domestic policies

The MPLA government took power in November 1975 committed to carrying out a social revolution, in addition to the political and economic ones, that would transform the lives of the vast majority of Angolans, who had been living in a situation of massive deprivation, ignorance and poor health under the Portuguese. Two major aims were the building of a national education system that would provide a uniform standard of basic education to all people and the creation of an effective health service for Angolans. Attempts had been made to set up embryonic education and health schemes in liberated areas and in countries of exile, but on independence the government and party were faced with the overwhelming task of establishing new and comprehensive services at a time of massive internal dislocation, economic decline and, most importantly of all, a dire shortage of skilled personnel.

Religion was a thorny problem for the MPLA. Many Angolans were Catholics or Protestants and missionaries had often played an important role in providing education to ordinary Angolans under colonialism—something denied to most Angolans by the colonial authorities. However, the MPLA's Marxist–Leninist ideology was inimical to the encouragement of religious activity. Although the party was not intent on pursuing strong anti-religious policies, its priorities in education and politicization stressed materialistic Marxism and implicitly opposed religion. In addition, the MPLA was suspicious of large organized groups, such as the Catholic Church, which had external links, were independent of party control and had not come out strongly against Portuguese colonialism.

Military policy was to be an overriding concern of the MPLA in the first decade of independence. A new national army had to be built from the MPLA guerrilla forces and this new army had to face the threat of conventional attacks, with sophisticated air support, from the South

African troops in Namibia and of guerrilla offensives from UNITA (and from the FNLA and FLEC in the early years of independence).

The MPLA's foreign policy, with its strong commitment to non-alignment combined with close and cooperative relations with the socialist states, was aimed primarily at ensuring the country's independence and territorial integrity, and secondly at supplementing domestic efforts to reconstruct the economy and prepare the foundations of a socialist system. An important factor in Angolan foreign policy since independence, and one that has been as influential as non-alignment or the commitment to socialism, has been the regional element which has involved conflictual interactions with South Africa and strong, cooperative relations with the independent states of southern Africa through the Southern African Development Coordination Conference.

Education

The MPLA had a massive educational task ahead of it following independence. Estimates put the level of illiteracy at between 85 and 90 per cent, while the shortages of teachers and facilities were severe. The all-important October 1976 plenum of the MPLA Central Committee studied the issue at length and set the elimination of illiteracy as the immediate task. Priority was to be given in the literacy drive in the countryside 'to benefit the peasant masses who were completely ignored and deprived by the colonialists' (MPLA, 1976, p. 17). The plenum also set the task of using schools as the 'strong revolutionary base for the creation of the New Man'. Of particular importance to all these aims, the Central Committee noted, was the training of cadres 'from the most exploited classes' who would be educated politically, technically and scientifically.

The plenum set the following priorities for education: literacy; primary education; secondary education; and intermediary and university education. The MPLA announced its intention of learning from the experience of the socialist and other friendly countries and of providing free education at all levels.

To cope with the literacy campaign, a National Literacy Commission was created, under the leadership of the Minister of Education.

The Minister of Education was given the sole task of dealing with immediate literacy and educational problems—a National Cultural Council and a Higher Council of Physical Education and Sports were established to deal with those areas. In the training of staff, priority was given to primary school teachers and the creation, with foreign assistance, of new teacher training colleges.

The primary sector was of vital importance, given the low educational level of the majority of the population. In 1973, the year before the Portuguese revolution, the primary school intake had been 500,000, of whom a third were Portuguese, and secondary enrolment was 72,000, of whom four-fifths were Portuguese. By 1977, the MPLA had increased primary school enrolment to 1,000,000 and secondary enrolment to 105,000 (Wolvers & Bergerol, 1983, p. 114). In the first year of the literacy campaign (November 1976–November 1977), 102,000 adults learned to read and write. By 1980, the figure had risen to 1,000,000.

At the MPLA congress in December 1977, the Theses on Education were discussed. The Theses stated that by the time of the congress 1,026,291 pupils were receiving primary education, 105,868 secondary education, and 1,109 higher education. The report pointed out that the improvement in educational services was not uniform nationally. Benguela and Luanda Provinces were very well served, while Cuando Cubango and Mocamedes were suffering from severe shortages of facilities. The structure of the school population was as depicted in Table 5.1.

The problems of building an educational system were multiplied by the shortage of qualified teachers. The MPLA congress was told that there were only 25,000 teachers available for the million primary school pupils (and 52 per cent of those teachers had only reached Class 4 themselves). Only 7 per cent of the primary teachers were considered to have the minimum teaching qualifications. The secondary sector had even more serious staffing problems—there were only 600 secondary teachers in 1977 and the only secondary schools were in towns.

One of the most important sections of the Theses on Education dealt with the colonial inheritance in the education sector and the need to build a system responsive to the needs of the MPLA's ideology and

Table 5.1 Structure of the school population

Pre-primary	402,306 (39.2%)*	Secondary	
Primary		Class 5	52,908
Class 1	297,624 (29.0%)*	Class 6	26,827
Class 2	161,128 (15.7%)*	Class 7	13,537
Class 3	95,445 (9.3%)*	Class 8	7,105
Class 4	69,778 (6.8%)*	Class 9	3,392
First pre- *univ. year*	769	Second pre- *univ. year*	830

* The figures for pre-primary–Class 4 are approximate.
Source: MPLA, 1977, p. 41.

its plans for socialist transformation. The colonial system had established schools which provided 'backward education from a backward country, imposed on a people living an entirely different reality'. The Theses added that the colonial education system was 'determined by the interests of the ruling class, reflecting and replicating the existing relations of production' (MPLA, 1977, p. 42). In rural areas the only education was that provided by Catholic and Protestant missionaries, who 'aimed to create a class of minor African cadres favourably disposed to their ideology and ready to cooperate in spreading religious obscurantism'. The colonial state only began providing education at a primary level to more than a privileged few following the start of the armed struggle in Angola. However, this form of education was limited to providing skilled labourers and trying to form an African petit bourgeoisie 'receptive to capitalist ideology' (MPLA, 1977, p. 43).

The MPLA congress was told in the Theses on Education that the MPLA's educational policies had been formulated during the liberation struggle, when the Department of Education and Culture was set up by the movement to provide education in liberated areas and on the borders. These educational services aimed at providing primary education and ideological instruction. The school students undertook political agitation and produced their own food, as well as taking part in military training. The education sector of the MPLA was part and parcel of the movement's political and military machinery—'in DEC schools one did not merely learn how to make revolution, but one participated actively in the revolution' (MPLA, 1977, p. 45).

The post-independence education system was, in the view of the MPLA, an extension and a development of the work carried out during the liberation struggle. The new educational system should be inextricably linked to the physical and mental task of building socialism and therefore 'must be at the service of revolutionary change so that it becomes a system responsive to the needs of the People's Republic of Angola and takes into account the development of productive forces'.

The congress resolved to institute an eight-year system of free, basic education. However, material and manpower problems would mean, according to the Theses, that initially four years of basic education would be provided. Vocational schools would assume greater importance than under colonialism, as they would become the basic means of training technical, scientific and other advanced cadres. An improved adult education system would be established to provide the basic education denied to the older generations by the colonial system.

One method used by the MPLA to assist the development of education, given the shortage of trained cadres, was close cooperation with the socialist countries, particularly Cuba. In 1976, Cuba offered 500 secondary school places in Cuba for Angolan students, and in 1978 a brigade of teachers was sent to Angola from Cuba—a total of 443 teachers from Cuba helped Angola's teachers in the 1978–81 period; they were then replaced by another 370 Cuban educators.

By 1981, 759,000 of the estimated 1.69 million illiterate adults in Angola were enrolled in 37,000 literacy classes and 70,000 literacy teachers had been trained; 1,980 post-literacy centres had been set up to provide more advanced adult education and their 11,000 classes were being attended by 276,300 students. Initially, literacy and post-literacy classes were organized purely in the official language, Portuguese, but in 1981 plans were drawn up to start pilot projects in Kikongo, Kimbundu, Chokwe, Umbundu, Mbunda and Kwanyama (*ACR*, 1981–2, p. B590).

The 1980 Special Congress of the MPLA noted the advances made in providing education but pointed out that the shortage of teachers and schools was unlikely to be overcome before the next congress—in five years' time. The congress stated that every effort should be made to maximize the contribution to education by the information media.

The Angola Combatante radio programme and the *Boletin do Militante* publication were said to have a particularly important role to play in assisting with education, both academic and political (MPLA, 1980, p. 21). Both types of education were vital to the overall development of the nation and to the development of the party. The Central Committee report to the congress noted that enhancing the political education of party cadres was hindered by 'the general educational level of party members, which is relatively low, making it difficult for them to assimilate the material given and lessening the extent to which theory is applied to the real conditions of everyday life'.

This problem was still serious in 1985, when President dos Santos told the MPLA national conference that more effort needed to be given to the 'theoretical shortcomings and education' of party members. More work should also be done, he said, to raise the political consciousness of the masses through the party's propaganda. However, in order for this to be effective, the general educational level would also have to be raised (MPLA, 1985, pp. 5-7).

Overall, the MPLA has not been unsuccessful in building a new educational system from the ruins of the wholly inadequate inheritance from colonialism. But for real progress to be made, time and more resources have to be made available and conditions created in which educational services can be provided in all areas of the country. As with political and economic tasks, the educational problems are only likely to be successfully tackled if and when the problems of South African and UNITA military activity are solved. The drain on manpower and funds deprives the educational system of teachers and the resources with which to build schools, print books and purchase equipment, while the war in the southern and central regions prevents the spread of the school system. In addition, schools and teachers have frequently been the targets for UNITA raids.

Religion

The basic attitude of the MPLA towards religion was, to some extent, ambiguous. It was not set on the destruction of organized religion or intent on thorough campaigns against religion. However, the movement's strong commitment to Marxism–Leninism meant that religion was generally viewed as an outdated hangover from colonialism that had no useful role to play in the building of a new society. The MPLA and its government were prepared to tolerate religious practices provided that the churches refrained from political activity and restricted themselves purely to spiritual matters.

This outlook was made plain at the October 1976 plenum of the MPLA Central Committee. In his speech to the meeting, President Neto said that there was a clear contrast between churches which carried out their work with 'social responsibility and political realism' and others which 'break the laws and step outside the specific realm of their activity by trying to create false contradictions . . . and turning their adherents away from the common national effort'. Neto added that the Central Committee was aware that there were religious believers among the masses of workers and peasants who had no intention of abandoning the struggle for national reconstruction under the leadership of the MPLA. But he added that the exploited classes were participating in the struggle for a prosperous and democratic state 'which is a patriotic duty, in no way compatible with religious creeds'. Neto's implicit warning to religious groups was directed not only at Christian groups, but also at African religions. He said that:

. . . the counterrevolutionary positions openly or covertly held by some religions are particularly counterproductive, anti-historical and politically suicidal . . . Such behaviour conflicts with the best and most legitimate traditions of such religions, whose opposition to certain religious teachings imposed by the colonialists gave them, in the past, an undeniable and essentially positive role in the development of our people's national consciousness. [MPLA, 1976, p. 9.]

As far as some of the African religions were concerned, there was the suspicion that their adherents supported Jonas Savimbi's UNITA. The greater strength of such religious groups in isolated rural areas meant that they could be of use to UNITA if they came out strongly against the secular, materialistic philosophy of the MPLA.

Neto reminded the meeting that Article 7 of the Angolan constitution laid down the right of religions to exist and to receive state protection as long as they stayed within the law. He concluded his remarks about religion by announcing that the Central Committee had recommended to the Revolutionary Council that it prepare the necessary measures to make illegal any attempts to oppose religious beliefs to the revolutionary transformation of society and to respect for the state and its institutions.

Criticism of religion and the way in which religious beliefs were used to oppose the MPLA were also dealt with extensively in the Central Committee's report to the MPLA congress in December 1977. The report stated:

Throughout history, religion has always been one of the weapons used by the exploiting class to keep the exploited away from the revolutionary struggle for their liberation . . . By posing the problem of religion correctly, Marxism–Leninism shows us that it is merely one of the forms of social consciousness . . . Its specific feature is the fact that by its very essence it is a distorted reflection of that reality . . . Following the guiding principles of Marxism–Leninism, the Party and State of the People's Republic of Angola are not going to prohibit religion. However, any views claiming that concessions should be made to religious ideas and leading the party to abandon its principled position towards religion must be combated . . . the religious question must be seen from two angles; on the one hand, there is the question of relations with churches and organisations formed by various religions . . . on the other hand, there is the question of the attitude to be taken towards religion as an ideology . . . As regards the first aspect, the party guides the state to guarantee freedom of conscience for each individual, that is, the right to profess a religion or not so long as he conforms with the law and the norms of socialist morality . . . with regard to religion as an ideology, the party will base its policy on the supposition that the struggle for a free, scientific, and materialistic consciousness is an integral part of the struggle to build a new society . . . a struggle in which it is indispensable that believers and atheists take part. [MPLA, 1977, p. 14.]

Shortly after the congress, the MPLA began to exert greater control over the activities of religious groups. In 1978, the Political Bureau ordered the registration of all 'legitimate' churches and religious organizations; the construction of new churches without permission was banned; and churches would no longer be exempt from tax. The Jehovah's Witnesses sect was banned by the MPLA on the grounds that the sect's members would not carry out military service and would regard the state as unimportant (Kaplan, 1979, p. 110). Identical policies towards the sect have been implemented by conservative regimes in Malawi and Zaïre.

At the time of the first congress, a dispute broke out between the party and the Catholic Church. In December 1977, the Catholic bishops of Angola met in Lugango and drew up a pastoral letter condemning what it called 'the frequent and lamentable violations' of religious freedom carried out by the government. They claimed that the constitution's articles on religious freedom were not being implemented. They also objected to the closing-down by the government of the Church's radio station, Radio Ecclesia. The MPLA reacted by accusing the Church of putting the honesty of the revolutionary process in question.

On 25 January 1978, after the distribution of the bishop's letter, Neto signed a decree stating that there was a compete separation between the state and all religous institutions and that the MPLA would hold a complete monopoly of the media—Radio Ecclesia was then dissolved irrevocably and its assets were nationalized. One point in the bishops' letter which angered the MPLA leadership was the statement that 'imposing atheistic materialism on a naturally spiritual people was a form of violence which could have the most evil consequences' (Kaplan, 1979, p. 110).

Despite its ideological opposition to religion and its suspicion of organized churches and religious institutions, the MPLA did not oppose religion out of hand and some of its activists were Catholics and some even priests. There was less hostility between the MPLA and the Protestant churches, as the latter had been less closely connected with the Portuguese colonial authorities (Neto's father had been a Methodist preacher). In February 1978, the state allowed a number of Protestant churches to form the Christian Council of Angola.

At the 1980 and 1985 congresses of the MPLA there was no basic change in party line towards religion. The Central Committee report to the 1980 congress summed up the basic MPLA stance by reaffirming the right to freedom of belief while warning that churches which took up reactionary positions as a result of lost privileges they had enjoyed under colonialism (a clear reference to the Catholic Church) would not be tolerated. The report called on the party to prevent the proliferation of churches and sects which had neither history or involvement nor following in Angola.

One very concrete way in which church influence was reduced in Angola and the power of the state was put in its place was in schools. Religious education was removed from the syllabus in schools, although churches were not stopped from giving religious instruction outside school hours.

Military Policy

The continuing military aggression by South Africa from its bases in Namibia, the constant guerrilla raids by UNITA, and the more infrequent activities of the FNLA and FLEC have meant that the MPLA government and the party have had to give a disproportionate amount of time and resources to military and security activities. The building of a national army from the guerrilla army, the formation of an air force and a navy, and the establishment of a militia organization to assist in combating the rebel movements have been vital aspects of the MPLA's work in the first decade of independence. Similarly, much time and effort have been put into the formulation of an effective strategy for defeating UNITA without alienating the peoples living in the areas in which the rebels are active.

During the liberation conflict, the MPLA had built its own armed wing—the Popular Forces for the Liberation of Angola (FAPLA)—whose role in fighting the Portuguese was to carry out guerrilla warfare tactics. The guerrillas received their arms and training from a number of sources, including Cuba, the Soviet Union, Eastern European states, Yugoslavia, Tanzania and the Organization of African Unity. FAPLA's period of greatest activity was between 1968 and 1972, when the guerrillas were fighting in the Dembos region, Cabinda and Moxico Province. FAPLA's capabilities declined somewhat after 1972 as a result of the split between the leadership of the party and the Eastern Revolt faction led by Daniel Chipenda.

A major concern of the MPLA leadership during the fighting against the Portuguese was the maintenance of political control over the guerrillas. It was the failure to ensure close supervision of the military and to maintain regular liaison between the political leadership and guerrilla commanders that led to the major problems with the guerrillas led by Chipenda on the eastern front. Attempts to subordinate the millitary to the political were accompanied by extensive political education for the guerrillas and the attachment of political commissars to guerrilla units (this was a policy also implemented with success by Frelimo in Mozambique and ZANU in Zimbabwe).

The Portuguese revolution of April 1974 led to major changes in the nature of the conflict in which the MPLA was involved. The growing competiton between the three liberation movements eventually became a military struggle that took on conventional rather than guerrilla warfare characteristics, especially with the early involvement of Zaïrean regular army units in support of the FNLA. Later in the civil war, South African armoured units and Cuban armed forces units became involved. The civil war ended up as a major conventional conflict involving the use of artillery, rockets and armoured vehicles.

The MPLA's defeat of its rivals and of the Zaïrean and South African interventions was made possible by the supply of substantial quantities of Soviet arms and the arrival of thousands of Cuban troops. Following the MPLA victory, the task of building FAPLA into a conventional-style national army was greatly assisted by Soviet arms supplies and the presence of the Cubans. By January 1976, the Soviet Union had sent the Angolans $200 million worth of arms including MiG-21 aircraft, T-34 and T-54 tanks, armoured personnel carriers, SAM-7 surface-to-air missiles and 122mm. Katyusha rockets. The Soviet Union also sent several hundred military advisers to Angola following independence to assist in building the national armed forces.

Another military force had grown up during the civil war which became an adjunct to FAPLA. This was the local militia force, formed by MPLA supporters to protect themselves against the reactionary Portuguese settlers who reacted violently to the Portuguese revolution, and against attacks by FNLA and UNITA military units. The militia was transformed into the People's Defence Organization (ODP) by the MPLA and was used to provide support to FAPLA for territorial defence and anti-guerrilla purposes. The ODP had the particular task of maintaining vigilance to detect the presence of UNITA and FNLA rebels.

Following independence there was a blurring of distinctions between political and military leaders, given that many of those appointed to leading positions in the party and government had been directly involved in organizing and fighting in guerrilla units. Similarly, many of the new commanders of the Angolan armed forces had held important political posts in the MPLA. The concept of blending the military with the political resulted from the MPLA belief that direct political control should be exercised over the armed forces, partly through the appointment of political commissars to all military units, and that the soldiers themselves should be politicized and made aware of their political as well as military duties.

The politicization of FAPLA was on the agenda of the MPLA Central Committee plenum of October 1976. The plenum passed a resolution stressing the urgent need to implant and organize MPLA structures within the armed forces and to intensify education work to politicize soldiers. A second resolution stressed the importance of the radio programme 'People in Arms', run by the FAPLA General Staff, in providing the correct political line for the armed forces. The resolution emphasized the vital importance of strong leadership over the National Political Commissariat of FAPLA (MPLA, 1976, p. 23).

Despite the Neto leadership's efforts to maintain close political control over the armed forces, the Alves coup of 1977 showed that the Alves faction had gained the support of sectors of FAPLA and had been able to infiltrate its supporters into leading political positions within the armed forces without hindrance from the central organs of the MPLA. Support for Alves was particularly strong in FAPLA's Ninth Brigade and it was this unit which led the attack on Luanda prison to free Alves. One reason for the ease with which Alves and his supporters were able to gain support in the military was the leading role in pre-liberation military affairs that Alves had played as commander of the MPLA's first military regon. One of his lieutenants in the military region had been Commander Bakalof (Ernesto Gomes da Silva), who after independence became General Political Commissar of FAPLA; from that position he was able to play a major role in mobilizing members of the armed forces to support Alves.

Apart from revealing splits within FAPLA, the coup attempt seriously damaged it because of the killing, by the Alves faction, of FAPLA's chief of security, Commander Njazi, of a leading member of the FAPLA General Staff, Commander Dangereux, of the Deputy Chief of Staff of FAPLA, Commander Bula Matadi, and of the head of personnel of FAPLA, Commander Eurico. Their deaths and the purging of FAPLA members suspected of support for or complicity in the coup led to a major reshuffle in FAPLA's structures after the coup and to more concerted efforts to ensure political control by the MPLA. Among the new appointees were David Antonio Moises as FAPLA Chief of Staff, and Juiao Mateus Paulo Dino Matross as FAPLA National Political Commissar (he was later promoted to the Political Bureau).

The Central Committee report to the December 1977 party congress made clear the integration of political and military activities and the political tasks assigned to FAPLA. The report stated that 'as revolutionary armed forces, FAPLA guards and defends the strengthening of the party's political line, improving and bettering political and ideological work among the combatants and ensuring that they are involved in production and the defence of the people's property'. The report noted that it had been through the armed struggle for independence and that a national consciousness had been instilled in the diverse ethnic groups of Angola. The report also expressed gratitude to Cuba for sending officers and soldiers to assist FAPLA in winning the struggle for independence and for the help given in strengthening FAPLA (MPLA, 1977, p. 20).

Between 1977 and the Special Congress of 1980, FAPLA's major task was combating the increasing number of attacks by UNITA and the aggression from South African troops based in Namibia. This gave the armed forces a dual role: preparing for a conventional war against the South African regular army and conducting a counter-insurgency campaign against UNITA. Extensive help in coping with these problems was provided by the Cubans (who in the late 1970s had around 25,000 troops in Angola) and the several hundred Soviet advisers attached to the Cuban armed forces. The Cubans were deployed chiefly to guard against UNITA or South African attacks on major economic installations such as the Cabinda oilfields, although UNITA claimed that they, rather than FAPLA, spearheaded offensives against the guerrillas. In March 1978, the government launched a major offensive against UNITA in Cuando Cubango Province, using five FAPLA battalions supported by helicopters—UNITA claimed that 9,000 Cubans supported the offensive (*ACR*, 1978,p. B489).

In the late 1970s and early 1980s, the Cubans more or less withdrew from the offensives against UNITA, concentrating on training and defence of major economic installations. FAPLA forces supported by the ODP took on the responsibility for fighting UNITA and dealing with South African incursions. There was certainly no evidence of fighting between Cubans and South Africans or of an unwillingness on the part of FAPLA to confront UNITA or the SADF.

Reviewing the military situation and FAPLA's role, the Central Committee report to the 1980 congress said that South African aggression and UNITA 'banditry' had affected areas inhabited by 2.5 million people and had caused damage totalling US$ 7 billion. In the three years preceding the congress, the report said, the SADF had carried out 1,400 reconnaissance flights, 290 bombing raids, fifty landings of troops by helicopter and seventy ground attacks against Angola, resulting in the killing of over 1,800 FAPLA soldiers and civilians. In June and July 1980, over 4,000 SADF troops with sophisticated support had invaded southern Angola. FAPLA, for its part, had shot down eleven Mirage, Buccaneer and Impala combat aircraft and two military helicopters. In the north, FAPLA and the ODP had neutralized the counter-revolutionary FNLA and FLEC forces (helped, no doubt, by the reduction of Zaïrean support for them following the *rapprochement* with Angola).

The congress placed major emphasis on strengthening FAPLA. The report said that 'building up of the armed forces in itself represents the sum total of economic, political, ideological, technical and military activities carried out by the state for the purpose of strengthening its military power'. Unfortunately for the MPLA, which would have preferred concentration on economic reconstruction and socialist transformation, the threat posed by South Africa and its UNITA proxy meant that defence was the top priority for the party and state. The report said that some improvement had been achieved in troop training and combat preparation and an air force, anti-aircraft defence unit and a naval force had been organized.

The congress also dealt with the organization of workers and peasants in the ODP, which could be used for military operations in conjunction with FAPLA and for defending factories, villages and farms. It was decided at the congress that military training should be compulsory for all sectors of the population (MPLA, 1980, p. 90).

One of the major problems in organizing the armed forces that was highlighted by the congress was recruitment. It was pointed out by the Central Committee that although there was compulsory conscription for two years' military service, there was no central organization assigned to the task of dealing with conscripts or with recruitment of volunteers. The Central Committee told the congress that the aggression against Angola had necessitated an increase in the size of the armed forces and therefore increased expenditure on military, 'to the detriment of national reconstruction' (MPLA, 1980, p. 91).

In the late 1970s, the size of the armed forces rose from around 30,000 to nearly 50,000 (although in 1980 the regular armed forces were reduced in size to 32,500, with 200,000 reserves in the ODP). At the time of the congress, the army consisted of 30,000 troops organized in seventeen infantry brigades, four anti-aircraft artillery brigades and two motorized infantry brigades (each with one tank and two infantry battalions). Most of the weaponry was of Soviet and East European origin, including I–34 and T–54 tanks, BRDM–2 armoured cars, rocket launchers, anti-tank rockets and surface-to-air missiles. The air force had 1,500 members and was equipped with MiG–17 and MiG–21 combat aircraft and a number of transport aircraft and helicopters. Senior FAPLA officers received training in Cuba and the Soviet Union, while Soviet and Cuban advisers assisted with training in Angola.

A major aspect of training was political education. The MPLA rectification movement was very active in FAPLA in the years leading up to the 1980 congress. MPLA-PT and JMPLA cells were established in the armed forces. During the rectificaton campaign, 2,150 militants, 854 aspirants, 847 sympathizers and 13,229 members of the JMPLA were registered during the campaign in armed forces units. Political education was viewed as vital in order to prevent infiltration of FAPLA by anti-government factions as happened during the Alves coup and to ensure that troops appreciated the necessity of combating UNITA guerrilla activity.

The increase in South African aggression in the early 1980s, notably Operation Protea in August 1981 which culminated in the occupation of much of southern Cunene Province by the SADF, enabled UNITA to step up its attacks on government installations and MPLA supporters. South Africa's creation of a safe rear area for UNITA in Cunene and its increased military and logistical assistance helped Savimbi's movement to spread its military operations to provinces further north and to stretch FAPLA resources.

The situation had become so serious by mid-1983 that President dos Santos and the MPLA Political Bureau decided to establish regional military councils throughout the country to coordinate all political, economic and military activities in the fight against UNITA. Speaking at the swearing-in of the Regonal Military Council of the Ninth Region in Malanje on 5 September 1983, dos Santos said that the region covered Cuanza Norte and Malanje and would

... lead all politico-military, social and economic activities in the provinces of Malanje and Cuanza Norte. We hope it will arouse all the energies of the working masses and cadres and correctly assess and solve the most pressing problems of the people. The adoption of this measure is designed to improve in the military field the efficiency of the fight against the armed gangs, and, on the other hand, to improve the operation of party and state structures at all levels ... [Luanda Radio, 6 September 1983.]

The president went on to outline the national military situation, pointing out that successes achieved by FAPLA against UNITA and the 'impossibility of the UNITA puppets' task of subversion in the field of military operations' had forced South Africa to intervene directly more and more frequently. Such interventions took place in December 1983 and January 1984, leading to major clashes between FAPLA and the SADF around Cuvelai and the bombing by SADF aircraft of military installations at Lubango. Despite the Lusaka accord of February 1984 on military disengagement in southern Angola, South African troops remained there until mid-1985, and even after the withdrawal announced by the South African government they intervened several more times in late 1985, notably at Mavinga, to prevent the success of major FAPLA offensives against UNITA.

Speaking at the closing session of the People's Assembly in Luanda on 21 February 1985, President dos Santos said that the Chief of the FAPLA General Staff had provided a report stating that despite the continuation of UNITA's terrorist actions and its massive propaganda effort, both supported by South Africa, FAPLA had taken 'decisive steps to hold the initiative in military actions' (Luanda Radio, 22 February 1985). Certainly, in mid- and late-1985 FAPLA had considerable success in drives against UNITA in Moxico and Cuando Cubango Provinces, only being stopped from moving against Savimbi's headquarters at Jamba by air and ground attacks by South African forces against the FAPLA units and SADF diversionary attacks in Cunene Province.

During his speech to the People's Assembly, dos Santos noted that because of FAPLA's successes against major guerrilla concentrations, UNITA had tried the tactic of avoiding military confrontation and infiltrating small units into urban areas to carry out sabotage and bombing missions, whose targets were generally civilians. The president called for stepped-up vigilance by the ODP to combat this new threat.

By early 1986, FAPLA was looking stronger than it had in previous years, particularly the air force (led by Iko Carreira, who had received several years' advanced military training in the Soviet Union) which began to apply a more effective role in anti-UNITA offensives and defence against South African attacks in late 1985. The army, too, appeared stronger: the drive for Mavinga in autumn 1985 was far more resolute than anti-UNITA operations between 1982 and 1984, when newly trained UNITA units looked like gaining the military initiative and FAPLA seemed unable to organize effective defensive or offensive operations in UNITA's main areas of activity. UNITA's success in marching foreign captives from Lunda Norte through Moxico into Cuando Cubango Province demonstrated FAPLA's shortcomings in those years. In 1985 and 1986, FAPLA looked more effective but the military situation remained unstable because of the South African factor. Mililtary assistance and direct military intervention by the SADF has enabled UNITA to attain a military position hitherto unthinkable, given the movement's limited activities before independence and its defeat during the civil war.

The only way that the military situation can improve significantly for the MPLA is through the withdrawal of all South African troops from Angola and the independence of Namibia (and the evacuation of

South African forces from there). Without that, FAPLA and the ODP will be unable to do more than limit UNITA's activities. Even if the South Africans do withdraw, FAPLA will have its work cut out to eliminate UNITA completely, as the extensive support given to Savimbi by Pretoria since independence (plus the possibility of American aid to the movement) means that it has built itself up into a much stronger and more organized movement and has the experience of ten years of guerrilla warfare plus that of political organizaton in the areas it has occupied with the help of the SADF.

Angola's Military Forces (1985)

The total size of the Popular Armed Forces for the Liberation of Angola is 39,500 (including an estimated 24,000 conscripts) with 50,000 reserves. The period of conscription is two years. The constituents of MAPLA are as follows:

Army: 36,000 (24,000 conscripts). Angola is divided into ten military regions. The army is equipped with 175 T–34, 200 T–54-55, 90 T–62 and 50 PT–76 tanks; 200 BRDM-1/-2 armoured fighting vehicles; 225 BTR-60/152 armoured personnel carriers; 200 howitzers of calibres between 76mm. and 152mm.; 500 82mm. and 120mm. mortars; 50 BM-21 122mm. rocket launchers; recoilless rifles, anti-tank rockets and anti-aircraft guns.
Navy: 1,500. Equipped with 6 Osa-II fast-attack craft armed with SS-N-2 surface-to-surface missiles and 4 Shershen attack craft; 12 patrol craft; and 3 Soviet amphibious landing craft.
Air Force: 2,000. Equipped with 141 combat aircraft and 12 armed helicopters. Aircraft include 78 MiG-21s, 12 MiG-19s, 20 MiG-17s, 25 MiG-25s and 5 Su-22s. Anti-aircraft defences include 20 SAM-3, 72 SAM-6 and 48 SAM-8 and SAM-9 surface-to-air missiles.
Para-military forces: 50,000 ODP, 7,000 border guards, and an unknown number of Popular Vigilance Brigades. (IISS, 1985-6, p. 91.)

Estimates of the Cuban troops in Angola vary between 19,000 and 26,000; the International Institute of Strategic Studies has put the number of troops at 20,000 and the number of civilian technicians/

advisers at 6,000. The Soviet Union is believed to have sent 700 military advisers to Angola, the German Democratic Republic 500 and Bulgaria, Portugal and other countries 1,500 between them. Angola has concluded military agreements with the German Democratic Republic, Bulgaria, Romania and Mozambique. The Soviet-Angolan Treaty of Friendship and Cooperation includes clauses on military cooperation and assistance. Angola and neighbouring Zaïre have signed a Treaty of Security of Defence, guaranteeing that each signatory will not allow its territory to be used for attacks or aggression against the other.

Angola provides bases and training facilities for the South West African People's Organization (SWAPO) and the African National Congress (ANC) of South Africa. During the liberation war in Zimbabwe it provided training facilities for Joshua Nkomo's Zimbabwe African People's Union (ZAPU).

Foreign Policy

In his speech on independence day, President Agostinho Neto announced the programme of the MPLA government, stressing that 'the foreign policy of the People's Republic of Angola will be based on the principle of total independence observed by the MPLA from the outset, will be one of non-alignment' (cited by Somerville, winter 1984, p. 297). The principle of non-alignment was also enshrined in the country's new constitution, as was a prohibition on the establishment of any foreign military bases in Angola. Neto's independence speech made it clear that the new government intended to base its domestic and foreign policies on socialism but that externally the country would not become embroiled in military blocs and would give emphasis to its non-aligned status. However, it was equally clear that relations with Cuba, the Soviet Union and other states of the socialist community would be an important facet of Angolan diplomacy. Soon after the end of the fighting in early 1976, Angola was recognized by and became a member of the OAU: part of the non-aligned stance was a commitment to the OAU, which tries to avoid becoming involved in East-West rivalries.

Another important factor in the shaping of Angolan foreign policy, and one which has not always been under the control of the MPLA government, is the regional situation in southern Africa and the aggressive stance of South Africa. Angola has, under the MPLA, supported other liberation movements in southern Africa politically and materially, and through its provision of direct support to SWAPO and the ANC it has become a target for South African military actions and destablization through UNITA. Cooperation with other southern African states through the front-line states group and the Southern African Development Coordination Conference (whose aims were chiefly economic) has also been a source of influence on foreign policy.

Although the MPLA leadership has constantly sought amicable if not over-close ties with the West (and trade relations are geared strongly towards the United States and Western Europe), problems have arisen with the United States because of its refusal to recognize the Angolan government while Cuban troops remain in the country; and further obstacles to normalization have been posed by the links maintained by successive governments in Washington with UNITA and the United States' unwillingness to put pressure on South Africa over Namibian independence. Relations with Western European countries, although not blossoming, are more cordial than Angolan–American relations and have been guided more by trade relations than by East–West factors.

MPLA Policy Guidelines

During the liberation struggle it became very clear that although the MPLA wished to cement cooperative relations with most states, the support of socialist, Third World and Nordic states for the liberation movements would have a far-reaching influence on the approach that would be adopted by the MPLA after independence. Similarly, the support given to Portugal by fellow members of the NATO alliance would be a hindrance to the establishment of cooperative relations, at least in the short term.

Following independence, the MPLA stuck to its principles of non-alignment, although the extensive support given to the movement by Cuba and the Soviet Union during the civil war and the MPLA's increasingly Marxist–Leninist stance meant that the commitment to non-alignment was combined with a commitment to friendship with the socialist states. Such a position was affirmed at the October 1976 plenum of the MPLA Central Committee. The Political Bureau declaration to the meeting noted that during the liberation struggle 'international imperialism' had attempted to prevent the liberation movement in Angola from 'assuming a clearly revolutionary character oriented by Marxist–Leninist principles', to keep the Angolan economy dependent on 'monopoly capital' and to maintain the status quo in southern Africa (MPLA, 1976, p. 19). Among the methods used to oppose the revolutionary movement in Angola had been 'the encirclement' of Angola with hostile regimes; an economic boycott and a propaganda campaign against Angola by the United States; the regrouping and arming of anti-MPLA forces; the refusal of the United States to recognize the MPLA government; and the use of the American veto at the UN to try to prevent Angola from becoming a member (MPLA, 1976, p. 20). However, the declaration went on, the friends of the Angolan people—the socialist states and the 'progressive forces and countries on every continent'—had come to Angola's assistance.

In the light of the Political Bureau's view of the international and regional situation, the declaration set out the following principles, which were then adopted by the Central Committee, for the conduct of Angola's foreign policy:

(a) The establishment and maintenance of diplomatic relations with all countries of the world on the basis of mutual respect for national sovereignty and territorial integrity, non-aggression and non-interference in the internal affairs of others, equality and mutal benefit and peaceful coexistence among states with differing social regimes;

(b) Respect for the principles of the Charters of the United Nations and the Organization of African Unity (OAU);

(c) The safeguarding of political independence and of the socialist option;

(d) A policy of non-alignment in relation to the global military blocs, acting together with the movement of non-aligned countries, supporting their anti-colonialist and anti-imperialist orientation . . .

(e) Rejection of all international agreements signed in the name of Angola by the Portuguese colonial government . . .

(f) Prohibition of foreign military bases on our soil . . .

(h) Strengthening the links of cooperation and friendship with the socialist community and with all anti-imperialist communities;

(i) Diversification of economic and techno-scientific cooperation;

(j) Support for the creation of a new international economic order . . .

(k) Maintenance of the traditional spirit of unity and struggle against imperialism and neo-colonialism among the former Portuguese colonies . . . militant solidarity with oppressed peoples and with movements of national liberation and support for armed struggle conducted by them for the reconquest of their rights;

(m) Solidarity with the workers of the world on the basis of proleterian internationalism;

(n) Support for the action conducted by the socialist countries and democratic and progressive forces at the international level for the implementation of détente and world disarmament and the elimination of areas of tension which imperialism creates or intends to create in different continents, to impede the progress of the people's struggle for liberation;

(o) Friendly relations with states bordering on Angola. [MPLA, 1976, pp. 20–1.]

Of these points, the most salient were: the safeguarding of the socialist option (as it was with this end in view that Angola sought extensive Cuban and Soviet help to defend Angola's independence and to replace some of the skilled Portuguese manpower which fled Angola on independence); the policy of non-alignment and anti-imperialism; the prohibition of foreign military bases (which meant that, despite its ties with the socialist countries and despite the accusations of the United States, the country did not become tied to the Warsaw Treaty Organisation and was able to maintain its non-aligned status); diversification of economic links (which meant that, although trade and other ties with socialist countries were increased, this was not to the exclusion of economic cooperation with the Western European states and even the United States); and support for national liberation movements (which led to the cross-border conflict with the South African forces in Namibia and South Africa's support for UNITA, without which the rebel movement would have had the same fate as the now ineffective FNLA).

Relations with the Socialist Countries

Although the MPLA's commmitment to Marxism has been flexible
and pragmatic in terms of policy formulation and the movement has
always been keen to keep open lines of communication to Western
states, including the overtly hostile Reagan administration, following
independence the new government was quick to cement good
relations with the Soviet Union. The Soviet Union had, after all, been
the movement's most consistent supporter during the long liberation
war and had, along with Cuba, been an important factor in the MPLA's
victory during the civil war. Thus, in May 1976, the Angolan Premier,
Lopo do Nascimento, visited Moscow for talks with the Soviet leadership on political, economic and military cooperation. Nascimento and
his Soviet counterpart, Kosygin, signed a declaration on peaceful
relations on 26 May. The final communiqué on the visit stated that
agreement had been reached on 'certain measures directed at providing the People's Republic of Angola with assistance in strengthening its
defence capacity' (*Pravda*, 1 June 1976). Among the agreements signed
during Nascimento's stay in the Soviet Union was one on Soviet
economic aid, which provided for financial assistance and help with
filling the vacuum left by the Portuguese both by training Angolans
and sending technicians, advisers and skilled workers from the Soviet
Union to Angola.

In October 1976, Neto paid his first post-independence trip to the
Soviet Union, where he signed a Treaty of Friendship and Cooperation
and an agreement on inter-party cooperation between the MPLA and
the CPSU (Communist Party of the Soviet Union). The treaty encapsulated a firm Soviet commitment to support the MPLA and a reciprocal commitment by the Angolans to establish close and cooperative ties
with the Soviet Union. The Treaty's clauses included ones dealing with
Soviet respect for Angolan non-alignment, consultations in situations
representing a threat to peace, and economic, scientific and technical
cooperation. The Treaty's tenth article stated: 'In the interests of
strengthening the defence capability of the High Contracting Parties,
they shall continue to promote cooperation in the military field on the
basis of corresponding agreements concluded between them' (*Soviet
News*, 26 October 1976). The inter-party agreement did not indicate a

Soviet recognition that the MPLA was a fully Marxist–Leninist party, but rather that it was, to use Soviet parlance, a party of 'socialist orientation' (this term has been used by Soviet leaders and commentators to describe those states in the Third World, such as Mozambique, the People's Democratic Republic of Yemen, Ethiopia and Angola, that have embarked on the formation of Marxist-Leninist parties and pledged themselves to build socialist systems).

Neto's talks with the Soviet leadership also led to the signing of further agreements on economic aid and military cooperation. However, Neto maintained a position of total independence during the visit. Speaking on Soviet television, he did not defer to his hosts and praised Cuban aid more than Soviet assistance. In an interview for Moscow Radio, he spoke very ambiguously about states that tried to bring pressure on other countries to adopt certain social and political policies—although no states were named, some observers in the West tried to suggest that this was a warning by Neto to the Soviet Union not to lean too heavily on Angola in order to push it towards socialism too quickly (Somerville, winter 1984, p. 298). But the overall effect of the visit was to strengthen bilateral relations and to confirm the socialist and anti-imperialist strand in Angola's non-aligned foreign policy.

After the Alves coup attempt, there was speculation in the West that the Soviet Union and the socialist countries had, at the very least, been sympathetic towards the plotters and might even have offered them assistance. The main evidence used to suggest links between the socialist countries and Alves was the latter's attendance at the CPSU congress in Moscow in February 1976 and the pro-Soviet speeches made by Alves on his return. Klinghoffer says that it is likely that the Soviet Union was aware of the plot and did nothing to alert the Neto leadership (Klinghoffer, 1980, p. 131). But the allegations of Soviet complicity with the coup ignore the racist and bourgeois nature of Alves's political outlook and the effects which support for an attempt against the internationally and OAU-recognized MPLA government would have on Soviet credibility in the Third World. The evidence of Soviet links with Alves are at best circumstantial. Following the coup Neto accused Alves of a 'feigned dedication to a friendly country' but he certainly did not even imply Soviet support for his opponents (Somerville, winter 1984, p. 299).

When the MPLA held its First Congress in December 1977, which confirmed the foreign policy guidelines adopted by the October 1976 plenum, the Soviet Union sent a high-ranking Politburo member, Andrey Kirilenko, to represent it. The congress pledged the MPLA's adherence to Marxism–Leninism and its transformation into a vanguard party—something urged on Third World countries and parties by Soviet party theorists. In his speech to the congress, Kirilenko said that the country had embarked on the path to 'people's democracy and socialism' and compared Angola flatteringly with Vietnam, a longstanding friend of the Soviet Union (*Pravda*, 6 December 1977).

Prior to his death in Moscow on 10 September 1979, Neto made efforts to balance the excellent ties with the Soviet Union and the other socialist states (particularly Cuba, which had tens of thousands of troops defending the country and thousands of civilian advisers, doctors and teachers helping with reconstruction) by increasing contacts, particularly economic ones, with the West. This dual policy was continued by the post-Neto leadership headed by President dos Santos, whose first foreign visit after becoming President was to the Soviet Union (where he and his Ministers of Defence, Interior, Foreign Affairs, Energy and Industry held talks with their Soviet counterparts with a view to increasing political, military and economic cooperation).

Political, military and economic ties with Cuba and a number of Eastern European states were strengthened by the MPLA under both Neto and dos Santos. Relations were exceptionally close between Angola and Cuba, not least because of the importance of Cuban military support in the face of South African destabilizaton attempts. All the socialist countries supported Angola staunchly in the face of South African raids and Pretoria's support for the UNITA guerrillas. The support took the form of diplomatic activity at the UN and other international forums, the supply of massive quantities of military hardware (mainly from the Soviet Union), and the provision of advisers (both civilian and military). The Soviet Union and its allies offered clear and unequivocal support to Angola in September 1981 following the major South African incursion into Cunene Province. Apart from publicly condemning the attack and supporting moves at the UN to penalize South Africa, the Soviet Union dispatched a number of warships to conduct military exercises off the Angolan coast—an obvious warning to South Africa that there was a limit to what the Soviet Union would would take in terms of aggression against a friendly state. Following the major South Africa incursion in December 1983, the Soviet Union arranged a meeting in Moscow with Angolan and Cuban representatives to discuss joint action to defend Angola and an agreement was reached 'on providing aid to the People's republic of Angola in the matter of strengthening its defence capacity, independence and territorial integrity', according to the Soviet news agency, Tass (Somerville, winter 1984, p. 302). At the time there were also reports that Soviet diplomats at the UN had contacted their South African counterparts and warned them that the Soviet Union would not stand idly by and watch the destabilization or destruction of the MPLA government in Angola.

The talks that were held in the early and mid-1980s between Angola, the United States and South Africa on possible formulas for Namibian independence were a point of divergence in Soviet–Angolan relations. Soviet comments on South Africa and on the Western Contact Group on Namibia (United States, Britain, France, West Germany and Canada) were strongly critical of the Western attitude over southern Africa and clearly opposed to talks with South Africa and any mediatory attempt by the United States. However, the MPLA authorities believed the talks to be to their advantage and several rounds of them were held in Cape Verde: despite the absence of diplomatic relations, several US State Department officials visited Angola in an attempt to reach agreement over a timetable for independence and to negotiate over the Cuban presence in Angola.

Despite the difference of opinion over Namibia, Angola continued to develop close relations with the Soviet Union and socialist states. The December 1985 congress of the MPLA-PT was attended by a high-ranking Soviet delegation led by Politburo member Geydar Aliyev. Two months later, President dos Santos himself led the Angolan delegation to the CPSU congress in Moscow, where he held talks with General Secretary Gorbachev.

During his attendance at the congress in the Soviet Union, Dos Santos held talks with a number of Eastern European party and state leaders and, most importantly, with Fidel Castro, the Cuban leader. Castro and dos Santos reaffirmed the closeness of their ties and also their determination not to allow South Africa and the United States to make the withdrawal of Cuban troops from Angola a precondition for Namibian independence. In 1984, following meetings with the Cuban leadership, President dos Santos had announced, in a letter to the Secretary General of the UN, that Angola and Cuba were willing to carry out a phased withdrawal of Cuban troops once South Africa had removed all of its troops from Angola and UN Security Council Resolution 435 on Namibian independence was implemented. The announcement was designed to counter the position adopted by the United States and South Africa that Cuba had to withdraw all of its troops prior to implementation of Resolution 435.

In early 1986, Angola was still seeking to negotiate over the future of Namibia, its role in talks on the future of the territory being necessitated by its hosting of SWAPO and by the Cuban presence. At the time of writing, in February 1986, the Cuban presence in Angola is estimated to be around 20,000 troops, with 6,000 civilian advisers and technicians. Apart from its military support for the MPLA, Cuba has played a major role in providing doctors, teachers, construction workers and skilled workers for a wide variety of industrial and agricultural sectors. Soviet, East German and Bulgarian technicians, advisers and skilled workers are also in Angola in their hundreds helping to train Angolans to run vital sectors of the economy. Soviet aid has been particularly important in the fields of fisheries, vehicle maintenance and hydroelectric-power generation (for example, the major dam project at Capanda).

Soviet aid disbursements to Angola have not been overly generous since independence, partly because of the Soviet Union's shortage of hard currency and its own economic problems. Western diplomatic sources put total aid disbursed between 1976 and 1978 at $17 million out of a total of $40 million offered between 1975 and 1982. However, diplomatic sources and the South African press report that the Soviet Union agreed to provide total aid amounting to $2,000 million between 1982 and 1990 (Somerville, winter 1984, p. 306). In January 1982, the then number one in the MPLA Political Bureau, Lucio Lara, visited Moscow and signed an agreement on aid to the end of the decade thought to refer to the £2 billion dollar package.

Trade between Angola and the socialist countries has still to exceed the 10 per cent of total trade position (see Chapter 4 on the economy), but considering that pre-independence trade was nil, some progress has been made in diversifying economic relations away from total dependence on Portugal, the United States and Western Europe. In addition, the MPLA has always followed a policy of continued trade with the West, provided it is in Angola's economic interest (as has certainly been the case in the petroleum sector).

The Angolan position on trade with foreign states was set out by President dos Santos in a speech in February 1982. He stressed the need for caution in agreeing to cooperate with foreign countries in order to bring about balanced development and went on to say that: 'In fundamental sectors of economic development, we must give priority to the consolidation of economic ties with the countries of the socialist camp. For they constitute the firm rearguard of our liberation struggle' (Luanda Radio, 5 February 1982).

The overall attitude of the MPLA towards the Soviet Union and other socialist states was encapsulated in a commentary put out in February 1982 by the Angolan news agency, ANGOP, dealing with the country's foreign policy. After reaffirming the Angolan commitment to non-alignment, the commentary said that foreign policy guidelines indicated

... the objective need to strengthen, in particular, the preferential relations with the parties and states of the socialist community and international workers' movement ... The first five years of the existence of the Friendship and Cooperation Treaty signed in Moscow ... attest to the major revolutionary achievements of these preferential relations with our natural allies' [Somerville, winter 1984, p. 303.]

Relations with Southern African States and the West

The crisis in the whole southern African region has been a major influence on all aspects of Angola's internal and external policies. The region is dominated militarily and economically by South Africa and Angola has taken a major role in opposing the regional and domestic policies of the apartheid-ruled state both through direct support for SWAPO and the ANC and the activities of the nine-nation Southern African Development Coordination Conference.

Support for SWAPO and the ANC, combined with socialist policies and the Cuban presence, has brought Angola into perpetual conflict (political and military) with South Africa and, at times, the United States. South African attacks against Angola have been designed to force the government to end its support for the two southern African liberation movements and to procure Angolan acquiescence in the face of South Africa's hegemonistic approach to the region. The internal contradictions in South Africa have led it into a policy of aggression and destabilization in southern Africa aimed at ending support for SWAPO and the ANC, weakening the independent African states and thereby buying time for the white minority in South Africa.

Angola, along with Mozambique, has been more forthright than other front-line states in supporting the anti-apartheid struggle and the fight for freedom for Namibia. Thus it in turn has been made to suffer by South Africa as a result of its policies. A major concern of Angolan regional policies and policies towards the West was an attempt to put pressure on South Africa to end its aggression against the country (both direct attacks and support for UNITA). Regionally, efforts have been carried out in the context of the informal front-line states grouping (Angola, Tanzania, Zimbabwe, Zambia, Mozambique and Botswana), whereby the countries involved seek to assist each other in fending off South Africa and in persuading Western states of the need to adopt a stronger position regarding South Africa's policy of regional destabilization and internal oppression.

The other main instrument for lessening the effects of South African dominance is the SADCC. This group, formed at the time of Zimbabwe's independence in early 1980, has as its objective the ending of economic dependence of the independent states on South Africa in terms of trade and transport in particular. Angola has played a major role in the SADCC and is responsible for coordinating the SADCC's ministerial committee on regional energy policy. Through the SADCC Angola has received some Western aid and the group was undoubtedly influential in the Angola decision in early 1985 to apply for membership of the Lomé III Convention between African, Caribbean and Pacific states and the European Economic Community (EEC).

Angolan policy towards Western states, with the exception of the United States, has been to increase trading and economic ties (French,

Portuguese, and British firms have been closely involved with the development of offshore petroleum resources). Angola has also to use cordial relations with Western European countries, notably France, as a means of gaining diplomatic support in the conflict with South Africa.

Relations with the former colonial power, Portugal, have been variable. At times the MPLA government has been furious with the leeway that successive governments in Lisbon have allowed UNITA for political and propaganda activities in the former colonial capital. However, President dos Santos was among the heads of state to attend the inauguration of Portugal's first civilian President, Mario Soares, in March 1986—perhaps presaging an improvement in relations.

Relations with the United States have never been more than luke-warm since independence. During the civil war, the United States actively supported the FNLA and UNITA and after independence referred to the MPLA government as a puppet of the Soviet Union and Cuba. Presidents Carter and Reagan both made the withdrawal of the Cubans the major condition for recognition and an improvement in relations. The Carter administration took a softer line in relations than its successor, but still failed to open official relations. The Reagan administraton has been generally hostile towards the MPLA and has been firm in its demand that the Cubans withdraw from Angola prior to the independence of Namibia and as a precondition for the opening of diplomatic relations. In March 1986, the Reagan administration and the US Congress were on the point of approving a $27 million aid package to UNITA, something made possible through the earlier repeal of the Clark Amendment which prohibited American aid to the anti-MPLA rebel movement. In a comment on the possibility of renewed American aid to UNITA, the Angolan news agency said that the United States should not confuse Angola with 'tiny Grenada' and added that such a move would have the effect of setting off an explo-sion with 'unforseeable consequences' (*Africa Now*, December 1985, p. 24). In his speech to the MPLA congress in December 1985, Presi-dent dos Santos was strongly critical of American support for UNITA and South Africa and said that the United States administration had become 'the faithful ally of the racist Pretoria regime'. He added that it was clear that Washington supported South Africa's campaign of destabilization against Angola and other southern African states. The President reaffirmed, though, that Angola was committed to its support for the ANC and SWAPO and to its ties with the Soviet Union and Cuba. The message of the comments was that Angola was not willing to abandon basic elements of its foreign policy in order to establish ties with the United States. Angola does, though, have excellent economic cooperation with a number of American companies, notably Gulf Oil. Trade has increased despite the refusal of the United States to recognize the MPLA government.

Relations with China

Although China supported the MPLA at times during the liberation war, by the time of the Portuguese revolution it was concentrating all of its aid on the FNLA and UNITA and had dispatched 450 military advisers to help the FNLA. Partly as a result of its close ties with President Mobutu, China supported the FNLA and UNITA during the civil war, though it took only a backseat role. After the MPLA's victory, China was strongly critical of the Soviet and Cuban role and effectively viewed the MPLA as Soviet puppets. Chinese military aid for Zaïre at the time of greatest tension between Angola and Zaïre during the two Shaba crises meant that little improvement took place in relations in the early years of independence. However, in the early 1980s, well after the Angolan–Zaïrean *rapprochement*, China began to soften its line towards Angola and, in January 1983, the two states established diplomatic relations and started talks on initiating trade. In February 1983, the Chinese Premier Zhao Ziyang said that China supported Angola's refusal to link the independence of Namibia to the withdrawal of Cuban troops—an almost complete reversal of China's position during the civil war. Something which clearly helped in the *rapprochement* between Angola and China was China's downgrading of vehement opposition to the influence of the Soviet Union in Africa and Angola's adherence to a non-aligned and pragmatic line in foreign policy despite its lasting friendship with the Soviet Union and Cuba.

Conclusion

From the foregoing account of post-independence developments in Angola, it can be seen that the MPLA leadership has implemented policies intended to reconstitute the broad-based national liberation movement into a disciplined and united vanguard party guided by Marxism–Leninism; to develop state control of the most vital areas of the economy; where possible, to set up state farms and agricultural cooperatives; and to launch mass health and educational campaigns, the latter being aimed at stamping out illiteracy and providing educated cadres for party, state and economic bodies. The commitment to Marxism–Leninism of the MPLA leadership under both Agostinho Neto and President Eduardo dos Santos is undeniable and it is evident that it intends to continue implementing policies, where the political, economic and military circumstances allow, aimed at creating the political, social and economic bases from which to embark on the formation of a new society.

But, and it is a very large but, a number of massive obstacles remain in the path of the MPLA and its socialist policies. So far, relatively little progress has been made in making socialist aims reality as a result of the devastation caused by the liberation and civil wars, the continuing military actions and sabotage by UNITA and its South African backers, and the crippling shortage of educated and politically conscious cadres to fill both party and state positions. Until at least the first two of these obstacles are removed, progress in reconstruction and towards socialist transformation is likely to be painfully slow.

The campaign of sabotage and destabilization carried out by UNITA and South Africa has forced the MPLA to devote a high proportion of its human and material resources to the war effort rather than to pressing polilical and economic tasks. Only the removal of South African military units from southern Angola and occupied Namibia and an end to Pretoria's support for UNITA will enable the Angolan armed forces to defeat UNITA militarily and enable the MPLA to combat its political influence on Ovimbundu areas. Without the massive assistance it receives from South Africa, UNITA would undoubtedly crumble into impotence, as did the FNLA and Holden Roberto following the withdrawal of extensive Zaïrean support. Until this battle is won, it will be impossible for the MPLA to make meaningful progress towards politicizing rural areas and winning the support of the bulk of the peasantry, particularly in the agriculturally important central and southern highlands.

The ending of South African and UNITA destabilization is also a precondition for real economic construction and the establishment of an economy capable of supporting the MPLA's plans for socialization of industrial and agricultural production. Until the 1973 levels of production have been reached, something that requires the drastic cutting of military expenditure (said now to be consuming 50 per cent of the government's financial resources annually), it will be impossible for the MPLA to go ahead with plans to expand production in the agricultural, fisheries and industrial sectors and increase the production of consumer and other goods necessary to improve living standards.

The military conflict in Angola has made it difficult for observers of developments there to gauge the real level of support for MPLA policies, the attitude of the mass of the peasantry (the overwhelming bulk of the population) towards cooperativization (a necessity for the socialization of the rural economy), and the likelihood of the MPLA being able to win over the peasants politically. These are major question marks hanging over the future of Marxism in Angola, but the questions cannot be fully or adequately answered because of the state of war in much of Angola and the embryonic nature of the measures taken so far to effect a transformation of society.

The cadre shortage, something which has been a serious hindrance to the attempts made so far to introduce party control over government activities and to mobilize the population and educate it politically, is a major problem that again cannot be tackled by the MPLA while it is preoccupied with fighting UNITA. At present, more effort has to be put into the political training of reliable officers and commissars for FAPLA than into politicizing Angolans at the urban and grassroots level because of the overriding need to ensure basic security and to defeat the government's internal and external opponents.

The conclusions that can be reached about Marxism–Leninism in Angola are that the ruling party has consistently held to its basic ideological position and has not compromised on its plans to work towards socialism. The party programme first outlined at the all-important plenum of the MPLA Central Committee in October 1976 has been approved and updated by successive party congresses in December 1977, 1980 and 1985, but without any real success having been achieved in realizing basic aims of defeating UNITA and restoring economic output to pre-independence levels. Success was attained in the rectification campaign and the fight against factionalism, though it remains to be seen whether the arrest of Ludy Kissassunda and Alda Lara and the removal from the Political Bureau of Lucio Lara will lead to the sort of factionalism rife in the MPLA prior to independence and at the time of the Alves coup attempt. The rectification campaign seemed to achieve considerable success in weeding out suspected opportunists who were using the party for personal advancement or gain, but it is questionable whether the party retains sufficient cadres from a broad section of the population and whether it has enough experienced cadres to carry out its policies effectively while generating popular support. A serious problem for the MPLA, and one that may well have been exacerbated by the rectification campaign, is the shortage of educated cadres in the MPLA, something highlighted by the December 1985 party congress. Although from the MPLA's point of view it was necessary to remove party members who were potential opportunists or opponents of the party line, there is some evidence (cited by President dos Santos in speeches since rectificaton) that many loyal party members were wrongly removed from the party. In addition, the reduction in the size of the party during the campaign and the failure of the MPLA to increase recruitment significantly will add to the problem of cadre shortages and mean that they are spread even more thinly than before.

Internationally, the MPLA has stuck firmly to its policy of anti-imperialist non-alignment combined with the expansion of cooperation and friendship with the socialist states. Increasingly closer ties have not meant, however, that the Angolans have become Soviet clients. They have guaranteed their independence in decision-making, something demonstrated by the clear divergence of views between the

MPLA and the Soviet leadership concerning talks with the United States and South Africa on the future of Namibia. On the other hand, the Luanda authorities have steadfastly refused to bow to American and South African pressure to agree to a withdrawal of Cuban troops from Angola as a precondition for Namibian independence and the withdrawal of South African troops from Namibia.

Cooperation with the socialist countries, particularly the Soviet Union and Cuba, has not prevented the MPLA government from developing excellent trade and economic relations with Western countries and multinational corporations. Although Angola has sought to increase trade and economic cooperation with the socialist countries, this has not been particularly damaging to cooperation with the West. It is a fact that, despite the poor political relations with the United States, Angola works very closely with the US Gulf Oil Company in the exploitation of oil resources.

Having briefly discussed the major points in the MPLA's domestic and foreign policies, there remain two questions about Angola's development that need to be answered in order to shed light on the position of Angola's political and ideological developments in relation to (1) African nationalism and the national liberation struggle, and (2) the international communist movement, and in particular, the Soviet Union.

(1) The commitment of the MPLA to Marxism–Leninism—and there can be little doubt that this commitment remains strong and is likely to be the salient feature of the party's future political orientation—did not develop as a result of the aid given to the movement during the liberation and civil wars by the Soviet Union, Cuba and other socialist states. Right from the formation of the movement, it had a strong Marxist element within it. The influence of the Marxists within the movement was strong both because many of the MPLA's founders were Marxists or were sympathetic to the ideology and because the Marxists in the MPLA were among the most highly educated of the members of the movement.

This opening statement begs the question: why did many of the leaders of the MPLA hold Marxist beliefs? The answer is that the early leaders of the national liberation struggle in Angola formed many of their ideas about the fight against colonialism while living outside Angola and they were influenced and guided by the ideological and political environment in which they began their political activities. In the case of Holden Roberto and the FNLA, they started their political struggle in Congo (Léopoldville)—later Zaïre—among the Kongo people and they were themselves members of the traditional Kongo hierarchy. It is not surprising, therefore, that their early ideas on freedom from Portuguese rule centred on Kongo nationalism and the resurrection of the old Kongo kingdom. Their ideas were modified by contacts with other African nationalists and developed into a conservative and Kongo-based form of nationalism. Incalculable influence on the course of the FNLA's political development was exerted by the political situation in Congo and by President Mobutu, in particular.

In the case of the MPLA, many of the early leaders received their political education as students in Fascist Portugal. Political activity was impossible except in clandestine groups. The effect of this political environment was to polarize politics more than in other colonial states (for example, in Britain and France, where African nationalists could imbibe political ideologies ranging from Marxism to liberalism and private enterprise capitalism). In Portugal, Angolan students and intellectuals found that political activity of a form that offered support for the aims of African nationalists was to be found almost wholly on the left of the political spectrum. The nature of the Portuguese Fascist state, and the opposition groups to which it gave rise, lent greater legitimacy to the Marxist-Leninist ideology of the Portuguese Communist Party in the eyes of African nationalists than, say, the British Communist Party did to nationalists from British colonies in Africa. In addition, the Portuguese Communist Party and related youth and trade-union organizations were more willing than other groups to accommodate and offer support to the liberation struggles and aspirations of African nationalists. Another important factor in bringing the Africans and the Portuguese communists together was the existence, in the years immediately following the second world war, of communist party cells in Luanda.

In this political and ideological environment it was hardly surprising that Angolan nationalists took on board Marxist teachings on political, social and economic analysis and Marxist-Leninist theories on political struggle. This is not to say that Marxism–Leninism was imposed on Africans in Portugal. The Portuguese Communist Party was, after all, illegal and the Salazar regime in Lisbon was intent on smashing it. The Fascist authorities did everything in their power to prevent Africans from the colonies from engaging in political activities in Portugal or in the colonies and were particularly keen to stop the spread of communist ideas. The adoption of Marxism by many Africans from the colonies—particularly from Angola and Mozambique—resulted from conscious decisions by the African nationalists that Marxism–Leninism offered not only an explanation of the nature of Portuguese colonialism and exploitation but also a reliable guide to political organization and action. As Barry Munslow has stated:

Access to Marxist literature and the presence [in Lisbon] of those gifted and committed cadres who were able to assimilate and creatively apply the theory to their own concrete situations were invaluable necessities ... It was the complex inter-action between the struggle and Marxist theory which formed them into a de facto revolutionary vanguard within the broader front [of the African nationalist movements in the African colonies]. [Munslow, 1983, p. 139.]

The MPLA and Frelimo were both broad nationalist fronts rather than Marxist parties, but they contained within them the nucleus of the later vanguard parties. In the late 1960s, Daniel Chipenda of the MPLA, as noted in a previous chapter, stated the intention of the MPLA to form itself into a vanguard party once the basic task of liberation was achieved.

During the liberation struggle, the Marxist cadres within the MPLA (and they were essentially the leading cadres) continued to develop their ideas on the Marxist transformation of Angola once independence had been achieved. However, in order to gain the widest possible support from the Angolan people, Marxism was not made a salient feature of the MPLA's liberation policies. Rather, emphasis was placed on the need to achieve political independence and to free Angola from the yoke of Portuguese colonialism. This was not a misleading policy on the part of the MPLA; it was a political necessity not just for the Marxists but for all the nationalists to form the broadest possible front of nationalists to defeat the Portuguese. Such a policy was also followed by Frelimo in Mozambique, ZANU and ZAPU in Zimbabwe, and is being followed by SWAPO in Namibia and the ANC in South Africa.

Following the achievement of independence, the Marxist vanguard within the MPLA declared its intention to transform the MPLA into a Marxist–Leninist party and to embark on a socialist transformation. There was no evident opposition to this within the MPLA; the factional struggles were centred on the exact ideology of the party and the nature of the future socialist system rather than socialism or Marxism *per se*.

We must now ask in what way the MPLA and its commitment differed from other socialist and nationalist parties in Africa. The answer is that the commitment of the MPLA leadership to Marxism–Leninism, which I have contended resulted from the political environment in which it conducted its nationalist struggle, incorporated ideas absent from other socialist theories applied by African parties. Partly as a result of the need to organize a broad front to fight an armed struggle and partly because of the particular nature of Portuguese colonialism and the political experiences of the Angolan nationalists, the MPLA developed adherence to Marxism as an integal part of its political development; whereas a country such as Tanzania was not forced to resort to armed struggle to achieve independence and did not suffer as oppressive and exploitative a system of colonialism as Angola and Mozambique. The Tanzanian nationalists, led by Julius Nyerere, had contact in Britain not only with Marxists but also with the largely non-Marxist Labour Party, which did not base its policies on class struggle and revolution as the communist parties did. Furthermore, in the last years of colonialism, clandestine political organization was not a necessity for the Tanzanians as it was for the Angolans and Mozambicans. These differences go some way towards explaining the differing conceptions of socialism held by some African nationalists. Nyerere and the nationalists in Tanzania developed a form of African socialism that eschewed class struggle in favour of a harking-back to perceived forms of cooperation and collective development from the African past. But the nationalists in Angola and Mozambique, partly guided by the experience of post-colonial developments in some African states, opted to reject what has been termed African socialism and to base their struggle and their policies for the future on Marxism–Leninism.

The MPLA leadership had seen the failure of the Sekou Touré regime in Guinea to achieve major advances in economic independence through African socialism, had seen the overthrow of Kwame Nkrumah's Pan-African socialism in Ghana and of Mobido Keita in Mali. These failures of African socialism to achieve what they set out to achieve must have played an important role in convincing the leaders of the MPLA of the need for a more radical approach; one that would get right to the heart of the problem of economic and political independence and provide a framework for dealing with external and internal opponents.

The Neto leadership of the MPLA decided, therefore, that its Marxist ideology provided a more realistic analysis of the problems facing Angola and a more efficacious guide to action than the ideas of African socialism. Marxism–Leninism provided an analysis of the international environment in which the Angolans had to operate, a critique of the international economic system, and a blueprint for party organization and the entrenchment of the political power of a movement committed to the foundation of a socialist system. One thing that it did not provide was an explanation of how Marxism–Leninism could be applied in Angola and the suitability of orthodox concepts of class struggle in a country with only the most embryonic working class and petty-bourgeois class.

In their study of what they term the rise of Afrocommunism in Angola, Mozambique and Ethiopia, the Ottaways argue that the adoption of the MPLA and Frelimo of class-conflict-orientated concepts was 'very artificial'. They see Marxism–Leninism as a useful guide for the MPLA in engineering social change and as 'an admirable instrument of rule in new nation states badly in need of a centralising institution' (Ottaway & Ottaway, 1981, pp. 199–200). While there is much to be said for this point of view, in terms of Marxist–Leninist theory—and one must remember that the leadership of the MPLA is firmly committed to Marxism–Leninism—the application of concepts of class conflict need not be so artificial in a peasant society such as that in Angola. The peasants in Angola live on the basis of subsistence farming and the production of a small surplus product with which to obtain cash in order to buy commodities they cannot produce. This mode of existence contains within it the seeds of a private enterprise approach and as such is, in Marxist–Leninist terms, the basis for the meta-morphosis of the peasantry into a petit-bourgeois class. Given the exodus of the Portuguese and the opportunity to assume control of land and the economic means of production abandoned by them, there existed in post-independence Angola the preconditions for the rise of a petit-bourgeois stratum and even a bourgeois class based on control of the means of production formerly controlled by Portuguese capitalists. In this sense, the MPLA commitment to class struggle was a means of preventing the rise of classes which by their very nature would be opposed to the transformation of society. Such classes would be eager to emulate countries such as Zaïre, Kenya and the Ivory Coast where capitalist-orientated regimes exist and where the means of production have been appropriated largely by indigenous capitalists. Further-more, such regimes have proved ideal sources of profit for Western capitalist multinationals.

It is in this sense that I believe one must recognize the MPLA commit-ment to class struggle. The struggle is not against an existing capitalist class, but against groups that adhere to a lifestyle and ideas that conflict with the party's socialist aims. Orthodox Marxism–Leninism supplies, in the MPLA view, a clear analysis of the dangers presented by petit-bourgeois tendencies, particularly in view of the existence of anti-Marxist movements such as the FNLA and UNITA who could harness petit-bourgeois groups to provide support for their efforts and the efforts of the South African regime and the United States to oust the MPLA. Marxist-Leninism also provides a coherent explanation of the role of 'international imperialism' in opposing the development of socialism in Angola. One must be careful not to see the situation inside Angola as isolation from the regional and global environment.

The MPLA view of the class struggle as an instrument for entrench-ing the power of the vanguard party and of the working class–peasant alliance it claims to represent is the direct development of Lenin's stric-tures on the fight against the petit bourgeoisie in post-revolutionary Russia. It would not be at all surprising to hear President dos Santos echoing the sentiments expressed in the following extract from Lenin's *The Peasantry and the Working Class*:

The very position of small farmers in modern society, therefore, inevitably transforms them into petty bourgeois. They are eternally hovering between the wage-workers and the capitalists. The majority of the peasants live in poverty . . . while the minority trail after capitalists and help keep the masses of the rural population dependent upon the capitalists . . . Only an independent organization of wage-workers which conducts a consistent class struggle can wrest the peasantry from the influence of the bourgeoisie . . . [Lenin, 1960–70, vol. 19, pp. 206–8.]

The sort of dangers outlined by Lenin in 1913, whereby he foresaw the problems of the countryside in post-revolutionary Russia, were clearly in José Eduardo dos Santos's mind when he warned the MPLA National Conference in January 1985 that the problems encountered by the cooperative movement in rural areas and its failure in some areas left poor peasants dependent on small transporters and traders and that this encouraged 'the growth of the rural petty bourgeoisie . . . greatly harming the consolidation of the worker peasant alliance' (MPLA, 1985, p. 4). He also anticipated the danger of 'socialist production relations' triumphing in the towns while the bourgeoisie took control of the country.

This danger is certainly real for the MPLA and explains the adherence of the party to concepts based on class struggle. However, what the party seems to ignore is that the peasantry formed the backbone of the MPLA's guerrilla forces during the liberation war and the civil war and that to embark on rigid and dogmatic campaigns in the countryside based on class struggle concepts is to risk alienating the very peasants who enabled the MPLA to win the struggle and launch the party's bid for socialism. The Angolan President admitted to the National Conference that the rectification campaign had failed to build party structures in the countryside. What he neglected to say was that one reason for this was the concentration of the campaign on recruiting members of the working class—a conscious effort was made to favour the working class through less rigorous periods of candidature. If the MPLA follows a policy of favouring the minute and embryonic working class (which is hardly an established and class-conscious proletariat in the normally understood sense), it will be effectively creating a rift between the town and the countryside and the worker and peasant. Far from strengthening the party, this will create a small urban elite remote from the overwhelming mass of the peasantry and operating in a vacuum as far as understanding of the needs of the peasants are concerned. In terms of the future of the MPLA, this would be placing in jeopardy the very existence of the party and its control over Angola through a misplaced insistence on dogmatic Marxist–Leninist policies that are not applicable to Angola in the way that they may have been applicable in Soviet Russia. While it was possible for Stalin to purge the countryside, at great human, social, politicial and economic cost, this option is clearly not open to the MPLA given the small size of the party, the reliance of the armed forces on peasants for manpower, and the threat posed by UNITA and South Africa.

It is perhaps with this situation in mind that dos Santos instituted a major reshuffle in the Political Bureau and Central Committee following the December 1985 congress. Although he did not announce any major policy changes, the demotion of chief ideologist Lucio Lara and the purging of party leaders connected with the former security police may indicate a change of emphasis to enable the party to conduct a more realistic policy towards the rural areas.

If the party insists on a rigid application of the class struggle in the countryside, it is very likely that this will push large sections of the peasantry into a position of outright opposition to MPLA policies. A hopeful sign was given by dos Santos when he told the National Conference that

... there is an imperative need for the Party effectively to reassume the promotion of revolutionary activity in rural areas, to define ways of stimulating the development of individual and family peasant production, to give new impetus to the formation of production associations and cooperatives ... and increase the number of the Party's base organisations in the countryside, in order that it may exercise its leading role in a consistent manner. [MPLA, 1985, pp. 4–5.]

The success of the party's policies in the rural areas will depend on whether by revolutionary activity the President means the sort of politicization which gained the support of the peasants during the liberation war or the imposition of the class struggle. The former could mark a turnaround in the MPLA's fortunes in the rural areas; the latter could mean disaster.

(2) As for the position of Angola and the MPLA in the international communist movement, both the MPLA and the Soviet Union regard developments in Angola as an integral part of the world revolutionary process. It is hard to disagree with this assessment and one can agree with Bogdan Szajkowski's conclusion that the process of establishment of Marxism states 'should be viewed as a series of related events that take their source in the Bolshevik revolution of 1917' (Szajkowski, 1982, p. 138). Certainly, in successive party documents emanating from congresses, the MPLA leadership has reaffirmed that it sees itself as part of a historical process stemming from the October revolution. But exactly what position does Angola occupy in the communist system?

The MPLA and its leaders are very forthright in maintaining that their party is a Marxist–Leninist vanguard party committed to the transformation of society along socialist lines. It does not claim to have established even the foundations of socialism let alone communism, but it does demand to be taken seriously as a party of the working class. In our analysis so far, we have suggested that the MPLA has been consistent in its adherence to and development of Marxism–Leninism and has implemented a concerted policy of ridding the party of non-Marxist elements and ensuring the adoption of democratic centralism and other vital components of Marxist–Leninist organizational and party work practice. Vast problems may remain in the building of the party and in the preparation of the foundations of socialism, but it is hard to deny that the MPLA has the basic credentials to be labelled a Marxist–Leninist party.

In the Soviet view, things are not as simple as that. Soviet party leaders and theoreticians have come up with a formulation known as 'socialist orientation' to describe the increasing number of parties and states in the Third World that adhere to Marxism–Leninism and have declared it their intention to create systems based on that ideology. Such countries include Angola, Mozambique, Benin, Congo and the People's Democratic Republic of Yemen. The formulation, used widely by CPSU leaders and by Soviet theoretical journals and the media, is a function not so much of developments in the Third World states concerned as of Soviet caution over pledging support for and recognizing as Marxist–Leninist parties and governments over which the Soviet Union has no controlling political influence and which may, in the Soviet view, be only temporary in their hold over power or their ideological commitment. The concept of socialist orientation correctly identifies the aims of the states concerned and lists certain basic policies which apply to them, but it falls short of recognizing the total commitment of the states to Marxism–Leninism. It is effectively a form of ideological fence-setting. The Soviet Union is willing to offer support to the states labelled as ones of socialist orientation and to applaud their development of vanguard parties, but it is not willing to accord them equal status as Marxist–Leninists.

The fence-sitting exercise undoubtedly resulted from the disappointment and ideological confusion in the Soviet Union over the failure of Nkrumah in Ghana, Keita in Mali, Sekou Touré in Guinea, Nasir in Egypt, and other Third World leaders of the 1960s who appeared to be moving steadily towards socialism but then were removed from power and replaced by anti-Soviet or at least anti-Marxist regimes or which, in the case of Sekou Touré and also of Siyad Barreh in Somalia, turned their backs on Marxism–Leninism or opted for a pro-Western international stance. The Soviet Union has been willing to provide extensive military and political support for Angola and Ethiopia, for example, but has not taken the step of recognizing the MPLA or the Worker's Party of Ethiopia as Marxist–Leninist parties. They remain parties and states of socialist orientation.

The essence of the socialist orientation formulation was set out by the late CPSU leader Leonid Brezhnev at the Soviet party congress in February 1981. He said of the states of socialist orientation: 'Their development along the progressive road is not of course proceeding uniformly, for it is taking place under complex conditions . . ..' He went on to say that socialist orientation meant the liquidation of imperialist monopolies, the restriction of the role of foreign capital, securing for the people's states the commanding heights of the economy, an increased role for the working masses in public life and the state apparatus, and the growth of the revolutionary party and an anti-imperialist foreign policy (*Pravda*, 24 February 1981). This analysis of what constitutes a state of socialist orientation certainly fits the conditions pertaining in Angola and the basic policies of the MPLA. However, the MPLA would not agree that it was merely a state of socialist orientation. It would demand to be taken serously as a Marxist state in its own right, and would reject the right of the Soviet Union to sit in judgement on whether or not it had the right to label itself Marxist–Leninist.

Angola's right to decide on its own future and to direct its developments free of outside influence was repeatedly stressed by Agostinho Neto prior to his death and has since been upheld by President dos Santos. In a statement in May 1977, Neto said that 'There is a lot of criticism of us abroad to the effect that Angola is subject to Soviet orientation, that it is the Soviet Union that commands in Angola. That is an absolute lie. And so long as the political leadership (of the MPLA) directs this country, we shall always defend our independence and non-alignment, (cited by Somerville, winter 1984, p. 301).

In conclusion, there are few better descriptions of the place of Angola and similar states in the world communist system than that given by Michael Waller and Bogdan Szajkowski in their opening chapter in *Marxist Governments: A World Survey*:

Even where, as in Angola, Vietnam, Cuba and Ethiopia, Soviet influence is particularly strong, the countervailing effects of cultural diversity and local circumstances make it increasingly difficult to make societies 'fit' a political model which draws overwhelmingly on Soviet experience. Moreover, there is ample evidence from all corners of the communist movement that the majority of the regimes that compose it are themselves not looking for the import of socialist practices from abroad. They aspire to their own original socialism. A socialism that will accord with their own circumstances. [Szajkowski, 1981, p. 15.]

For Angola, what now remains is to ensure that the form of Marxism–Leninism it applies to its own situation accords rather than conflicts with circumstances.

Bibliography

Books and Articles

Africa, 1985. July.

Africa Contemporary Record, 1976–84 (annually). New York and London, Holmes and Meier.

Africa Now, 1985. December.

Africa Research Bulletin, 1875. 1–30 April.

African Business, 1985. April.

Anglin, D. and Shaw, T. M., 1979. *Zambia's Foreign Policy*. Boulder, Colorado, Westview Press.

Barnett, D. and Harvey R., 1972. *The Revolution in Angola*. New York, Bobbs-Merrill.

Bender, G. J., 1978. *Angola Under the Portuguese: The Myth and the Reality*. London, Heinemann.

Bhagavan, M. R., 1980. *Angola: Prospects for Socialist Industrialisation*. Uppsala, Sweden, Scandinavian Institute of African Studies.

Birmingham, D., 1965. *The Portuguese Conquest of Angola*. London, Oxford University Press.

—— 1978. 'The Twenty Seventh of May: An Historical Note on the Abortive Coup Attempt in Angola', *African Affairs*, vol. 77, no. 3.

Burchett, W., 1978. *Southern Africa Stands Up*. New York, Urizen Books.

Carr, E. H., 1966. *The Bolshevik Revolution 1917–1923*, Vol. 1. Harmondsworth, Pelican.

Central Intelligence Agency (CIA), 1983. *The World Factbook 1983*. Washington, DC, US Government Printing Office.

Davidson, B., 1975. *In the Eye of the Storm: Angola's People*. Harmondsworth, Penguin.

—— 1976. 'The Politics of Armed Struggle: National Liberation in the African Colonies of Portugal' in B. Davidson, J. Slovo and A. R. Williamson (eds), *Southern Africa: The New Politics of Revolution*. Harmondsworth, Pelican.

—— 1977. 'Angola Since Independence', *Race and Class*, vol. 19.

De Braganca, A. and Wallerstein, I., 1982. *The African Liberation Reader*, Vols. 1, 2 and 3. London, Zed Press.

Duffy, J., 1959. *Portuguese Africa*. Cambridge, Mass., Harvard University Press.

Hallet, R., 1978. 'South African Intervention in Angola', *African Affairs*, vol. 77, no. 308.

Henderson, L. W., 1979. *Angola: Five Centuries of Conflict.* Ithaca and London, Cornell University Press.

Hill, R. J., 1985. *The Soviet Union: Politics, Economics and Society.* London, Frances Pinter.

Hough, J. F. and Fainsod, M., 1979. *How the Soviet Union is Governed.* Cambridge, Mass., Harvard University Press.

Ignatyev, O., 1977. *Secret Weapon in Africa.* Moscow, Progress Publishers.

International Institute of Strategic Studies (IISS), 1985–6. *The Military Balance, 1985–86.* London, IISS.

International Monetary Fund (OMF), 1985. *Directory of World Trade Yearbook 1985.* Washington, DC.

Jane's Defence Weekly, 1985. 16 November.

Kaplan, I., 1979. *Angola: A Country Study.* Washington, DC, The American University.

Klinghoffer, A. J., 1980. *The Angolan War.* Boulder, Colorado, Westview Press.

Legum, C., 1981. 'Angola and the Horn of Africa' in S. Kapla (ed.), *Diplomacy of Power: Soviet Armed Forces as a Political Instrument.* Washington, DC. Brookings Institute.

Lenin, V. I., 1960–70. *Collected Works*, 45 vols. Moscow.

McGowan, P., 1962. 'Politics of a Revolt' in *Angola: Views of a Revolt.* Institute of Race Relations. London, Oxford University Press.

Marcum, J., 1969. *The Angolan Revolution, Vol. 1: The Anatomy of An Explosion (1950–1962).* Cambridge, Mass., MIT Press.

—— 1978. *The Angolan Revolution, Vol. 2: Exile Politics and Guerrilla Warfare (1962–1976).* Cambridge, Mass., MIT Press.

—— 1979. 'Angola: Perilous Transition to Independence' in G. Carter and P. O'Meara (eds), *Southern Africa: The continuing Crisis.* London, Macmillan.

Marquez, G. G., 1977. 'Operation Carlota', *New Left Review*, no. 101–2.

MPLA, 1962. 'Major Programme' in T. Ikuma, *Angola in Ferment.* Boston, Mass., Beacon Press.

—— 1965. 'Boletin do Militante' in De Braganca and Wallerstein, op. cit., Vol. 1.

—— 1969. 'MPLA–Information' in De Braganca and Wallerstein, op. cit., Vol. 2.

—— 1976. *Documents of the MPLA Central Committee Plenary*, 23–29 October 1976. London, Mozambique Angola and Guinea Information Centre.

—— 1977. *MPLA First Congress: Central Committee Report and Theses on Education.* London, Mozambique, Angola and Guinea Information Centre.

—— 1980. *Angola Special Congress: Report of the Central Committee of the MPLA-Workers' Party.* London, Mozambique, Angola and Guinea Information Centre.

—— 1985. *Angola Information Bulletin*, no. 107. London.

Munslow, B., 1983. *Mozambique: The Revolution and Its Origins.* London, Longman.

Newitt, M., 1981. *Portugal in Africa: The Last Hundred Years.* London, C. Hurst and Co.

Ottaway, D. and Ottaway, M., 1981. *Afrocommunism.* New York, Africana.

Somerville, K., 1984. 'Major Defeats for UNITA', *New African*, January.

—— 1984. 'The USSR and Southern Africa', *Journal of Modern African Studies*, vol. 22, no. 1, March.

—— 1984. 'Angola: Soviet Client State or State of Socialist Orientation?', *Millenium Journal of International Studies*, vol. 13, no. 3, winter.

—— 1985. 'Angola Looks to Oil and Lomé', *Africa Now*, July.

Southern African Development Coordination Conference (SADCC),1981. *Southern Africa Toward Economic Liberation.* London, Rex Collings.

Staar, R. F., 1985. *Yearbook of International Communist Affairs.* Palo Alto, Calif., Stanford University Press.

Stockwell, J., 1978. *In Search of Enemies.* London, André Deutsch.

Szajkowski, B., 1981. *Marxist Governments: A World Survey*, Vol. 1. London, Macmillan.

—— 1982. The *Establishment of Marxist Regimes.* London, Butterworth.

—— 1985. 'Socialist Orientation Revisited', *Coexistence*, no. 22.

US Department of Agriculture, 1981. *Food Problems and Prospects in Sub-Saharan Africa.* Washington, DC, Department of Agriculture.

Van der Post, L. and Taylor, J., 1984. *Testament to the Bushmen.* London, Viking.

Vneshnaya Torgovlya, 1980–84 (annually). Moscow, Statistica.

West Africa, 1981. 7 December.

Wheeler, D. L. and Pelissier, R., 1971. *Angola.* London, Pall Mall.

Wolfers, M. and Bergerol, J., 1983. *Angola in the Frontline.* London, Zed Press.

World Bank, 1981. *Accelerated Development in Sub-Saharan Africa.* Washington, DC.

Zafiris, N., 1982. 'The People's Republic of Angola: Soviet-type Economy in the Making' in P. Wiles (ed.), *The New Communist Third World.* London, Croom Helm.

Newspapers and Radio

Guardian
Lisbon Radio (This and all other references to radio stations are taken from
   the *BBC Summary of World Broadcasts*, Part 4.)
Luanda Radio
Pravda
Soviet News
Sunday News (Tanzania)
The Times (London)
Voice of the Resistance of the Black Cockerel (radio)

Index

Marxist Regimes
Politics, Economics and Society

A series of 36 multi-disciplinary volumes each examining and evaluating critically the application of Marxist doctrine to the respective societies, assessing its interpretations, its successes and failures. Each book includes: Basic Data, History and Political Traditions, the Social Structure, the Political System, the Economic System, and the Regime's Policies. The series draws upon an international collection of authors, each an expert on the country concerned, thus ensuring a unique depth and breadth of analysis.

ANGOLA

This book describes the development of the Popular Movement for the Liberation of Angola (MPLA) as a Marxist-Leninist party, its policies and its attempts to implement them. There is a brief survey of the pre-colonial and colonial history of Angola and a more detailed description of the liberation struggle and civil war.

Since independence in 1975 and the establishment of MPLA control, the movement and its government has had to conduct a war against the South African backed UNITA forces, while at the same time struggling to rebuild an economy shattered by the war and the mass exodus of the Portuguese.

This war, coupled with a crippling shortage of educated and politically conscious cadres, has impeded progress in implementing socialist policies. Internationally, the MPLA has followed a blend of non-alignment which incorporates close friendship with the Soviet Union, Cuba and other socialist states, and trading relations with advanced capitalist states.